WOMEN'S
LIVES
WOMEN'S
WORK

Project Staff

SUE DAVIDSON, *Editor*

SHIRLEY FRANK, *Associate Editor*

MERLE FROSCHL, *Field-Testing Coordinator*

FLORENCE HOWE, *Director*

MARY MULROONEY, *Production Associate*

ELIZABETH PHILLIPS, *Editor*

SUSAN TROWBRIDGE, *Designer and Production Director*

SANDY WEINBAUM, *Teaching Guide Editor*

Out of the Bleachers

Writings on Women and Sport

Stephanie L. Twin

The Feminist Press
OLD WESTBURY, NEW YORK

The McGraw-Hill Book Company
NEW YORK, ST. LOUIS, SAN FRANCISCO

Photo Research by Flavia Rando

**Library of Congress
Cataloging in Publication Data**

Main entry under title:
Out of the bleachers.

    (Women's lives / women's work)
    Includes bibliographical references
    and index.
    1. Sports for women. 2. Sex discrimination
in sports. 3. Feminism. I. Twin, Stephanie.
II. Series.
GV709.095   796'.019'4   78–16531
ISBN 0–07–020429–2

Grateful acknowledgment is made for permission to reprint the following copyrighted material:
    Bernikow, Louise, "Confessions of an
Ex–Cheerleader." © 1973 by Louise Bernikow.
Reprinted from *Ms.* Magazine by permission of
the author.
    Connolly, Olga, "Last Word." Reprinted by
permission from *womenSports* Magazine, June
1974. Copyright © 1974 by womenSports Pub-
lishing Company.
    Crittenden, Ann, "Closing the Muscle Gap."
Copyright © Ms. Magazine Corporation, 1974.
Reprinted with permission.
    Edwards, Harry, "Desegregating Sexist Sport,"
Intellectual Digest, July 1972. Copyright © 1972
by Harry Edwards. Reprinted with permission.
    Fasteau, Brenda Feigen, "Giving Women a
Sporting Chance." Copyright © Ms. Magazine
Corporation, 1973. Reprinted with permission.
    Franks, Lucinda, "See Jane Run." Copyright
© Ms. Magazine Corporation, 1973. Reprinted
with permission.
    Franks, Lucinda, "Women in Motion." Re-
printed from the book *Woman in the Year 2000*,
edited by Maggie Tripp, by permission of the
publisher, Arbor House Publishing Company.
Copyright © 1974 by Maggie Tripp.

(Acknowledgments continued on page 229)

Table of Contents

Publisher's Acknowledgments

EARLY IN 1973, Mariam Chamberlain and Terry Saario of the Ford Foundation spent one day visiting The Feminist Press on the campus of the State University of New York/College at Old Westbury. They heard staff members describe the early history of The Feminist Press and its goal—to change the sexist education of girls and boys, women and men, through publishing and other projects. They also heard about those books and projects then in progress; they felt our sense of frustration about how little we were able to do directly for the classroom teacher. Advising us about funding, Terry Saario was provocative. "You need to think of yourselves," she said, "in the manner of language labs, testing and developing new texts for students and new instructional materials for teachers." Our "language" was feminism, our intent to provide alternatives to the sexist texts used in schools. The conception was, in fact, precisely the one on which the Press had been founded.

Out of that 1973 meeting came the idea for the *Women's Lives / Women's Work* project. This project, which would not officially begin for more than two years, has allowed us to extend the original concept of The Feminist Press to a broader audience.

We spent the years from 1973 to 1975 assessing the needs for a publication project, writing a major funding proposal, steering it through two foundations, negotiating with the Webster Division of McGraw-Hill, our co-publisher. We could not have begun this process without the advice and encouragement of Marilyn Levy of the Rockefeller Family Fund from which we received a planning grant in 1973. In 1978, The Feminist Press received funds from the Edward W. Hazen Foundation—and a second grant from the Rockefeller Family Fund—in order to help complete the project.

For one year, Phyllis Arlow, Marj Britt, Merle Froschl, and Florence Howe surveyed the needs of teachers for books about women, reviewed the sexist bias of widely used history and literature texts, and interviewed editorial staffs of major educational publishers about their intentions to publish material on women. The research accumulated provided a strong case for the grant proposal first submitted to the Ford Foundation in the summer of 1974.

During the winter of 1974–75, Merle Froschl, Florence Howe, Corrine Lucido, and attorney Janice Goodman (for The Feminist Press) negotiated a co-publishing contract with McGraw-Hill. We could not have proceeded without the strong interest of John Rothermich of

McGraw-Hill's Webster Division. Our co-publishing agreement gives control over editorial content and design to The Feminist Press; McGraw-Hill is responsible for distribution of the series to the high school audience, while The Feminist Press is responsible for distribution to colleges, bookstores, libraries, and the general public.

In the summer of 1975, the final proposal—to produce for co-publication a series of twelve supplementary books and their accompanying teaching guides—was funded by the Ford Foundation and the Carnegie Corporation. Project officers Terry Saario and Vivien Stewart were supportive and helpful throughout the life of the project.

Once funding was obtained, The Feminist Press began its search for additional staff to work on the project. The small nucleus of existing staff working on the project was expanded as The Feminist Press hired new employees. The *Women's Lives / Women's Work* project staff ultimately included eight people who remained for the duration of the project: Sue Davidson, Shirley Frank, Merle Froschl, Florence Howe, Mary Mulrooney, Elizabeth Phillips, Susan Trowbridge, and Sandy Weinbaum. Two other people, Dora Janeway Odarenko and Michele Russell, were on the staff through 1977, and we wish to acknowledge their contributions. Helen Schrader, a Feminist Press staff member, participated on the project during its first year and kept financial records and wrote financial reports throughout the duration of the project.

The *Women's Lives / Women's Work* project staff adopted the methods of work and the decision-making structure developed by The Feminist Press staff as a whole. As a Press "work committee," the project met weekly to make decisions, review progress, discuss problems. The project staff refined the editorial direction of the project, conceptualized and devised guidelines for the books, and identified prospective authors. When proposals came in, the project staff read and evaluated the submissions, and made decisions regarding them. Similarly, when manuscripts arrived, the project staff read and commented on them. Project staff members took turns drafting memoranda, reports, and other documents. And the design of the series grew out of the discussions and the ideas generated at the project meetings. The books, teaching guides, and other informational materials had the advantage, at significant stages of development, of the committee's collective direction.

Throughout the life of the project, The Feminist Press itself continued to function and grow. Individuals on staff who were not part of the *Women's Lives / Women's Work* project provided support and advice to the project. All major project policy decisions about such matters as finance and personnel were made by The Feminist Press Board at its monthly meetings. The Board includes all Feminist Press staff, and other individuals who have an ongoing relationship to the Press: Phyllis Arlow, Jeanne Bracken, Brenda Carter, Toni Cerutti, Ranice Crosby, Sue Davidson, Michelina Fitzmaurice, Jeanne Ford, Shirley Frank, Merle Froschl, Barbara Gore, Brett Harvey, Ilene Hertz, Florence Howe, Paul Lauter, Carol Levin, Corrine Lucido, Mary Mulrooney, Dora Janeway Odarenko, Ethel J. Phelps, Elizabeth Phillips, Helen Schrader, Barbara Sussman, Susan Trowbridge, Sandy Weinbaum, Sharon Wigutoff, Jane Williamson, Sophie Zimmerman.

The process of evaluation by teachers and students before final publication was as important as the process for developing ideas into books. To this end, we produced testing editions of the books. Field-testing networks were set up throughout the United States in a variety of schools—public, private, inner-city, small town, suburban, and rural—to reach as diverse a student population as possible. We field tested in the following cities, regions, and states: Boston, Massachusetts; Tucson, Arizona; Seattle, Washington; Los Angeles, California; Tampa, Florida; Greensboro, North Carolina; Eugene, Oregon; Martha's Vineyard, Massachusetts; New York City; Long Island; New Jersey; Rhode Island. We also had an extensive network of educators— 350 teachers across the country—who reviewed the books in the series, often using sections of books in classrooms. From teachers' comments, from students' questionnaires, and from tapes of teachers' discussions, we gained valuable information both for revising the books and for developing the teaching guides.

Although there is no easy way to acknowledge the devotion and enthusiasm of hundreds of teachers who willingly volunteered their time and energies, we would like to thank the following teachers— and their students—with whom we worked directly in the testing of *Out of the Bleachers: Writings on Women and Sport*. In New York City: Lynn Kearney, Mary McAulay, Beth Millstein. In North Carolina, Sandra Powers, Professor of Education at the University of North Carolina / Greensboro—with the assistance of Anita Hawkins— helped to contact teachers in and near Greensboro: Joanie Anderson, Mary Anderson, Marilyn Z. Cotten, Patricia L. Gottlieb, Annie N. Thompson. In Florida, Mary Bullerman, Director of Instructional Services for the Hillsborough County School System, and Ellen Kimmel, Professor of Education at the University of South Florida / Tampa, helped to contact teachers in the Tampa Bay area: Gayl E. Davis, Edie Edwards, Miriam Katz, Sylvia Lampert, Pam Livingston, Sara Kate Milledge, Katie Sible, Catherine A. Steinker. We would also like to acknowledge the participation of Eloise M. Fells of the Federal Sex Desegregation Center at the University of Miami.

Three times during the life of the *Women's Lives / Women's Work* project, an Advisory Board composed of feminist educators and scholars met for a full day to discuss the books and teaching guides. The valuable criticisms and suggestions of the following people who participated in these meetings were essential to the project: Millie Alpern, Rosalynn Baxandall, Peggy Brick, Ellen Cantarow, Elizabeth Ewen, Barbara Gates, Clarisse Gillcrist, Elaine Hedges, Nancy Hoffman, Susan Klaw, Alice Kessler–Harris, Roberta Kronberger, Merle Levine, Eleanor Newirth, Judith Oksner, Naomi Rosenthal, Judith Schwartz, Judy Scott, Carroll Smith–Rosenberg, Adria Steinberg, Barbara Sussman, Amy Swerdlow. We also want to express our gratitude to Shirley McCune and Nida Thomas, who acted in a general advisory capacity and made many useful suggestions; and to Kathryn Girard and Kathy Salisbury who helped to develop the teacher and student field-testing questionnaires.

One person in particular whom we wish to thank for her work on *Out of the Bleachers* is Flavia Rando for her exhaustive photo research and her unbounded enthusiasm for the job. Indeed, her research unearthed so many excellent photographs that it was with great difficulty that we limited ourselves to the ones that we finally selected for this volume.

Others whom we want to acknowledge are Ruth Adam for restoration of the historical photographs; Charles Carmony, who prepared the index; Hester Eggert and Carlos Ruiz of McGraw–Hill for administrative assistance; and Emerson W. Madairy and Linda Petillo of Monotype Composition Company for technical assistance.

The work of the many people mentioned in these acknowledgments has been invaluable to us. We would also like to thank all of you who read this book—because you helped to create the demand that made the *Women's Lives / Women's Work* project possible.

THE FEMINIST PRESS

Author's Acknowledgments

FOR THE MATERIALS in this volume, two sources deserve special mention. One is the New York Public Library, whose excellent collection of historical resources provided most of the information in the introduction, and whose careful preservation of an original copy of Frances Willard's 1895 ode to the bicycle enabled me to excerpt portions for this book. Secondly, I would like to thank the former staff of *womenSports* Magazine for generously allowing me use of their facilities, especially their library.

Next, I wish to single out my editor, Elizabeth Phillips, whose skilled and intelligent editing was matched by an unusual sensitivity to the needs of both the author and the book. Her carefully crafted section introductions have particularly enhanced this volume.

Credit goes to The Feminist Press as a whole for including a book on sports—which the burgeoning field of Women's Studies has largely ignored—in its *Women's Lives / Women's Work* project. The several staff members who read potential selections as well as successive drafts of the introduction contributed enormously to the final shape of this book.

Thanks, too, to the writers who took the time to give me much of the information contained in the headnotes, and to the athletic women of the past one hundred years, whose physical and emotional strength and social nonconformism have broken down both subtle and overt barriers of all sorts for all women.

Finally, I wish to thank two individuals whose assistance greatly facilitated my work on this volume: Florence Kapovich, for her wonderful care of Alexandra; and Richard Smuckler, for the same, as well as for his overall support and egalitarianism.

STEPHANIE L. TWIN

Introduction

IN 1970, WHEN THE STUDY OF SEX ROLES was accelerating, a
member of the Association for Humanistic Psychology challenged her newsletter's male readers to imagine life in a female-
dominated society. Language would be feminine; *woman* and
she would refer to human beings of both sexes. Women would
be the political and economic powerbrokers, and men would
naturally fulfill themselves as husbands and fathers—"naturally" for the obvious biological reason of men's physical and
emotional passivity. "By design," the writer explained,

> female genitals are compact and internal, protected by her body. Male
> genitals are so exposed that he must be protected from outside attack
> to assure the perpetuation of the race. His vulnerability obviously
> requires sheltering. . . .[A boy] remembers his sister's jeering at his
> primitive genitals that "flap around foolishly." She can run, climb and
> ride horseback unencumbered. Obviously, since she is free to move,
> she is encouraged to develop her body and mind in preparation for her
> active responsibilities of adult womanhood. The male vulnerability
> needs female protection, so he is taught the less active, caring virtues
> of homemaking.[1]

This particular rendering of "anatomy is destiny" may strike
us as ridiculous, certainly laughable, because it reverses the
actual conceptions of the body with which each sex is raised.
Yet it is no more ridiculous than those "real" conceptions.
Girls learn from a young age that their bodies restrict their
range of behavior. The way sports are encouraged and organized
for boys is perhaps the most impressionable way girls observe
that males are to be active while females are not. Psychological
theories, custom, and popular prejudice combine to measure
women negatively against men.[2] The fact that females generally
grow to be shorter, lighter, and less muscular than males is
exaggerated to mean that femininity equals weakness, softness,
and inertia. Athletic women are thus seen as masculine. In
1912, Harvard's famous Dr. Dudley Allen Sargent went so far
as to suggest that women who excelled at competitive sports
might have inherited masculine characteristics.[3] A contemporary variation is that muscular, first-rate female athletes

take male hormones (steroids). The implication, both in 1912 and today, is that true females are physically limited.

The Beginnings

This perception of the female form goes back centuries. Despite speculation about matriarchal (female-dominated) cultures and the existence in mythology of female hunting, fertility, and athletic goddesses, in most known cultures physical contests have been primarily for men. In numerous societies, male economic activities evolved into sports—as with hunting, fishing, riflery, and archery—but female ones did not.

Beyond sport's relation to men's work, however, many cultures have linked athletics with male physical energy in an almost mystical bond. The classical world's conviction that vitality was exclusively masculine is found in Aristotle's theory of human conception. The fetus was a mixture of semen and menstrual liquid, he believed, and the semen was actually purified blood and the active, critical "germinating fluid." In the formation of life, man was to woman what the carpenter was to a block of wood: the creative shaper of a passive substance. Indeed, the word *semen,* meaning seed, reflects this view, as does the adjective *seminal,* meaning germinative or original.

If men biologically monopolized vitality, then excluding females from the Greek Olympics was logical. Women were permitted neither to watch nor to participate in the ancient games which, along with literature and music competitions, formed a religious festival dedicated to Zeus. The winners emerged as political and religious heroes. They were honored with civil privileges and titles and, in Athens, supported for life at public expense. One writer noted that a "beautiful and good woman for wife" was often promised as a reward for winning the running high jump. "History does not relate," she sardonically added, "whether or not the Spartan girls were awarded a 'beautiful and good man for husband' in their competitions."[4]

The women of the Greek city-state Sparta were only partial exceptions to the classical world's faith in male physical energy. They were trained from girlhood in running, jumping, wrestling, and javelin and discus throwing to enhance their future role as breeders. Their sports were designed to build the health and emotional stamina needed to bear great warriors for the state; their athletics held no wider political or religious significance. Most Grecian women were denied even this minimal justification for sports. Thought weak and timid, they were assigned to indoor, domestic tasks, the more difficult of which fell to slave women. "The oddity" of the Greek woman's life was striking, the classicist Emily James Putnam remarked in 1911. "She lived in the house among a people that lived out of doors. . . . Among a people who gave great importance to physical training she was advised to take her exercise in bedmaking."[5] Plato referred to females as "a race that are used to living out of the sunlight."

Sparta remains one of the few patriarchal (male-dominated) states to have associated birthgiving with female physical strength. In most cultures, the belief in female passivity and bodily inferiority—or the ideal of feminine fragility—has existed alongside the physically strenuous reality of childbirth. Modern estimates are that the uterus exerts the equivalent of 100 pounds of pressure in expelling a full-term fetus. The paradox of actual biological and physical strength interpreted as feminine weakness casts an ironic perspective on the past, as one historian has noted. In his study of early seventeenth-century France, David Hunt described childbirth as that period's most demanding physical activity:

> Ironically, in a society which put such a high premium on bravery and endurance, and in which masculine prerogatives were so aggressively formulated, childbearing was probably the single experience which made the heaviest demands on the courage and fortitude of the participant. For all their vainglorious pretentions, men were obliged to watch helplessly from the sidelines as women faced this ultimate trial.[6]

This paradox suggests that traditional notions of female limitations have seriously underestimated women's actual physical experience and capacity.

Female Frailty in the Nineteenth Century

Though long-held, the belief in feminine physical frailty reached its peak, perhaps, in nineteenth-century America. It became a self-fulfilling prophecy for numbers of middle-class women. The "woman on the pedestal," whose strengths were moral and emotional and nonphysical—indeed antiphysical—emerged as the ideal by the 1830s. Popular and scientific opinion alike upheld physical inertia as both natural and desirable for women. Physicians warned that too much activity unnerved females, creating everything from hysteria to dyspepsia. Since the uterus, they thought, was connected to the nervous system, nervous shocks induced by overexertion threatened reproduction and might lead to "weak and degenerate offspring."[7] Women were to conserve the little energy that they had. By 1850, these notions had crystallized into a cult of ill health in which women proved their femininity with invalidism.

A logical extension of this perception of females as weak was a belief in girls' and women's recreational passivity. Furthermore, sports were believed irrelevant to girls' future roles. Ball playing was encouraged among boys because it tested speed, strength, skill, and agility but discouraged among girls, who were thought to need none of those qualities. Girls might occasionally toss a ball or, for health's sake, go "bathing." Horseback riding was permitted as transportation; the gentry considered it appropriate recreation for both sexes. Young women sometimes rolled hoops or ice skated, but an historian has related how, during the 1850s skating revival, at least one woman was urged to hold her partner's coattails so as to have fun without "incurring any of the fatigue of the exercise."[8]

Though articulated for all women, this standard of delicacy pertained in reality to a minority. As Barbara Ehrenreich and Deirdre English have explained in *Complaints and Disorders: The Sexual Politics of Sickness* (1973), "For the affluent women, society prescribed lives of leisured indolence; for the working-class women, back-breaking toil."[9] On farms, where most Americans lived, women worked long, hard hours. In mills, factories, and private homes farmers' daughters and immigrant women labored as industrial workers and domestic servants. Slave women provided the most flagrant disproof of supposed female debility, as the freed slave Sojourner Truth reminded a women's rights audience in 1851:

The man over there says women need to be helped into carriages and lifted over ditches, and to have the best place everywhere. Nobody ever helps me into carriages or over puddles, or gives me the best place—and ain't I a woman? Look at my arm! I have ploughed and planted and gathered into barns, and no man could head me—and ain't I a woman? I could work as much and eat as much as a man—when I could get it—and bear the lash as well! And ain't I a woman?[10]

While she roused her listeners to a standing ovation, not all Americans would have agreed that she was, indeed, a woman. That is, they would have concurred in her being anatomically female, but not feminine. Lacking femininity, she was not really a woman: genuine women were physically weak. Thus working women, who were the majority, used their bodies at the price of their sexual identity—at least the identity determined by orthodox opinion. Athletic women in the twentieth century have suffered the same penalty.

In a 1901 *Harper's Bazar*, Dr. Grace Peckham Murray analyzed women's dilemma in this way:

Women were strong enough for the drudgery of life—men never disputed that—but when it came to entering fields of labor which yielded the crops of dignity and remuneration, women who were pioneers received great reprobation and were accused of unsexing themselves.[11]

In other words, women were permitted to do certain kinds of hard physical labor—someone had to. But if women demanded recognition or payment for their labor, took pride in their physical ability, or tried new kinds of work, they were chided for defying nature and social norms.

This attitude hindered pioneer educators' and health reformers' attempts to strengthen women physically. Until the late 1800s, even the mildest female exercise regimens won little public approval. The earliest known experimenter with female gymnastic instruction was William Bentley Fowle, who in 1826 vainly searched for precedents:

You know the prevailing notions of female delicacy and propriety are at variance with every attempt to render females less feeble and helpless. . . . I read all the books I could find, but met with very little applicable to the instruction of females. It seemed as if the sex had been thought unworthy of an effort to improve their physical powers.[12]

Some female seminaries and colleges required housework as a form of exercise. Reformers such as Catharine Beecher, Dio Lewis, and Dr. Dudley Allen Sargent devised calisthenic and dumbbell routines which, despite denials, were hardly different from or more invigorating than dance quadrilles.

In stark contrast, males were regarded as repositories of energy. One historian has found that "energy was one of the most frequent and most characteristic terms associated with male activity" in the middle third of the nineteenth century.[13] As in the ancient world, men's physical vitality was traced to sperm and seen as the basis of both their work roles and their aggressive social roles. Men were warned that masturbation and nonprocreational intercourse wasted their precious energy supply. In other words, women, lacking energy themselves, might also drain men of theirs and debilitate them in the work world.

An anthropologist noted in 1975 that many cultures, sharing this view, have isolated men from women before important male rituals such as hunting, warfare, or, in our society, sports. He compared twentieth-century male athletes' pregame sexual abstinence to the Cheyenne feeling that male sexuality was "something to be husbanded and kept in reserve as a source of strength for the great crises of war."[14] Victorian America felt this way apart from war and before the rise of organized sport: male sexuality energized men for business and work.

The Evolution of Sport

To grasp American women's changing relation to sport over the last 150 years, we must understand the evolution of sport itself in the United States. The media-popularized, multibillion-dollar spectator and sporting goods industries which shape athletics today were barely discernible even 100 years ago. In the predominantly rural, small town society that America was up through the Civil War, games were casual, occasional, and usually work-related. This does not mean that hunting, trapping, and the like comprised all play. An assortment of bat and ball games did exist. Puritan men and boys played an informal version of football, using inflated pigs' bladders filled with peas. However, unlike modern games, such play lacked fixed rules and varied dramatically by region and class.

After the Civil War, industrialization transformed American life. The factory replaced the farm, the worker the entrepreneur, the clock the sun, and the city the town. Work and play were divorced, as life became compartmentalized. As people worked in set places for a set time, play had to be conducted separately. In this way, industrialization encouraged the development of organized athletics, which also benefited from emerging national communication and transportation networks.

As industrialization proceeded, long-standing but casually played games acquired formal rule structures and permanent teams. College football and professional baseball, having unfolded in the late 1860s, steadily gained popularity throughout the 1870s. In that decade, sports journalism materialized, A. G. Spalding and Brothers opened, the first bicycle was invented, and national associations were founded for various sports. These trends continued in the 1880s, which also witnessed the construction of the modern "safety" bicycle that created a sensation in the 1890s. Besides the bicycling fad, the 1890s gave rise to basketball and volleyball, as well as the first public sports scandals and an increasingly aggressive physical education movement. In 1900, America's first mass circulation sports magazine, *Outing*, appeared.

Sports were considered increasingly important for men as changes in the work world brought about by industrialization created the fear that effeminacy was sapping male vitality. People were disturbed by the decline of outdoor farm life. Sedentary urban occupations were interpreted as passivity and lethargy overtaking an earlier dynamic frontier virility. In addition, the once sex-segregated work world was steadily encompassing women, as females moved into professions and grew visible as industrial laborers. As the new century turned, articles proliferated with titles like "The Effeminization of the United States," "The Feminizing of Culture," "Feminizing Our Schools," and "Feminization in School and Home." Observers worried especially about the effect on boys of women's predominance as schoolteachers. Since urban jobs separated men from their families for most of the day, many people feared that boys were losing role models both at school and at home. Organizations such as the Boy Scouts were meant to serve as compensation, and, in large measure, so were sports.

Americans believed that sports revitalized "masculine" instincts, which were loosely referred to as virility. In 1893, nearly a decade before he became president, Theodore Roosevelt delivered his famous address, "The Value of an Athletic Training," in which he used the word "manly" at least a dozen times to describe the sort of national character and lifestyle athletics created. In a key passage he warned:

In a perfectly peaceful and commercial civilization such as ours there is always a danger of laying too little stress upon the more virile virtues—upon the virtues which go to make up a race of statesmen and soldiers, of pioneers, and explorers by land and sea. . . . These are the very qualities which are fostered by vigorous, manly out-of-door sports. . . .[15]

Writers, educators, psychologists, reformers, priests, and politicians endorsed sport as a solution to social problems attributed to male energy imbalances. Crime and fornication, the products of too much energy, were thought to afflict lower-class boys; effeminacy and homosexuality, the products of too little energy, were believed to threaten males of the upper class. To refine yet preserve boys' supposed "animal nature," civic leaders and private promoters founded numerous summer camps and religious, community, and school athletic leagues. Many of these, such as the Police Athletic League, survive today and still administer sports mainly to boys.

If sports were regarded as an expression of male sexuality, they were also believed to teach men values that were especially important in the post–Civil War era. The labor struggles and urban poverty growing from rapid industrial change showed class tension and unequal opportunity to be realities of American life. Scores of middle-class Americans came to believe that sports called forth the very qualities long held to be prerequisites for success: hard work, ambition, diligence, perseverance, humility, and respect for authority. By playing sports, they claimed, disadvantaged males could acquire attributes and attitudes which would help them strive toward the American Dream. Rich men, they continued, could learn the virtues of effort and equality since sports were a social leveler; on the playing field, wealth and status gave no advantage. Spectators could supposedly absorb all these lessons. In inspiring character as well as virility, the argument concluded, sports might thus blunt the malaise arising from tumultuous change. This theory did not hold up in practice. Yet the contention that "sports build character" has enjoyed a long, little-criticized life, although public scandals, open corruption, and colorfully "uncouth" players have convinced numbers of people otherwise.

Women's Evolving Athleticism

Since the sort of character sports were believed to build was thought irrelevant to womanhood, women were deprived of a philosophical basis for sports participation as well as a biological one. Hard work, ambition, diligence, and perseverance were considered unfeminine and so were women who displayed them. Women's evolving athleticism, beginning in the 1880s and strengthening with each succeeding decade, therefore came from other sources.

One source was the rise of an industrial leisure class. The "captains of industry" and their families, like most social elites, pursued sport as a form of art; it was a "refined" way for the sexes to spend time together. Aristocratic women in the Middle Ages had sometimes engaged in fox hunts and early forms of tennis and golf. When the modern versions of those games appeared in the late 1800s, elite women immediately took part. A woman, Miss Mary Ewing Outerbridge, is credited with bringing tennis to the United States from abroad. Women's colleges rapidly adopted it, and in 1887, the first female tournament occurred. (The earliest in golf was in 1895.) Thus, though numerically few and socially remote from the larger population, upper-class women contributed to the budding athleticism of their middle-class sisters.

Middle-class women's introduction to sports came primarily as a consequence of female higher education. Ironically, it was the critics of female education who were partially responsible for this development. These opponents, backed by the period's dominant medical opinion, considered intellectual effort physically harmful to women, especially to their reproductive systems. In 1873, Harvard Medical School's eminent Dr. Edward H. Clarke published his controversial *Sex in Education; or, A Fair Chance for the Girls.* In it he blamed college education for a range of female ailments, among them neuralgia, uterine disease, and hysteria. Female educators and proponents of women's education strongly disagreed and countered the next year with *No Sex in Education; or, An Equal Chance for Both Girls And Boys.* However, because of the popularity of Clarke's position, they made efforts to guard against possible female invalidism. Advocating mild physical activity as a way of keeping the female body—especially the sedentary, intellectual one—healthy, women's and coeducational colleges carefully included physical departments to ensure female students' physical health.

By the early 1890s, studies showed college women to be healthier than their noncollege counterparts, and female physical education spread. Popular magazine articles on these programs encouraged a wider audience to view women's sports more positively. In addition, numbers of native-born white protestants became interested in female physical strength through the eugenics movement. The leaders of this movement claimed that because the immigrant population was growing as the native-born white protestant birth rate was declining, the survival of the native-born white protestants as a race was threatened. The healthier female body would, it was hoped, be able to bear more, healthy children and "save" the race.

Although there were advances in the early 1900s, contemporaries exaggerated the extent of women's pre–World War I athleticism because the sight of even a few women cycling, rowing, exercising, and playing golf, tennis, basketball, and field hockey was a startling deviation from the nineteenth century. Supporters hailed the era of the tomboy and pronounced the sickly, corseted Victorian woman dead. Critics blamed everything from divorce to delinquency on women's growing physical assertiveness and judged the selfless, maternal Victorian woman dead. The truth was somewhere in between:

the tomboy was not a favored ideal; most women still wore layered, corseted clothing, remained physically undeveloped, and aspired primarily to marriage and motherhood. Even college women's athletic involvement was nominal, a *Collier's* writer claimed in 1910. Jane Addams, the social work pioneer who would one day win a Nobel Peace Prize, charged correctly, in 1908, that Americans still refused to acknowledge the energies of girls.[16]

The dominant perception of the female body had not changed dramatically. In 1907, the University of Chicago sociologist William I. Thomas published *Sex and Society; Studies in the Social Psychology of Sex*, a compilation of his scholarly articles from the past decade. He saw the "emergence of the adventuress and the sporting-woman" as a negative reaction to society's insistence on passivity. Women needed exercise, he agreed, but athletics were beyond their physical capacity. He explained that females were physically inferior to males because their reproductive function arrested their development early. Woman "resembles the child and the lower races, *i.e.*, the less developed forms," he wrote, in having "relatively" shorter limbs and a longer trunk than man. Such proportions constituted "a very striking evidence of the ineptitude of woman for the expenditure of physiological energy through motor action."[17]

Dr. Dudley Allen Sargent offered a somewhat more liberal interpretation of female physiology in 1912. The sexes, he said, were structurally similar. Therefore, women not only needed exercise, but could even be quite capable athletes. However, he added, sports broadened and strengthened women, making them more "masculine" physically, and only women with such acquired or else inherited masculinity could excel at men's sports. Since this was socially undesirable, he concluded, women's sports should be modified versions of men's: shorter and less strenuous, like the female body itself.

This line of thinking had already won a wide following, especially among the first generation of female physical educators. In 1899, a group of them had created special women's basketball rules, designed to minimize exertion and physical contact. Believing women more vulnerable than men to heart

strain, exhaustion, and jarred reproductive organs, the educators had divided the court into three sections and confined
certain players to each. A five-person team (nine were also
permitted) had two forwards in one section, two guards in
another, and a center in the middle. A player could not grab
or strike the ball from another player's hands, hold it longer
than three seconds, or bounce it more than three consecutive
times or at a height lower than her knee. In other words, the
game allowed only brief, broken movements in a small space
with too many people who could not touch one another. It
undoubtedly eliminated overexertion. In 1908, a permanent
panel was formed to enforce acceptance of the separate rules.
With the growth of national women's sports organizations after
World War I, the women's game became standard in most
schools and colleges. Its main feature, the divided court,
generally lasted until the early 1970s.

Other sports were similarly modified to conform with
women's assumed or desired physical limitations. In 1902,
female tennis tournaments were reduced from three of five
sets to two of three, despite players' protests. In bicycling and
field hockey, clothing reinforced rules to modify movement.
The absence of competition had made bicycling more of an
outdoor gymnastic exercise than a sport among women. Yet
"lady cyclists" had been mercilessly ridiculed for their necessarily loose attire, especially their bloomers, and had eventually stopped cycling altogether. In field hockey, which became a favorite team sport in women's schools and colleges in
the early 1900s, women clad in long-sleeved, petticoated,
ankle-length dresses attempted to wield hockey sticks force-
fully and dash across a field. Their uncorseted, ankle-rather-
than-ground-length costume was widely considered a reform.

Hopelessly "masculine" sports were thought beyond mod-
ification. Baseball, boxing, football, and track, except for short
sprints, were unanimously opposed for women by physical
educators and publicists. Competition was likewise discouraged, even in "feminized" sports, because its essential elements—contention, ambition, and exertion—were believed
unfeminine. Women were not to play seriously; they were not
to win, which was masculine, but to play for fun, companion-

ship, and health. As late as 1917, the New York City Board of Education's Inspector of Athletics for Girls characterized dancing as the best female sport. The most widely approved form of female physical activity was physical culture: mild calisthenics designed to strengthen, beautify, or correct various parts of the body.

In nurturing women's athleticism, then, the late 1800s and early 1900s lifted some but not all of the Victorian constraints on female physical expression. Although more restraints would vanish after World War I, the groundwork for women's twentieth-century sport participation was laid in the prewar period. Women's physicality was acknowledged in those formative years, but was assumed and hoped to be limited. Her body, a means to social ends—beauty, motherhood, education—rather than something to be mastered in itself, simply needed to be kept healthy. Some educators argued that a healthy body was the basis of women's new work and community roles, but most women's sports sympathizers only cared that the body be kept healthy to strengthen the old roles of wifehood and maternity. Few suggested that, through sports, women might gain mastery over their bodies, and most doubted even that they could.

The First Wave of Athletic Feminism

The second generation of female physical educators and their allies built on this ambivalent legacy after World War I. Through various national organizations, they persuaded innumerable school districts and colleges to use separate rules and sponsor only certain sports for women. They campaigned hard against female interscholastic competition and in favor of "play days": regional, one-day meets in several sports between shifting, temporary teams. Baltimore physical educators decided that girls could participate in state basketball championships after "building up to it" for nine years with dodge ball, captain ball, and volleyball. Other cities warded off or eliminated girls' tournaments for mildly competitive intramurals. The justification was that strenuous, highly competitive athletics undermined women biologically and socially. In

1923, a *Ladies' Home Journal* writer insisted that, despite women's growing competitiveness in sports, "physiological necessity . . . decidedly stands in the way of unrestricted physical achievement." Menstruating females were believed particularly handicapped, which was why women's teams were to be larger than men's.[18] A Texas physical educator described the "ideal girl" in 1927 as "one who is active, graceful, skillful in at least one sport, but at the same time a girl who is mentally alert and socially attractive, who does not make her athletic ability her chief hobby. . . ."[19] As late as the early 1960s, national women's sports groups maintained that most out-of-gym competition was unnecessary and undesirable.

Not everyone, of course, agreed. Competitive female athletics blossomed in the 1920s and 1930s. American women entered the Olympics in 1920, and in 1922, the Fédération Sportive Féminine Internationale hosted the first Women's World Games. In the "feminine" sports of tennis, swimming, ice skating, and golf top female competitors became popular personalities. They were admired for their skills, imitated in advertising, and discussed in magazines. Even in the less "feminine" sports of softball and basketball, companies sponsored successful, profit-making, spectator-oriented leagues. In some regions, women's softball outdrew men's during the 1930s. In 1936, a knowledgeable observer claimed that basketball, played by a million girls and women, was the most common female game.[20]

To some extent, the emergence of popular competitive female athletes represented a liberalized perception of women's bodies. During World War I, women had assumed many of the heavy industrial jobs vacated by men. This fact was not lost upon the public, although women lost these jobs after the war. Dr. Clelia Duel Mosher had observed that women were performing tasks thought beyond their capability. This prompted her to study the comparative strength of physically active but nonathletic college women and athletic college men, and conclude that "there is no difference in the muscular strength of women and men which is due to sex as such." Differences resulted from cultural limitations, such as restrictive clothing, poor eating habits, and inadequate training.[21] Educators who would not go that far did agree that the war had shown women physically capable of more than expected. At their postwar conventions, educators increasingly tied sports to women's roles as citizens and workers, not simply to motherhood as in the past. Government and military leaders, also impressed with women's wartime contribution, established the National Amateur Athletic Federation in 1922. They hoped to include "men and women and boys and girls . . . on equal footing, with the same standards, the same program, and the same regulations."[22] However, Girl Scouts President Mrs. Herbert Hoover opposed equal standards. Reflecting the still-dominant belief in female physical limitations, she presided over a Women's Division within the NAAF which took the lead in anticompetition efforts.

This growing awareness of women's physical potential had, significantly, another dimension. The female form was becoming a marketable item, used to sell numerous products and services. It emerged as a staple of American life in the 1920s, part of what sociologist Martha Wolfenstein later called "fun morality."[23] The old fear of having too much fun gave way to the new fear of having too little and was exploited by advertisers to create consumer demand for products. The message, "Sex is fun, and so is my product (body)," made women physically profitable.

The commercialization of women's bodies provided a cultural opening for competitive athletics, as industry and ambitious individuals used women to sell sports. Leo Seltzer included women in his 1935 invention, roller derby, with "one eye to beauty and the other on gate receipts," according to one writer. It was a novelty, a successful publicity gimmick, since athletic marathons were usually for men.[24] Similarly, money-making sports ventures benefited from women's shortened postwar clothing. Colonel Melvorne McCombs, the insurance company women's basketball coach who "discovered" Babe Didrickson, claimed that a 1920s Dallas press controversy over players' shorts had increased regular game attendance from 150 to 5000.

While women's physical marketability profited industry, it also allowed females to do more with their bodies than before.

It allowed them to become not merely athletic but athletes—as long as they underscored their femininity with the right sports and attire. No longer condemned as masculine or "Amazons," competitive female tennis players, ice skaters, and sprinters were called goddesses, and swimmers were referred to as mermaids. Helen Wills, the top female tennis player between 1923 and 1935, was praised for upholding "the wonderful womanhood that uses sports to enhance its womanly charm instead of to affect an artificial masculinity."[25] Producer Flo Ziegfield and Hollywood agents regularly scouted swimming and tennis meets in search of attractive females for nonathletic, nondramatic stage and film roles. And Marty Fiedler, promoter of women's softball teams with names like Slapsie Maxie's Curvacious Cuties and the Balian Ice Cream Beauties, was called sport's Ziegfield—"to wit, the glorifier of the American girl athlete."[26] The beauty queen, movie star, and athlete were related examples of the nature of women's expanded postwar physical freedom. In fact, the beauty queen and the woman athlete were officially recognized within a year of each other: 1921 introduced the first Miss America pageant and 1922, the first "Women as Athletes" category in the *Reader's Guide to Periodical Literature* (an annual index of magazine articles).

Female physical educators saw these cultural connections and protested. Competition was exploitation, they charged, cheap prostrations of women for publicity and money. They claimed that women were being pushed beyond themselves physically and emotionally to satisfy crowds. They predicted that nervous instability, premature pelvic ossification, narrowed vaginas, difficult deliveries, heart strain, and spinsterhood were the high prices women would pay for being serious contenders. Furthermore, educators agreed, competition turned play into work.

The Women's Swimming Association of New York, which trained most of the top Olympic swimmers in the 1920s and 1930s, was critical of an overemphasis on competition and had as their motto, "Sportsmanship is more important than winning." However, they also believed that contention did not inherently contradict health and fun, and they refused to separate the basics of racing from recreational swimming:

A stroke succeeds in all-round competition because it exploits ... human strength and stamina; because it enables contestants to draw greater speed, or endurance from their physical resources. It will be obvious then that such a stroke must afford the same advantages to those who swim for recreation, physical improvement or to save their lives.[27]

Didrickson's coach, McCombs, similarly argued that certain techniques were necessary to play sports well, whether for recreation or recognition. He said colleges' restrictions produced inferior women's teams.

Educators and allied civic leaders grew particularly outraged over women's participation in the Olympics and Women's World Games. Disapproval was nearly unanimous, a 1923 *Ladies' Home Journal* writer observed, among physicians, physical educators, and national organizations involved in women's sports. Many of these groups and persons joined in a formal protest after the 1928 Olympics, asking officials to suspend the newly added female track and field competition and, if possible, women's participation altogether. Their petition noted that Pierre de Coubertin, the founder of the Olympics, had not wanted females included and that, as a male organization, the Olympics should not conduct sports for women.

Actually, women's involvement was strictly supervised. The Olympics Medical Sub-Commission decided in 1925 that women's "special functions" and "special organization" necessitated "carefully chosen" events "reduced considerably from those arranged for men." Women were medically examined more frequently than men, and clothing regulations existed "to prevent regrettable exhibitions." In addition, the Olympic Congress partially acceded to the educators' wishes by dropping the women's 800-meter race.

Though rooted in physiology, female physical educators' objection to competition had other dimensions. It attacked both men's athletics and American culture. "It isn't the competition which so many of us decry," insisted Barnard College's prominent Agnes R. Wayman, "but the highly intense type of do-or-die play, . . . a desire to 'defeat someone.'" Competition was the vital "soul" of sport, she continued, but Americans' compulsion to win "tends to tear down real values and set up false ones."[28] She and her colleagues characterized men's intercollegiate athletics as joyless, elitist, exploitive, money-making enterprises without educational value. Men's sports were the overcoached, intensive training of the few instead of the democratic, extensive training of the many.

In 1929, the Carnegie Report's famous "Bulletin 23" similarly indicted intercollegiate sports for exclusivity, excessive commercialism, corrupt practices, and overspecialized training. The NAAF Women's Division flourished its motto, "A Game for Every Girl and a Girl for Every Game," in contrast. In 1937, the National Section on Women's Athletics of the American Physical Education Association composed a statement of principles, the Standards Report, affirming the superiority of nonprofit, noncompetitive women's sports. Sportswriter John Tunis called it "a clear definition of what sport should be in a democratic regime. It ought to be studied by all those charged with supervising men's athletics."[29] Others involved in men's athletics praised women educators' emphasis on "the right to participate." One coach wrote that college women were half a century ahead of college men. "The co-ed is blazing a modern trail through the educational wilderness for her brother, one that he must ultimately follow. . . ."[30]

As a cultural critique, organized women's opposition to competitive athletics reflected their feminism. Feminism is said to have died with the victory of the suffrage movement in 1920, but in reality, a feminist perspective survived among professional women educated in preceding decades. Early twentieth-century feminists had turned antifeminist arguments inside out by describing women's limitations as virtues. Were women too pure for politics, or too inexperienced for government? On the contrary, feminists had argued, government was just enlarged housekeeping and women's higher morality would clean it. Essentially, postwar female physical educators did the same thing, first declaring women incapable of competition and then calling "play for play's sake" superior. They consciously converted a physiological argument into an alternative philosophy of sport.

This philosophy was vigorously trumpeted by *The Sportswoman*, an "amateur magazine . . . by and for women who love sport for sport's sake." It was published between 1924 and 1936 by the U.S. Field Hockey Association, a women's organization. The magazine had its own staff consisting largely of college students and teachers, and included high school students as contributors.

The Sportswoman did not oppose all competition. It endorsed nonprofit, medically supervised amateur competition, played by women's rules. It reported standings and results of tournaments and meets, and ran profiles on female athletes. In 1931, it even disputed American Physical Education Association (APEA) President Mabel Lee for saying intercollegiate sports equaled "throwing women's ideals to the winds." Intercollegiate competition, the editors countered, was "highly beneficial as a broadening and character-developing influence" if not overdone.

However, the magazine applauded whenever a school district or urban area substituted intramurals or field days for championship structures. It energetically promoted play days, minimized Olympic coverage, and denounced professionalism and scholastic "semiprofessionalism." Calling the latter a "perverted form of enthusiasm," it periodically editorialized against spectator-oriented basketball programs and tournaments. "Women desire the promotion of sport for recreation rather than for commercialism," the editors explained. A 1927 writer categorized fierce personal competitiveness and striving as "infantile characteristics" which experienced female teams and athletes outgrew.

The athletes themselves thought otherwise. In 1931, former Women's Swimming Association Olympian Ethel McGary suggested, to The Sportswoman readers, that "since there always exists a certain amount of competition, it really seems more logical to work for improved conditions in this through education" instead of alienating athletes by opposing competition. Other prominent athletes wrote similarly.

Egalitarian as it sounded and accurate as the physical educators' perception of American sports was, "play for play's sake" was a problematic alternative. It could hardly have succeeded in such a highly competitive society. But beyond that, modified stakes in modified games did not inspire girls to participate, nor schools to provide facilities and funding. Wayman's denial aside, most female physical educators were hostile to competition itself, not just to its excesses. The play days they advocated were trivial and boring. Why, asked a dissenting teacher in 1939, did college women hate gym class and shun sports in their spare time? "Heretical as it sounds," she answered, slogans such as "A Game for Every Girl and A Girl for Every Game" were meaningless "theme songs" which had failed. Not every girl wanted a game, she claimed, especially the games educators liked.[31]

Three Decades of Inactivity

The Sportswoman's dissolution in 1936 ended the first wave of athletic feminism. The second, beginning in the early 1970s, came after more than three decades of inactivity. Between the 1930s and the 1970s, the basic premises of women's athletics remained unchanged. Player pressure steadily forced educators to liberalize basketball rules, but modified games and play days continued at least through the early 1960s. In 1967, an article in *Today's Health*, published by the American Medical Association, advised for "sound reasons" that girls refrain from contact sports. "The female breasts and other organs can be injured seriously by a sudden blow. The danger of scars, broken teeth, or other results of injury probably are more of a psychological hazard for girls than for boys."[32] Two years later, Yale philosopher Paul Weiss suggested, like countless educators before him, that women be viewed as "truncated males" capable of men's sports in "foreshortened versions."[33]

Athletic women from the 1930s through the 1960s had few options if they wanted to avoid the masculine stereotype. Sportswriter Paul Gallico had wryly remarked in 1936 that women looked beautiful in only eight of twenty-five sports. Some sports, including ball games, were out for making women perspire. The acceptable included archery, shooting, fishing, riding, flying, and skating because women moved gracefully, if at all, and wore "some pretty cute costumes."[34] Thirty years later, a similar attitude prevailed. A majority of the people interviewed by *Today's Health* writers thought most sports unfeminine except the traditional ones of swimming, tennis, golf, girls' basketball, and a little track. Even these sports were considered unfeminine if serious competition was involved.

One 1934 study had found athletic high school girls no different—no more "mannish" though perhaps more outgoing—than their nonathletic peers.[35] However, the work of psychologist Lewis M. Terman later in that decade showed otherwise, and it was the Terman study that was widely publicized. In 1939, *Good Housekeeping* reported that Terman had devised a Masculinity-Femininity Quotient test for his book *Sex and Personality*.[36] By conventional standards, male engineers and college athletes had responded the "most masculinely" and female athletes and physicians the "least femininely" to the questions. Both Terman and the magazine observed that such judgments could change as society's standards changed. But neither noted that mastery or total control of the body was a power shared by athletes and physicians and was what probably made them equally "unfeminine."

In the post–World War II era, athletic women improved their skills and records, but not their numbers or image. A 1950 estimate was that merely five percent of professional athletes were female.[37] Athletic women's "masculinity" became popular and academic dogma, with Terman's study setting the tone for postwar analyses. Sports sociologist Gregory Stone observed, in 1955, that little was known about the female player except that she was masculine.[38] In 1967, a psychiatrist writing on "The Superior Athlete" paused to consider women:

Someone is bound to ask: "What about female athletes?" Female athletes, no less than female nonathletes, present special problems in evaluation. I am aware of no one who claims any special competence in assessing either group. . . . The real enigma is in the reconciliation of the soft, physiologically, socially and culturally determined maternal inclinations with the harsh phallic requisites of competitive sports at a superior level.[39]

The Seventies and Beyond

Throughout the twentieth century, women's growing autonomy, education, and economic productivity have blurred the once clear distinction between masculine and feminine. The changes in work and family relationships begun by industrialization a century ago have intensified since World War II. Forty percent of the workforce was female in 1975, double the 1920 figure. Between 1965 and 1975, women accounted for three-fifths of the expansion in nonmilitary fields of work. In 1976, the Department of Labor announced that the two-income family had become the norm. Other statistics confirm an increase in single-parent households. This blurring of sex roles has left some people frightened and confused, although others see it as a healthy development for both sexes.

In his 1967 "psycho-social" study of sport, psychiatrist Arnold R. Beisser observed that the athletic world's traditional ordering of relationships has helped blunt the impact of change elsewhere:

It is small wonder that the American male has a strong affinity for sports. He has learned that this is one area where there is no doubt about sexual differences and where his biology is not obsolete. Athletics help assure his difference from women in a world where his functions have come to resemble theirs.

Beisser concluded that "sports represent the cultural safety valve . . . the great arena in which the historical traditional roles of the sexes can be played."[40] If so, then attempts to unplug the valve by altering roles inside this last bastion of tradition understandably meet strong resistance.

The changes of recent years have not, however, bypassed athletics; today's women's movement has revived sports as a feminist issue. The athletic feminism of the seventies is different from that of the past in its legal, equal-rights orientation and its appeal to female athletes. The two go together. Though all women involved in sports and physical education in the 1920s and 1930s complained of having less staff, funding, and facilities than men, top players could hardly have joined in the demands of women's sports organizations for less competition. A sisterly alliance between athletes and educators was thus impossible.

Today's athletic feminism is different because feminism is different. Unlike their predecessors, contemporary feminists rarely argue for goals on the basis of women's moral superiority or physical inferiority. The roots of modern feminism lie in the civil rights and antiwar movements of the 1960s—hence the emphasis on equality and the search for legal solutions. In sports, this has led to a rash of court cases invalidating sex segregation in Little League, and to Title IX, the 1975 HEW directive prohibiting sex discrimination in sports conducted by federally assisted institutions and organizations. Almost all schools and colleges receive some federal assistance, and so Title IX applies to a huge number of institutions. Some schools, such as Stanford University, have merged the men's and women's athletic departments, a controversial move that any previous generation of physical educators would have opposed, and that many still question. Noticeably, today's athletic feminism is more the work of lawyers and athletes than of physical educators. *The Sportswoman* was published by the U.S. Field Hockey Association, a women's organization dominated by educators. *WomenSports*, the major women's athletic magazine of the 1970s, was published by athlete Billie Jean King and advocated total sexual equality in competitive sports.

Attitudinal gains lag behind the legal ones. Despite favorable decisions, few girls participate in Little League and related organizations because females are still discouraged from team and contact sports. Those who attempt involvement are frequently harassed. In 1975, a suburban Little League in Michigan insisted that a female player comply with regulations by wearing an athletic supporter. In his 1976 *Sports in America*, novelist James Michener considered the "problems" of sex-integrated teams, especially for girls and boys aged eleven to twenty-two. He shared the concern of coaches who had "warned [him] that they would not wish their thirteen- and fourteen-year-old boys to compete against girls in public situations in which a defeat might be interpreted as a failure in manliness."[41]

Athletics are still largely viewed as an expression of male sexuality and power, a world in which women are intruders but not rightful heirs. In 1973, the authors of a three-part series in *Sports Illustrated* on female athletics found physicians, educators, and athletic personnel across the country indifferent or hostile to the subject. Most claimed that sports did not provide the same educational and physical benefits for women as for men, that women did not want sports, and that women's sports were economically unprofitable. The writers painstakingly refuted each point: if sports were educationally valid, then they were as valid for women as for men; women's physical capabilities were unknown, untested, and submerged in myths; and the popularity of women's tennis, girls' basketball in Iowa (where it is a major spectator sport), and roller derby (a violent sport and the only one in which women have numerical parity) proved women's athletic marketability. A year later the writers reported that many of the schools and colleges had improved their resource allocations and their attitudes, though not enough.[42] Zealously guarding the status quo, a well-financed male college sports lobby successfully diluted the final version of Title IX in 1975. Their desire to share athletic budgets with women was, to understate it, minimal. The vagueness of the guideline makes meaningful program reform, let alone equality, unlikely.

Still, activists have done much to open sport's professional and material rewards to women. They have won larger budgets, staffs, and programs in many schools and colleges. They have provided role models and helped foster an atmosphere supportive of women's athleticism. They have promoted "unfeminine" and contact sports as well as the traditional ones. In 1976, the New York Times reported that about 10,000 American women were weight lifting, compared to a few hundred in 1974. Weight lifting has always been among the most masculine of sports, though female athletes have done it moderately for conditioning. The Times quoted a California YMCA instructor who said the sport was growing fastest among housewives and office workers, "women under twenty-five who weren't crushed by the old stereotypes" and accepted "the idea that there is no such thing as a masculine or feminine sport."[43]

At some point, however, activists will have to regain earlier generations' awareness of the limitations of equality. In transcending their restricted past, women are uncritically courting an athletic structure which heaps enormous resources on a few participants and underserves most of the populace. A growing number of male athletes have deserted or denounced the sports world in recent years, charging that its exaggerated pursuit of victory and profit leaves players overworked, underpaid, and physically subservient to coaches and owners. "I would never say that athletes are exactly like slaves were," former New York Jets player George Sauer has claimed. "But there is something about organized athletics that treats an athlete somewhat as a slave. The attitude still exists that we are a body and that we are property. . . ."[44]

For these reasons, some feminists are urging women to reject athletic scholarships. A 1972 writer described the scarcity of women's athletic scholarships not as discrimination but as "a blessing in disguise, since without athletic scholarships the possibility of maintaining sport as an experience to enhance the individual exists to a greater degree for women than for the male collegiate athlete."[45] Female physical educators traditionally made this claim; it was a staple of athletic feminism in the past. Its truth is debatable, given most women's limited economic resources. And its parallels with "play for play's sake," which activists today blame for holding women back, make it unpopular.

Women's effort to liberalize the sports structure that exists rather than to oppose it or forge an alternate one is momentarily their best option. Like all discriminated-against groups, women stand to gain more from equality than they would lose. If they can erase sport's masculine identity, as blacks have changed sport's earlier racist character, and acquire athletic habits, as men do from childhood through adolescence, women will have gained a great deal. In fighting for equality, however, women ideally would keep in mind what Jack Scott, director of the Institute for the Study of Sport and Society and former physical education chairperson of Oberlin College, calls sport's "radical ethic": the belief that athletic excellence is obtainable within a humane, democratic, and widely accessible structure.[46] Women can work to avoid the most authoritarian, alienating, and corrupt aspects of men's sports, while still striving for mastery and achievement.

Sport is part of a larger movement for female physical autonomy, a movement in which efforts to gain control over pregnancy, birth, family size, and individual safety figure prominently. As this movement proceeds, athletics may well form its backbone.

Notes

1 Theodora Wells, "Woman—Which Includes Men, of Course . . . , An Experience in Awareness," *Association for Humanistic Psychology Newsletter* 7, no. 3 (December 1970).
2 For a humorous reversal of this, see the K.N.O.W. publication by psychotherapist Joyce Jennings Walstedt, "Corporeal Orgasm and Personality Development in the Human Male (A Spoof in the Manner of Freud)," (September 1970).
3 Dr. Dudley A. Sargent, "Are Athletics Making Girls Masculine?" *Ladies' Home Journal* 29 (March 1912): 71. See p. 52 of this book.
4 Sophie C. Elliott-Lynn, *Athletics for Women and Girls: How to Be an Athlete and Why* (London: Robert Scott, Roxburghe House, 1925), p. 65. She was the vice president of England's Women's Amateur Athletic Association.
5 Emily James Putnam, *The Lady: Studies of Certain Significant Phases of Her History* (Chicago: University of Chicago Press, 1970), p. 13.
6 David Hunt, *Parents and Children in History: The Psychology of Family Life in Early Modern France* (New York: Basic Books, Inc., 1970), p. 88.
7 Carroll Smith-Rosenberg and Charles Rosenberg, "The Female Animal: Medical and Biological Views of Woman and Her Role in Nineteenth-Century America," *Journal of American History* 60, no. 2 (September 1973): 335.
8 Foster Rhea Dulles, *A History of Recreation: America Learns to Play*, 2nd ed. (New York: Appleton-Century-Crofts, 1965), p. 96.
9 Barbara Ehrenreich and Deirdre English, *Complaints and Disorders: The Sexual Politics of Sickness* (Old Westbury, N.Y.: The Feminist Press, 1973), p. 11.
10 Eleanor Flexner, *Century of Struggle: The Woman's Rights Movement in the United States* (New York: Atheneum, 1970), pp. 90–91.
11 Dr. Grace Peckham Murray, "The Health of Professional Women," *Harper's Bazar* 34, no. 17 (27 April 1901): 1117.
12 Thomas Woody, *A History of Women's Education in the United States*, vol. II (New York: The Science Press, 1929), pp. 109–110.
13 Ben Barker-Benfield, "The Spermatic Economy: A Nineteenth-Century View of Sexuality," *Feminist Studies* 1, no. 1 (Summer 1972): 46.
14 William Arens, "The Great American Football Ritual," *Natural History* (October 1975): 79–80.
15 Theodore Roosevelt, "Value of an Athletic Training," *Harper's Weekly* 37, no. 1931 (23 December 1893): 1236.
16 Florence E. Canfield, "Give the Girls a Chance," *Collier's* 44, no. 25 (12 March 1910): 20; Jane Addams, "Some Reflections on the Failure of the Modern City to Provide Recreation for Young Girls," *Charities and the Commons* 21 (5 December 1908): 365–68.
17 William I. Thomas, *Sex and Society; Studies in the Social Psychology of Sex* (Chicago: University of Chicago Press, 1907), chapter 1, based on an 1897 article.
18 Sarah Addington, "The Athletic Limitations of Women," *Ladies' Home Journal* 40 (June 1923): 144.
19 Josephine Schmid, "Some Sport Activities at the University of Texas," *The Sportswoman* 3, no. 10 (June 1927): 23.
20 Frank G. Menke, sports encyclopedist, gave the figure and ranked swimming second.
21 Mary Roberts Coolidge, "Clelia Duel Mosher, the Scientific Feminist," *Research Quarterly* 12, no. 3, supplement (October 1941): 640–41.
22 Alice Allene Sefton, *The Women's Division, National Amateur Athletic Federation: Sixteen Years of Progress in Athletics for Girls and Women* (Palo Alto: Stanford University Press, 1941), p. 2.

[23] Martha Wolfenstein, "The Emergence of Fun Morality," in *Mass Leisure*, ed. Eric Larrabee and Rolf Meyersohn (Glencoe, Ill.: The Free Press, 1958), pp. 86–95.
[24] Quentin Reynolds, "Round and Round," *Collier's* 98, no. 8 (22 August 1936): 15.
[25] "Sketches from Helen: A Novel from Suzanne," *Literary Digest* 89, no. 3 (17 April 1926): 66.
[26] Frank J. Taylor, "Fast and Pretty," *Collier's* 102, no. 8 (20 August 1938): 23.
[27] *Women's Swimming Association News* 7 (March 1927): 3.
[28] Agnes R. Wayman, "Let's Take It in Our Stride," *The Sportswoman* 10, no. 7 (March 1934): 14; Sefton, *The Women's Division*, p. 29.
[29] John R. Tunis, *Democracy and Sport* (New York: A. S. Barnes & Co., 1941), p. 42.
[30] H. W. Whicker, "Growing Up to Play," *The North American Review* 235, no. 5 (May 1933): 469–70.
[31] Mary C. Baker, "The 'Love of Strenuous Activity Among College Women' Myth," *School and Society* 49 (18 February 1939): 208–12.
[32] Rose and Hal Higdon, "What Sports for Girls?" *Today's Health* 45, no. 10 (October 1967): 21.
[33] Paul Weiss, *Sport: A Philosophical Inquiry* (Carbondale & Edwardsville, Ill.: Southern Illinois University Press, 1969), p. 215. See p. 62 of this book.
[34] Paul Gallico, "Women in Sports Should Look Beautiful," *The Reader's Digest* 29 (August 1936): 12–14.
[35] Dr. Edwin G. Flemming, "Personality and the Athletic Girl," *School and Society* 39 (10 February 1934): 166–69.
[36] Amram Scheinfeld, "A Test for Femininity," *Good Housekeeping* 108 (February 1939): 59–60.
[37] Gregory P. Stone, "American Sports: Play and Dis-Play," in *Mass Leisure*, ed. Larrabee and Meyersohn, p. 260.
[38] *Ibid.*, p. 260.
[39] Stephen D. Ward, "The Superior Athlete," in *Motivations in Play, Games and Sport*, ed. Ralph Slovenko and James A. Knight (Springfield, Ill.: Charles C. Thomas, Publisher, 1967), p. 311.
[40] Arnold R. Beisser, *The Madness in Sports: Psycho-Social Observations on Sports* (New York: Appleton-Century-Crofts, 1967), pp. 198, 225.
[41] James A. Michener, *Sports in America* (New York: Random House, Inc., 1976), p. 126.
[42] Bil Gilbert and Nancy Williamson, "Women in Sport" (3-part series), *Sports Illustrated* 38, no. 21 (28 May 1973); 38, no. 22 (4 June 1973); 38, no. 23 (11 June 1973).
[43] Sharon Johnson, "A Little Weightlifting to Get into Feminine Shape," *New York Times*, 13 December 1976, p. 46.
[44] Paul Hoch, *Rip Off the Big Game: The Exploitation of Sports by the Power Elite* (Garden City, N.Y.: Anchor Books, 1972), p. 111.
[45] Darlene Kelly, "Women and Sports," *Women: A Journal of Liberation* 3, no. 2: 16.
[46] Jack Scott, "A Radical Ethic For Sports," *Intellectual Digest* 2, no. 11 (July 1972): 49–50. See p. 182 of this book.

Out of
the Bleachers

Writings on Women and Sport

To Alexandra

ONE: Physiology and Social Attitudes

Separating Fact from Fiction

"SPORT IS MALE TERRITORY," writes female physical educator M. Marie Hart. When women invade that territory, they are often confronted with passionate arguments that are variations on two themes: women are physically inferior to men; sports

are not feminine. These criticisms of women's full participation in sports are not generally based on fact, but they have had a powerful impact on women's lives nonetheless. Some of the selections in this section set forth these arguments: they discourage or propose limits to female athletics. Significant historically, they also illustrate the persistence of such attitudes into the present, despite strong scientific evidence that would seem to refute them. They are important, too, because, as Hart notes, one must understand current practices and social attitudes in order to change them. Other selections in this section present facts about physiology that clearly support

women's full participation in sports; some pieces also analyze
the social attitudes that have limited such participation.

Although sex-related differences probably have some bearing
on women's athletic potential, Dr. Thomas Shaffer and Ann
Crittenden indicate that differences of strength, endurance,
and athletic ability are greater within each sex than between
the sexes. Further, because physical conditioning greatly affects
athletic performance, and because women have not had the
same kind of physical conditioning as men, we cannot know
exactly how significant sex-related differences are for athletic
achievement. We do know that certain traditional beliefs about
women's alleged physical limitations are no longer valid:
women have won Olympic medals during all phases of their
menstrual cycles, for example. Similarly, pregnant women have
competed successfully; at the 1964 Olympics in Australia, ten
out of the twenty-six Soviet women champions were pregnant.

If women are physically capable of performing and excelling
in all sports, what is stopping them? The answer, frequently,
is social attitudes and social conditioning. Discussing women
who have become athletes, M. Marie Hart states that, "for
longer than one can remember, women in sport have known
and experienced rejection due to their failure to live up to a
particular concept of 'feminine.'" In her 1899 article, Dr.
Arabella Kenealy does not doubt that women are physically
able to participate in sports. She warns her readers, however,
that if women spend too much time on athletics, they will not
fulfill their "womanly duties"—taking care of home and family.
Kenealy is also concerned with the athlete's new physical
appearance: "In her evening gown she shows evidence of joints
which had been adroitly hidden. . . ." When Dr. Dudley Allen
Sargent wrote "Are Athletics Making Girls Masculine?" in
1912, he was responding to arguments like Kenealy's. Although
Sargent was instrumental in encouraging female athletics in
the late nineteenth and early twentieth century, he, too, was
concerned with the social implications of women's participation in sports. He would have viewed Kenealy as an alarmist,
though: "Much of the reading matter put forth . . . so utterly
disregards truth and reason that we are in danger of half

believing that womankind has already become a distorted Amazon creation, to be talked about and wondered at, but no longer to be loved and admired."

In spite of women's increased sports participation and their demonstrated ability to excel in a wide variety of sports formerly considered beyond women's physical capabilities, philosopher Paul Weiss, writing fifty-seven years later than Sargent, is no more progressive in his views. He implies that all differences between the sexes—in thought, action, and attitudes—are biologically determined and thus unchangeable. His analysis rests on undocumented assertions like, "Young men are restless and exuberant . . . while women are content to move smoothly, using their energies to improve the union of body and mind that is natural to them."

Although opposition to women's full participation in sports continues, as evidenced by the Weiss selection, the view that athletic ability is individual rather than sex-linked is slowly gaining acceptance. Ann Crittenden explains: "The physically inferior, it turns out, are not women, but any human beings who do not develop the body's potential—exactly what women have been taught not to do for centuries. Just how much that indoctrination has cost them is only now being revealed, as more and more girls challenge the age-old prejudices defining their physical capacities."

Closing the Muscle Gap

By Ann Crittenden

Ann Crittenden, a former Newsweek *correspondent, is currently a financial writer and reporter for the* New York Times. *She has won several journalism awards and lectured at Yale University. In this article, which appeared in* Ms. Magazine *in 1974, Crittenden reviews women's athletic gains and the state of female physiology research. She emphasizes the importance of physical conditioning and training, and suggests how the gap between women's and men's athletic performance can be narrowed.*

The author of nature gave man strength of body and intrepidity of mind to enable him to face great hardships, and to woman was given a weak and delicate constitution, accompanied by a natural softness and modest timidity, which fit her for sedentary life.—Aristotle, "Physiognomics" (4th century B.C.)

Woman is "defective and accidental ... a male gone awry ... the result of some weakness in the [father's] generative power. ..."—St. Thomas Aquinas (13th century)

I will make you acquainted with the proportions of a man; I omit those of a woman, because there is not one of them perfectly proportioned.—Author (unknown) of a Renaissance treatise on painting (16th century)

One way of dealing with these disparities between the athletic promise and achievement of men and women is to view women as truncated males. As such they should be permitted to engage in such sports as men do ... but in foreshortened versions.—Paul Weiss, Professor of Philosophy at Yale (1969)

Of all the repressions visited on woman by the heavy-handed centuries of paternalism, perhaps the most insidious has been the denial of her physical powers. Despite the fact that the average man is larger, heavier, and stronger than the average woman, it is now clear that those differences are far less than it formerly appeared. Evidence shows that the difference in strength between trained male and female athletes is far less than that between average or untrained men and women. And it is equally clear that the differences of strength within either sex are far greater than the differences between them.

The male's "overwhelming" superiority of strength and endurance may be, as Dr. Jack Wilmore of the University of California at Davis has written, more an "artifact of social or cultural restriction imposed on the female ... than a result of true biological difference in performance potential between the sexes." The physically inferior, it turns out, are not women, but any human beings who do not develop the body's potential—exactly what women have been taught not to do for centuries. Just how much that indoctrination has cost them is only now being revealed, as more and more girls challenge the age-old prejudices defining their physical capacities.

Nowhere is the narrowing gap between young men and women so well demonstrated as in the record books of international competitions. Twenty-five years ago the women's outdoor world record for the 100-meter dash was 11.5 seconds, compared with a men's record of 10.2. Today men can cover the 100 meters in 9.9 seconds, an improvement of .3 seconds, while women have shaved a full .7 seconds off their time—now 10.8, or only .9 seconds off the time of the men.

Even more dramatic gains have been made in swimming, where women have been competing on an international level for a longer period, and therefore come closer to fulfilling their potential. In the 1924 Olympic games, for example, the men's winning time in the 400-meter freestyle was 16 percent faster than the women's. This lead was reduced to 11.66 percent by 1948, and cut to only 7.3 percent in Munich in 1972. Today's stars, like Debbie Meyer and Shane Gould, could have driven Tarzan back into the trees; Gould's current women's world record for the 400-meter freestyle is 4:21.2, a pool-length ahead of Johnny Weismuller's men's record of 4:52.0 in 1927.

Track experts expect that the present 15.9 percent faster performance of men in the mile run will soon be reduced just as impressively. A few physiologists, such as Dr. Jerry Mogel at Queens College in New York, even refuse to rule out the possibility that a woman might eventually turn out to be the fastest runner in the world, at least in the distance runs, where brute muscle strength counts for less. At the very least, as more women compete and stay in competition until full maturity, the gap between the sexes in most physical tests could well be narrowed to 10 percent or less.

For the moment, however, such speculations about women's athletic potential remain just that, for the truth of female power still lies buried under centuries of sexist dogma. Even today the secrecy and ignorance surrounding the subject of female physiology are staggering, if not surprising. Only a fraction of physical education research deals with women's performance or compares men and women under conditions of maximum effort. "It's almost as if there were a cultural or professional taboo against designing a research study involving women," comments Dr. Clayton L. Thomas, vice-president of medical affairs for Tampax and one of the few experts on female physiology in the male-dominated medical field. (Only 7 percent of American doctors are women, and of some 250 exercise physiologists in the country, fewer than 10 are female.)

There are almost no studies of the long-range effects of strenuous conditioning programs on women. There is virtually no information on the physical capabilities of older women, and little is known about the physical advantage that girls aged 12 to 14 have over boys of the same age. The influence of sexual activity on women's performance has never been studied. (Masters and Johnson found it had no effect on the muscular performance of men.) Nor has anyone studied the influence of menstrual cramps (dysmenorrhea), although, as Thomas points out, "If men had cramps, we'd have had a National Institute of Dysmenorrhea for years." Worst of all, the effects of birth-control pills on a woman's strength, coordination, timing, endurance, and emotional stability are still a mystery, although one 1969 experiment indicated that the additional estrogen in most pills might cause women to be less physically active.

"All in all, what we know, compared to what we don't know, is a drop in the bucket," according to Dr. Dorothy Harris, whose new Center for Women in Sport at Penn State University in College Park, Pennsylvania, is attempting to dispel some of the uncertainties.

What we *do* know is that throughout childhood, boys and girls are roughly similar in size, strength, and reaction times. Girls aged 9 to 12 are, if anything, larger and stronger than their male peers because their bone structure and musculature begin developing earlier and mature by age 12 or 13. Boys do not generally achieve the same stage of development until age 14, 15, or 16.

At adolescence, however, a sharp divergence between untrained male and female performance begins and continues until well after middle age. When physical maturity is reached, young men are on the average about 10 percent larger than young women, and their muscle mass is about twice that of girls. They perform two to four times as well in tests of strength, according to Dr. Thomas Shaffer, pediatrics professor at Ohio State University. In sum, the skimpy evidence that exists indicates that adult men are at least 30 percent stronger than women until both subside into a more or less equally feeble old age.

The question is, why?

Much of the answer lies in the male hormone, androgen, which produces denser bones and stimulates the growth of muscle tissue. As a result, men are not only larger and heavier than women in general, but a normal man of any given size will have more muscle, or lean body mass, than a woman of similar build (or than a man with a lower androgen level). Athletes know all this very well, and those dependent on brute strength, such as football players and weight lifters, frequently (and illicitly) beef themselves up with male hormones in the form of anabolic steroids. Even a few female athletes have been known to indulge in order to perk up a performance. But no one takes female hormones for the same purpose—they simply wouldn't do the job.

From infancy, males also display a smaller amount of fat tissue than females, a distinction which increases after adolescence. Apparently no amount of conditioning can make women as lean, proportionately, as men. College-age men in the United States, for example, average 15 percent body fat; women some 25 percent. In trained athletes, however, the difference is far less, although males are still lower on the average than females. (One national study of 27 female track stars showed that seven had less than 10 percent body fat. Two had fat values of less than 7.5 percent, which was the average for 114 male competitors at the 1968 U.S. Olympic Marathon Trial.) Despite the exceptions, even most women athletes are like racehorses with a heavier handicap; that extra load of fat they have to carry around has a direct and negative effect on their work capacity and stamina.

(It is important to note, however, that fatty tissue gives

women extra buoyancy and an added insulation against cold. It is no accident that women hold the records for swimming the English Channel, and that the daring food divers off the coasts of Korea and Japan are predominantly women.)

Women's stamina—their ability to perform at maximum capacity and over an extended period of time—may be genetically less than men's for two other reasons. Endurance depends on the ability to take oxygen from the air and then send it to the muscles. Men have proportionately larger hearts and lungs, enabling them to pump more blood to the tissues, and they have higher concentrations of hemoglobin, the oxygen carrier in the blood. It is still unclear to what extent these factors limit female endurance, or if they actually do at all, but it is at least true that in all comparisons so far between men and women with equal degrees of conditioning, the men's maximum oxygen intake is higher.

Nevertheless, an athletic woman will have a much greater oxygen intake capacity than an untrained man—by 25 percent in one study. And there is a broad overlap between the sexes in all tests of strength and stamina, even though women's opportunities for physical development are still pitifully limited.

But far more significant than the "anything you can do I can do better" comparison game is the fact that when encouraged, women can shatter all the stereotypes about the gentle, weaker sex. Young 14- to 17-year-old female athletes are handling weights of up to 40 pounds without reaching maximum capacity, and female swimmers are covering 8,000 to 12,000 yards in two two-hour sessions a day. Women distance runners, limited in the Olympics to nothing longer than the 1500-meter race (approximately one mile), chalk up 100 miles a week in training sessions. And after a few weeks in a conditioning course at Queens College in New York, sedentary coeds can do 200 sit-ups and run a half hour without stopping. "Women have been babied in the past," says Dr. Frank Katch, their instructor. "They've never been pushed hard enough or given strenuous training. I predict there'll be a revolution in the next five years in what women can do."

There may well be, for women are discovering that the secret of their physical intimidation by men is as simple as a saying of Mao and as close as the nearest gym: conditioning. By developing her powers to the fullest, any woman, from Olympic star to the weekend tennis player, can be a match for any man she chooses to take on. More importantly, she will inherit the essential source of human self-confidence—pride in and control over a finely tuned body. That alone would be a revolution.

Physiological Considerations of the Female Participant

By Thomas E. Shaffer, M.D.

Dr. Thomas E. Shaffer, professor of pediatrics at Ohio State University, presented this paper at a 1972 conference on Women and Sport at Pennsylvania State University. Reviewing recent studies in biology, he concludes that sex-related differences in physical performance exist, but that they are less significant than differences among individuals of the same sex.

In preparing this paper I have had to consider whether guidelines for women's participation in sports should differ from those for men simply on a basis of sex or whether there are more pertinent criteria, such as size, strength, vital capacity, etc. What is the extent of sex differences, and are they important, aside from the reproductive function? I have concluded that the relevant issues are sex-related, directly or indirectly.

Very real physiological differences between the sexes exist and they are established at the very earliest stage of life, when spermatozoon meets ovum. At this time genetic sex is established. Whether an individual's sex chromosome constitution includes two X chromosomes or one X and one Y (and this is decided almost entirely by chance) determines later sexual differentiation. An individual's sex will be female when the fertilized egg contains two X chromosomes (male when there is one X and one Y). Research tells us that many more males than females are conceived, the ratio being about 130 males to 100 females. These data, obtained from examinations of fetuses, stillborn, and living infants, suggest that the determination of sex is not entirely on a 50–50 chance. Apparently spermatozoa bearing the Y chromosome have greater speed or other capability in reaching the unfertilized egg in the fallopian tubes than do those carrying the X variety. Theoretically there are equal numbers of each type.

The sexual development of the fetus is undifferentiated during the early weeks. However, when there is a Y chromosome on the scene, testes develop in the fetus. In the absence of the male or Y chromosome, the embryonic genital tract develops in the female pattern and this will occur even when there is no X chromosome, in experimental studies. It seems that a substance produced within the embryonic testis suppresses the more basic tendency for development along female lines. When the fetal testis has been removed experimentally, a fully developed female genital tract will result even in a genetically male embryo. In such experiments, the fetus is born with fallopian tubes, uterus, vagina, and vulva of essentially normal type. These observations indicate that there is a basic inclination for early embryologic development to follow the female pattern unless inhibited by a fetal testis, and give some backing to Dr. Ruth Pick's statement that "a male is simply an imperfect female." Ashley Montagu points out that no fertilized ovum can survive unless it contains at least one X chromosome and thus males exist only because they are endowed with an X chromosome by their mothers.

There are additional facts to support Dr. Pick's views. Starting with the ratio of 130:100, the male:female ratio at the time of birth is 106:100, indication that there is a considerable loss of life in the male population in utero. This trend persists after birth, with significantly more mortality among males throughout life. Life expectancy for males at birth is 66.6 years and for females it is 74 years. Starting off with a ratio of 106:

100, males are outnumbered in the population after the second decade of life.

Of 365 diseases listed by one observer more or less at random, 245 occurred predominantly in males.[1] Another writer reports that of 88 diseases, 59 occur preponderantly in the males while 29 are more common in females.[2] It is a shocking fact that two-thirds of the married women in the United States are widows by the age of 65. The evidence seems clear that from a constitutional standpoint woman is the stronger sex, and presumably this is all due to a second X chromosome.

How can we account for this phenomenon? One explanation might be that the Y chromosome, being smaller, contains fewer genes than the X variety. This could be a serious handicap if deficiencies of enzymes, antibodies, and other constitutional qualities would result. . . . Furthermore, antibodies to certain bacteria have been found to be slightly higher in female infants, and the antibody response of female children to German measles vaccine was found to exceed the response by male children, slightly but consistently, in each of ten field trials involving 15,000 children.[3] A decided advantage in having two X chromosomes is that one of them can protect a woman against defective genes of the other. Here take hemophilia as an example, and recall that women transmit but do not manifest the disease.

From conception on throughout the life cycle the female has many physiological characteristics which differ from the male. Prenatally there are differences in development which result in the female infant being smaller but more physiologically mature at birth.

The ovary is the hub of female physiology. This small organ has two important functions: to produce ova and to produce hormones. The full quota of ova, to last throughout the reproductive years, is produced early, being present in the ovary at birth, waiting for hormonal stimulus at puberty. This situation of being ready for stimulation, but remaining dormant, applies to the entire reproductive system.[4]

The pituitary gland is believed to be capable of producing hormones very early in life which stimulate sexual development but the system is quiescent until puberty. . . . At that time, a year or more before the first menstruation, a pituitary hormone causes estrogen to be produced in the follicles around some ova and the results are very obvious changes in a pubertal girl. There is accelerated growth in height, rapid development of breasts, typical changes in the pelvic bones, along with a different typically feminine pattern of fat distribution. Axillary and pubic hair appear and increase at the same time under the influence of newly-produced adrenal hormones. The menarche, or first menstrual period, concludes the pattern of female pubertal development, occurring after all sex characteristics are well developed.

There is a definite trend for pubertal development to appear about four months earlier in each successive generation. The menarche which once occurred around the age of 17 years now appears typically at 12½–13 years, although there is a wide difference in the time of normal sexual maturation. Earlier sexual maturation signifies also an earlier onset of physical growth and physical development, because these are under hormonal regulation. Linear growth (height) is almost completed by the time menstruation begins.

The trend toward earlier sexual maturation is not the only evidence that growth has been speeded up in the past 100 years. Cone[5] and Tanner[6] have summarized impressive evidence for earlier growth and development in successive generations. There has been an average increase in adolescents' height and weight, amounting to about one-half inch and three pounds per decade. Maximal height in girls, now attained at 16–17 years of age, probably was not reached until the third decade fifty years ago. The reasons for these changes are obviously better nutrition, fewer illnesses, improved living standards and the general results of health education. The significance for our consideration is that strength, endurance, and motor coordination are related to maturation, and thus the age of participation in sports has dropped and will continue to do so for a while at least.

Although there is no significant difference in size of boys and girls of the same age during the first ten years of life, girls are ahead of boys in maturation throughout this period. There is a slight difference in bone age at birth and by ten years the girls are definitely 12 to 18 months ahead of boys of the same age in this particular aspect of physiological development. Girls begin their adolescent growth spurt in the period between 10½ and 13 years of age, and it is terminated at the onset of menstruation by virtual cessation of skeletal growth. About two more inches of growth occur after the menarche, total growth being completed by about 16 years of age.

Boys' growth spurts occur between the ages of 12½ and 15 years. These extra years of physical growth, under the influence of growth hormone, prior to sexual maturity, account for the greater size of males. Young men generally are about 10 percent larger than young women when growth ends. This applies to height, weight and other external measurements. Union of all epiphyses to the main portion of the bones has occurred by the age of 16 years in girls and 18 years for boys. Late maturing girls would have a longer period of skeletal growth and thus greater height and longer legs and arms than would occur on the usual schedule.

The amount of muscle is almost identical in children of either sex in the first decade of life. Muscles, like other tissues, increase during adolescence, their peak growth occurring a few months after the greatest increment of height growth. At maturity, however, the muscle mass in women is about one-half that of men. The reason for this is the effect of androgens (male sex hormone) on muscles.

In girls the most rapid increase in strength occurs before the menarche, with a diminishing increment for a few years thereafter. Jones[7] has pointed out that the "early maturing individuals are on the average superior in strength to the late maturing. This is most marked in boys at about the age of 14½ years and in girls at 13." Early maturing girls show a characteristically early arrest in development of strength as well as height. Espenschade[8] found that the motor skills of girls do not improve after the age of 14 years.

Body Composition. Body composition in children shows a significant sex difference at 9 years of age with boys being leaner than girls. Girls from 13 to 14 are less fat but soon after the menarche women consistently have more fat than do males. All studies indicate that from the pre-adolescent period on, boys are leaner than girls, and men leaner than women. The greater amount of fat and its distribution in the human female is regulated by estrogen, an ovarian hormone. Fat in females is distributed to the pelvic girdle, buttocks, thighs, shoulders and breasts. Being sex-determined and a source of energy stored for future needs, the fat would appear to be related to pregnancy needs. Body fat may be determined by measuring the thickness of skinfolds at various sites on the body. Appraised by this method, boys are leaner than girls. Girls show a steady increase of body fat from six years on, with an acceleration at the time of the menarche. . . .

The significance of the amount of fat in the female body is that there is more fat and less muscle per unit volume, and this has significance for a woman's work capacity, endurance, and athletic performance, in which strength is a factor. . . .

Muscle. Women's peak growth in strength occurs at the chronological age of 12½ years and, when related to the menarche, invariably peak strength is obtained in the year before that event. The inception of the strength spurt is correlated with maturational indices such as maximum increase in height, sex maturation and bone age rather than with chronological age. By the seventeenth year, males excel females two to four times in tests of strength, because of the greater muscle mass in males. This larger muscle mass is attributed to the effects of the male sex hormones, and to the greater ratio of muscle to fat in males. There is no evidence that there is a difference in neuromuscular efficiency or in quality of the muscle in males.

Although women's maximal strength capacity is about one-half that of men, male and female are equally efficient at all ages in skilled work of mild intensity. . . .

Cardiovascular. Maximal physical performance depends on capacity to deliver energy, and on mechanical efficiency (skill and technique). The superiority of an athlete lies in her ability to meet the demand for oxygen.

As has been mentioned, during puberty the longer period of growth in males permits increase in size of the body components before cessation of growth. Thus the male's heart is larger, as are the lungs, liver, and other organs.

In general, at all ages females have a faster pulse rate than males, at rest and exertion. After puberty, females have lower blood pressure than males.

Brouha[9] states that during exercise the heart rates of women are higher than those of men and their recovery to the pre-exercise level is slower. In both sexes the maximum increase in heart rate with increasing work follows a straight line. Exhaustion is reached at a lower work load for women than for men.

Pulmonary Physiology. The lungs, like most organs, in mature females are smaller than those of males. When related to age and height or weight lung vital capacity of females is less. Predictions of physiologic performance really should be based on age, considerations of height, weight, and body surface area, rather than on any one single property. There is a question whether there is a real sex difference in pulmonary function when allowances are made for body size, although there are definite differences in vital capacity beginning around 14 or 15 years of age.

Endocrinology. The important differences in female and male physiology are sex-determined, either related to the reproductive organs, or to the hormonal effects on other parts of the body from gonadal hormones.

As mentioned earlier, genetic sex is determined at conception and differentiation appears at six weeks post-conception. Minor developmental characteristics are related to genetic sex during infancy and prepubertal periods. Females are slightly advanced in maturation throughout early life and adolescence. Farsightedness persists in boys longer than girls; dentition may be slightly advanced in girls; there are minor differences in the total body fat. For general purposes, however, the physiologic and anatomic differences are of minor importance throughout infancy and latency.

Puberty is brought about by the production of gonadotropins in the anterior pituitary gland, and these in turn stimulate the ovaries or testes to produce their own hormones. This process begins about 18 to 24 months earlier in girls, although the time of onset in a particular girl varies widely according to familial and racial background. At no other time in life is chronologic age such a fallacious measure of development and function, as during puberty. The female pituitary secretes two potent gonadotropic hormones, the follicle-stimulating hormones and luteinizing hormones and a third, luteotrophic hormone. The follicle-stimulating hormone, which causes maturation of ova and estrogen production, is detected in serum and urine at least a year before menstruation begins. Effects of estrogen are manifested some months before the menarche in widening of the pelvis and in the development of the breasts. The output of estrogen is cyclic during the 18 months prior to the menarche, which is an interesting sign of immature but functional ovaries. The occurrence of first menstruation varies greatly but the age at which it occurs is of considerable help establishing physiologic age. When girls are given a "post-menarchal age" many subsequent physiologic functions are seen more clearly than when related to chronologic age.

The effects from estrogen are not limited to the reproductive tract, although growth and development of the uterus are readily appreciated as are changes within the vagina. Other more distant effects concern stimulation of growth of the long bones, and eventual end to growth through sealing of the epiphyses.

The relationship of estrogen to the cyclic menstrual function is maximal during the first two weeks of the cycle. Ovulation occurs 14 days after the onset of the previous menstrual period, at which time a new hormone, progesterone, is produced in the ovary. Ovulation produces a slight but noticeable temperature elevation which persists until menstruation.

Progesterone has a primary role in producing changes within the uterus in anticipation of pregnancy. When fertilization does not occur, progesterone is no longer needed and the amount being produced decreases rapidly. This hormone has unpleasant systemic effects by having a part in causing dysmenorrhea, premenstrual tension and retention of fluids.

Physical Performance. The physical performance of girls up to the menarche is equal to that of boys. Morehouse[10] points out that in females the development of performance ability stops or even declines after puberty. The maximum endurance declines rapidly in girls after the age of 14 as well.

Women are said to be less responsive to training and require more time and work to increase their strength, but others have stressed that pubertal girls respond to training in the same fashion as adolescent and adult males.

A characteristic of women's response to moderate exercise is a greater and more rapid elevation in pulse rate than noted in men under similar conditions. Limitations on women's responses to strenuous activity and to tests of endurance are the more rapid heart rate, fewer red blood cells and less hemoglobin, smaller maximal pulmonary ventilation, lung capacity less than that of males, lower maximal oxygen uptake, and less muscle mass. The latter has an indirect effect on endurance because readily available carbohydrate, glycogen, is stored in muscles and in the liver.

The total body sweat rate is higher in men and increases to a greater degree during acclimatization to heat.[11] Apparently females do not begin sweating until the internal body heat has risen to a slightly higher degree than is the case in men. Thus, there is lessened ability to react to unfavorable heat and humidity conditions in females than in males and this could well become a major problem under unfavorable environmental conditions, or heavy work by those who are not acclimatized and conditioned.

Iron and Anemia. The delivery of oxygen depends on hemoglobin which is somewhat deficient in all females and may become a major problem. Iron is required to synthesize hemoglobin and the requirement is considerably higher in females because of iron loss during menstruation.

Physical performance depends in large part on the ability to take in and utilize oxygen. Oxygen consumption depends not only on pulmonary and cardiac function, but also on the transport of oxygen from the lungs to the tissues. The delivery of oxygen from the heart and lungs depends on hemoglobin which is synthesized from iron and proteins within the body. Females may easily become deficient in iron and in hemoglobin because the requirement for iron is considerably higher because of loss during menstruation. On the average, 15 milligrams of iron are lost at each menstrual period, approximately 200 milligrams per year. This incremental loss, augmented by the usual borderline or insufficient iron intake in the diet, places women in a critical situation when there is unusual loss of blood, or the demands for stored iron are increased during pregnancy. The amount of stored iron in women is minimal, amounting to 250 milligrams compared with 850 or more milligrams in the average adult male. Iron stores of 115 white college women who had never experienced abnormal menstrual bleeding or been pregnant were found by Scott and Pritchard to be scant-to-absent in two thirds of the subjects.[12] There were no consistent laboratory findings, although hemoglobin was slightly lower than that of the typical male. These young women seemed to be in good health but were definitely below par as determined by careful studies. These investigators attributed the iron deficiency in healthy young women to low intake of iron, and increased need due to menstruation. They concluded that young women needed extra iron even if not anemic or subject to profuse menstrual bleeding.

Menarche, Menses, Pregnancy. The two principal considerations involved in programming sports activities for girls and women relate to the size and the efficiency of the female organ systems which are related to earlier puberty and lack of androgen stimulation, and secondly to the real or fancied effects of strenuous activity on the female reproductive system and vice versa. In spite of the opinion of observers 40 or 50 years ago that girls who started intensive sports training before menarche showed a higher percentage of menstrual disorders than those who started strenuous activities after the menarche, current opinion based on careful observations leads us to believe that participation in active sports does not delay the onset of the menarche or contribute to the rather common menstrual irregularities which occur to most girls during adolescence. Stress or anxiety about anything at all, including competition, might cause temporary cessation of the menstrual function but this is not physically harmful nor does it leave lasting effects.

Dysmenorrhea (menstrual cramps) is very common among adolescent girls, particularly in the period between 16–19 years of age. There are many causes for dysmenorrhea some of which are related to anatomical-physiological changes in the reproductive organs and others which are related to psychological factors. Regardless of cause, physical activity almost always has a beneficial effect.

Progesterone secreted in the ovary during the second half of the menstrual cycle has systemic effects as mentioned previously. One of these is to stimulate contractions in the uterus which undoubtedly cause appreciable sensations whether or not they are sufficient to be incapacitating. Another effect of progesterone is to produce fluid retention during the week before the menses and to create some emotional tension in many women. None of these conditions is of such magnitude that physical activity should be suspended or would be affected.

Another question which is frequently raised concerns the advisability of participation in sports during menstruation. There is abundant opinion and data to support the recommendation that menstruation need not interrupt performance of most games and sports. Menstruation does not interrupt performance of acrobats, or other entertainers.

Whether or not a girl exercises during all phases of a menstrual cycle should be decided by her rather than a physician, nurse, or other adviser. She should not be forced to participate, but she should not be prevented from doing so. Generally, most female athletes are able to achieve their average sports performance throughout the entire menstrual cycle including menses. Dalton[13] has shown that there were adverse effects of menstruation on routine school work of a large group of menstruating girls he studied in schools in England. In these schools where weekly examinations are given to all students, one of every four girls had a lower weekly mark during the week preceding menstruation with an apparent rise in ability after menses.

Many authorities have prohibited swimming during menstruation, but there is no evidence that this is justified in our era when vaginal tampons are so commonly accepted and used for menstrual hygiene.

Contrary to time-honored opinions that a record of participation in competitive sports has harmful effects on pregnancy and delivery, Erdelyi[14] and a host of others have found that complications of pregnancy are less, including toxemia and difficult labor, in those who have participated in competitive sports. Some of Erdelyi's subjects had continued their sports during the first three or four months of pregnancy without apparent harm to participant or the infant. Duration of labor was considerably shorter for those who participated in sports, frequency of caesarean section was less than in non-athletes, and there were no apparent ill effects upon the muscles of the pelvic floor and perineum from intensive sport activity.

No observer has found evidence that physical exercise by young girls has had any ill effect on growth and development of the pelvis or the ovaries, fallopian tubes, uterus, and adjacent ligaments and soft tissues. The uterus is well protected by the pelvis and firmly anchored by the broad ligaments and is not nearly as susceptible to injury as is the partially filled bladder or the sigmoid region of the colon.

Casper[15] made a study of the course of pregnancy in women who had previously engaged in strenuous sports. Fifty subjects who had previously averaged 14 years of athletic life and averaged 26 years of age at time of delivery had only one premature birth. There were no complications of labor. Twenty-five of the fifty had engaged in sports up until the sixth month of pregnancy. This is not always advisable and would not be a recommendation.

The opinions of Erdelyi and Casper have been reiterated on

many occasions by others during recent years. There seems to be no reason to restrict the physical activity of women because of the reproductive organs and no need for concern about later effects of sports competition on pregnancy, labor, and later health.

Summary. Evidence has been presented that from the sixth week of embryonic life there are anatomic and physiologic differences which affect physical growth and development. In the female, her pattern of growth and development leads to certain characteristics such as smaller body size and dimensions of organs, more body fat, leading to proportionately less muscle mass, reduced hemoglobin mass, physiologic variations related to the reproductive system after puberty. All of these require special consideration in programming physical activities and sports for women. However, while there are very significant sex-related differences between males and females, it should be borne in mind that there are undoubtedly greater differences between the third and the ninety-seventh percentile in each sex than there are differences between the average female and the average male in terms of physical performance.

[1] Sprague, H. B. Unpublished data, 1954.

[2] Montagu, A. *The Natural Superiority of Women,* New York, MacMillan Co., 1968.

[3] Michaels, R. H. and Rogers, K. D. *A Sex Difference in Immunologic Responsiveness,* Pediatrics 47:120, 1971.

[4] Tanner, J. M. *Growth at Adolescence,* 2nd ed., Oxford, England, Blackwell Scientific Publications, 1962.

[5] Cone, T. E., Jr. in Gallagher, J. R. *Medical Care of the Adolescent,* 2nd ed., New York, Appleton, Century, Crofts, 1966, Chapter 4.

[6] Tanner, *Growth at Adolescence.*

[7] Jones, H. E. *Motor Performance and Growth,* Berkeley, University of California Press, 1949.

[8] Espenschade, A. "Development of Motor Coordination in Boys and Girls," *Research Quarterly,* 18:30, 1947.

[9] Brouha, L. A. "Effect of Work on the Heart" in *Work and the Heart,* Ed. by F. F. Rosenbaum and E. L. Belknap, New York, Paul B. Hoeber, Inc., 1959, Chapter 21.

[10] Morehouse, L. E. and Miller, A. T. *Physiology of Exercise,* Ed. 4, St. Louis, C. V. Mosby, 1963.

[11] Morimoto, T. et al. "Sex Differences in Physiological Reactions to Thermal Stress." *J. Applied Physiol.* 22:526, 1967.

[12] Scott, D. E. and Pritchard, J. D. "Iron deficiency in Healthy Young College Women." *JAMA* 199:897, March 20, 1967.

[13] Dalton, K. "Effect of Menstruation on Schoolgirls' Weekly Work." *Br. Med. Journ.* 326, June 30, 1960.
[14] Erdelyi, G. J. *Women in Athletics.* Proceedings of Second Nat'l. Conf. on Medical Aspects of Sports, Chicago, Am. Med. Assoc., 1961.
[15] Casper, H., *Deutsch Med.* Wochenschr. 54:25, 1928.

On Being Female in Sport

By M. Marie Hart

M. Marie Hart is a prominent and widely published physical educator who is currently head of the Health and Movement Studies Department at Mills College in California. In this essay, she analyzes the influence of social attitudes on women's participation in sport. An earlier version of "On Being Female in Sport" appeared in Psychology Today *Magazine in 1971. It is also included in Hart's anthology,* Sport in the Socio-Cultural Process.

The topic of social and sexual roles in sport is a complicated one about which Americans seem particularly sensitive. The sexually separated facilities and organizations that often accompany sport and physical education activities may be an extension of certain problems in this area. There is an urgent need to consider these questions if we are concerned about the quality of the experience for all those who engage in sport. Many times it seems that people find it difficult to consider such problems with any degree of objectivity. To remove the personal self from the social process being examined requires a thorough grounding in knowledge of self and a deep understanding of one's own personal sport involvement.

This article is particularly concerned with being a woman and being in sport. Although we have isolated and studied "Women in Sport," we have not so separated "Men in Sport" as a special topic. This is because the latter is the accepted, rather than the exception, in sport discussions. It seems well established that sport is male territory; therefore participation of female newcomers is studied as a peripheral, non-central aspect of sport. If one aspect of sport is social experience it seems appropriate to study it in total context and to note the differences of role and reaction in the variety of people taking part. The separation and alienation of women in sport is not the healthiest of situations. It is only through interaction that we can gain awareness and acceptance of differences. Why is it that in most of the rest of the Western world women co-exist with men in sport with less stigma and more as accepted and respected partners?

Being female in this culture does not necessarily mean that one is perceived or accepted as "feminine." Each culture has its social norm and sex roles within which one must live, but in the United States this definition seems especially rigid and narrow. For longer than one can remember, women in sport have known and experienced rejection due to their failure to live up to a particular concept of "feminine." It has been an unpleasant and painful memory for many.

Why has it been difficult for women to stay "woman" and be an athlete, especially in games emphasizing physical skill? Games of physical skill are associated with achievement and aggressiveness which seem to make them an expressive model for males rather than females. Women are more traditionally associated with high obedience training and routine responsibility training, and with games of strategy and games of chance which emphasize those qualities supposedly desirable in women.[1] This all begins so early that the young girl in elementary school already begins feeling the pressure to select some games and avoid others if she is to be a "real" girl. If she is told often enough at eleven or twelve that sports are not ladylike, she may at that point make a choice between being a lady and being an athlete. Having to make this choice has potential for setting up deep conflict in female children, which continues later into adulthood.

The concept of conflict-enculturation theory of games is developed in an essay by Sutton-Smith, Roberts and Kozelka. They maintain that "conflicts induced by social learning in childhood and later (such as those related to obedience, achievement, and responsibility) lead to involvement in expressive models, such as games. . . ."[2] This process can be applied also to the game involvement of adults. Cultural values and competencies are acquired in games. It would appear that games operate on various levels as expressive models to ease conflict, with the exception of the case of the woman athlete. As girls become more and more proficient in sport, the level of personal investment increases which may, due to the long hours of practice and limited associations, isolate her socially. Personal conflict and stress increase as it becomes necessary for her to assure others of her femininity, sometimes requiring evidence. This level of tension and conflict may increase dramatically if a girl makes the choice to be intensely involved in a sport which is thought of as male territory.

In an interview Chi Cheng, who holds several world track records, was quoted as saying, "The public sees women competing and immediately thinks that they must be manly—but at night, we're just like other women."[3] Why does a woman need to comment about herself in this way and how does this awareness of stigma affect her daily life? Chi goes on to say: "I'm gone so much of the day and on weekends. I give a lot of public appearances—where I can show off my femininity."[4]

Numerous occasions have occurred in college discussion groups over the past few years that convince one that we have imposed a great burden on women who are committed to performing or teaching sport. As an example, several married women students majoring in physical education confided to a discussion group that they had wanted to cut their hair but felt they couldn't. Members of the group asked why this was so, if their husbands objected, if they would feel less feminine, if they were in doubt about their own femaleness. In every case they responded that they simply didn't want the usual stereotype image and comments from friends and family in their social lives. Even when hair styles are short women in sport are judged by a standard other than fashion. If the married sportswoman experiences anxiety over such things, one can imagine the struggle of the single woman. Unfortunately, this often results in a defensive attitude developed as a shield against those who poke and probe.

When young women do enjoy sport what activities are really

open to them? A study done in 1963[5] shows recommendations made on sports participation by 200 freshman and sophomore college women from four Southern California schools. Although their own background had been strong in the team sports of basketball, softball and volleyball, they did not recommend that a girl, even though highly skilled, pursue these activities at a professional level. They strongly discouraged participation in track and field activities. The sports they did recommend for a talented young woman were those that they had not necessarily experienced personally. They were ranked as follows: tennis, swimming, ice skating, diving, bowling, skiing and golf. All of these recommended sports are identified with aesthetic considerations, social implications, and fashions for women. Physical strength and skill may be components of some but are not their primary identifications.

Some may argue that the past decade has seen great change in the acceptance of women in a larger variety of sports. That is no doubt true, at least to a degree, but some limited observation would indicate that there has been no radical change. In fact, the wave of enthusiasm for women in gymnastics only reinforces the traditional ideal of the striving for aesthetic form as "appropriate" for women in sport—an aesthetic that emphasizes poise, smooth and rhythmic movement. Form is the ultimate criteria, not strength and speed. Could this be indicative of the status quo?

In contrast to the findings of the 1963 study is the situation of the black woman athlete. In the black community, the woman can be strong and achieving in sport and still not deny her womanness. She may actually gain respect and status as evidenced by the reception of women like Wilma Rudolph and other great performers. The black woman seems also to have more freedom to mix her involvement in sport and dance without the conflict expressed by many white women athletes. This in itself could be the subject for research study.

The limitations on sport choices for women have been instituted largely by social attitudes about women in sport as previously discussed. These attitudes have a long history which is revealed in the sport literature. Early sport magazines reinforced the idea of women being physically inferior to men in sport and furthermore inferred that their female emotionality rendered them incompetent. As an example, in response to a strong desire of women to be involved in the new and exciting sport of flying in 1912, the editor of *Outing Magazine* was outspoken in his bias:

Other things being equal, the man who has had the most experience in outdoor sports should be the best aviator. By the same token, women should be barred. . . . Women have not the background of games of strength and skill that most men have. Their powers of correlation are correspondingly limited and their ability to cope with sudden emergencies inadequate.[6]

The social process by which women had arrived at this helpless state of being was never mentioned or discussed.

In 1936 the editor of *Sportsman*, a magazine for the wealthy, commented about the Olympic Games that he was " . . . fed up to the ears with women as track and field competitors." He continued, "her charms shrink to something less than zero" and urged the organizers to "keep them where they are competent. As swimmers and divers girls are beautiful and adroit as they are ineffective and unpleasing on the track."[7]

More recent publications such as *Sports Illustrated* have not been openly negative, but the implication is sustained by the limitation in their coverage of women in sport. Content is small and consists mostly of a discussion of fashions and of women in traditionally approved activities such as swimming, diving, ice skating, tennis and golf. The emphasis in periodicals is still largely on women as attractive objects rather than as skilled and effective athletes.

The magazines *Sportswoman* and *womenSports* have been dedicated to presenting a full and fair coverage of women in sport. The efforts of the editors and writers are excellent even though one occasionally gets the impression that the message is "see we're just as good, skilled and tough as the men but still attractive."

Granted the image is somewhat exaggerated but again care must be taken not just to accept and act out the traditional

model of sport developed by and for men. There may be more
alternatives and dimensions to be explored which would benefit
a greater variety of personalities and social groups.

Attitudes toward women in sport have been slow to change
because of misunderstandings like the muscle myth. It has
been difficult to allay the fear that sport activity will produce
bulging muscles which imply masculinity. Young girls are
frightened away from sport by "caring" adults who perpetuate
this false idea. The fact, well documented by exercise physiologists, is that "excessive development (muscles) is not a
concomitant of athletic competition."[8] Klafs and Arnheim
further affirm this situation, reporting: "Contrary to lay opinion, participation in sports does not masculinize women.
Within a sex, the secretion of testosterone, androgen, and
estrogen varies considerably, accounting for marked variation
in terms of muscularity and general morphology among males
and females."[9] Participation in sport cannot make changes in
the potential of hereditary and structural factors of any individual.

Perhaps what occasionally gives observers the impression
that the muscle myth is true is the reality that some girl
athletes are indeed muscular. However, it is due to their
muscularity that they enter sport; it is the reason why they
participate in sport rather than the result of their participation.
This is further explained by Klafs and Arnheim:

Girls whose physiques reflect considerable masculinity are stronger
per unit of weight than girls who are low in masculinity and boys
who display considerable femininity of build. Those who are of
masculine type often do enter sports and are usually quite successful
because of the mechanical advantages possessed by the masculine
structure. However, such types are the exception, and by far the
greater majority of participants possess a feminine body build.[10]

Some of the most important considerations of women have
been written by Simone de Beauvoir. In her book, *The Second
Sex*, she discusses sport as a way of experiencing oneself in the
world and of asserting one's sovereignty. She says that outside
of participation in sport, a girl must experience most of her

physical self in a passive manner.[11] De Beauvoir makes one point that is worth the serious consideration of all who are concerned about the dilemma of the woman athlete. She states:

And in sports the end in view is not success independent of physical equipment; it is rather the attainment of perfection within the limitations of each physical type; the featherweight boxing champion is as much of a champion as is the heavyweight; the woman skiing champion is not the inferior of the faster male champion; they belong to two different classes. It is precisely the female athletes who, being positively interested in their own game, feel themselves least handicapped in comparison with the male.[12]

Americans seem not to be able to apply this view of "attainment of perfection within the limitations of each" to the woman in sport. Women have been continually compared to males and have had male performance and style set as model and goal for them. Repeatedly young girls and women athletes listen to, "Wow, what a beautiful throw. You've got an arm like a guy." "Look at that girl run, she could beat lots of boys." Father comments, "Yes, she loves sports. She's our little tomboy." It would seem strange to say of a young boy, "Oh, yes, he is our little marygirl." We have ways of getting messages to boys who don't fit the role, but we haven't integrated it into our language terminology so securely.

These kinds of comments carry with them the message of expected cultural behavior. When well learned it results in girls losing games to boys purposely, avoiding dates which show her sports talent or risking never dating the boy again if she performs better than he does.

The male performance standards and the attending social behavior have extended into even more serious problems. In the early international competition of the 1920s women were not subjected to medical examinations. After doubt arose over one or two competitors, each country was asked to conduct medical examinations to determine if indeed the performer was female. Countries did not trust the honesty of nonsupervised tests so additional tests began to be employed. In international events a woman must now pass the "Barr Sex Test" perfected by a Canadian doctor. The test consists of scraping cells from the inside of the cheek and then analyzing them for "Barr bodies." The number fluctuates normally during a month but all women have a minimum percentage of Barr bodies all the time. In the test, if the percentage drops below the minimum for females then the femaleness of the performer is suspect and she is dropped from the competition.

In 1968, the "Barr Sex Test" was administered for the first time at an Olympic Game, causing quite a stir. The scene was described by Marion Lay, a Canadian swimmer performing in both the 1964 and 1968 Olympics. The line-up awaiting the test in Mexico erupted in reactions ranging from tension-releasing jokes to severe stress and upset. Some performers suggested that if the doctor were good looking enough, one might skip the test and prove one's femininity by seducing him. At the end of the test the women received a certificate verifying their femaleness and approving their participation in the Games. Many were quite baffled by the necessity of the test, feeling that their honesty as much as their femininity was in question. Most could not imagine anyone wanting to win so badly that they would create a disguise or take drugs that might jeopardize their female identity.

In addition to the concern over proof of sexual identity, there has been much discussion about the use of "steroid" drugs by some women performers, particularly those from Russia and Eastern bloc nations. These drugs are derived from male sex hormones and tend to increase muscle size. The subject of the use of these drugs by women has been somewhat muted with the result that there is not much literature describing the effects of this drug on women performers. There have been strong and continued warnings against its use by men because of its dangerous effects but there is very little published about the effects of the "steroid drug" on women. It is known to increase body size and also to produce secondary male characteristics such as increasing of facial hair and lowering of the voice.[13] Why would a woman take such a drug? Because the values are on male records and performance, and she will attempt to come as close to this goal as possible. This kind of performance and attending social behavior have caused serious problems for women athletes. If the performance of

women could be recognized on its own merit without comparison to male records and scores, many painful social and
"medical" experiences for women would be avoided.

If women in sport feel outside of the mainstream of social
life in this country, perhaps another question could be posed
to representatives of the new movements. Where has the
feminist platform been in relation to women athletes? When
the role of women is no longer limited to mother, secretary,
or Miss America, isn't it about time that women were given
not only freedom to be but respect for being successful in
sport? Granted that the early 1970s have been a time of
increased interest and recognition from women's organizations,
but more support, understanding and coverage are still needed.

It seems apparent that the female athlete in general has
much, if not more, to contend with than any other women in
the American way of life. To entertain doubts about one's
sexual identity and role results in more than a little stress. An
editorial in *Women: A Journal of Liberation* states: "In America, dance is a field for women and male homosexuals. There
is the dancer's cult of starving and punishing one's body."[14] In
contrast, one might think of sport as a field for men and female
homosexuals, or so the image seems often to be interpreted.
The need to change the environment of sport and dance from
symbolic cultural territory for the establishing of sexual identity and acceptance to an environment of valued personal
experience and fulfillment is long past due.

The aforementioned editorial goes on to say: "My dream is
that dance will not have to be an escape from America's sick
sexuality but a celebration of all of our bodies, dancing."[15]
What else could one wish for both men and women in sport?
Why could not sport be a celebration, both personal and
mutual, of the body-self? A celebration—rather than a conflict
over best scores and most points, over who is most masculine
and who is least feminine—a celebration of one's body-self
whoever he or she is. The jokes, stories and oppression are old
and far too heavy to be carried along further. The present-day
woman athlete may soon demand her female space and identity
in sport.

Today women *have* begun to enter sport with more social acceptance and individual pride. After World War II the increase in women athletes and their success became more apparent and better received. In 1952 researchers from the Finnish Institute of Occupational Health conducted an intensive study of the athletes participating in the Olympics in Helsinki. Their findings were of major importance in the study of women athletes. After studying their athletic achievements, physiological and clinical data, age, fitness and social status, the researchers stated that "women are about to shake off civic disabilities which millennia of prejudice and ignorance have imposed upon them."[16] The researchers concluded that the participation of women was a significant indication of positive health and living standards of a country.

In addition to the physiological and clinical data, the researchers observed other factors apparent in the performance of women athletes. Criteria for describing the performances expanded to include aesthetic considerations because it "added itself" to the researchers' data. They stated:

A third criterion for the evaluation of women's athletics is an aesthetic one. Parallel with the growth of athletic performance standards there has taken place during the past fifty years or so a display of new dynamic patterns of motion and form which contain elements of artistic value and of creative beauty. The great woman hurdlers and discus throwers, fencers, and divers, gymnasts and canoeists have introduced, unwittingly, of course, features of elegance and of power, of force and of competence such as had previously not been known. That sports and athletics should be able to elicit in women categorical values of this kind and that performance and beauty should thus be correlated is a surprising and highly relevant experience.[17]

In the same vein, Ogilvie, a professor of psychology, stated:

The review of the data upon San Jose State College women swimmers presents evidence that there has been no loss of the feminine traits most valued within our culture. There was strong evidence that at least this small sample of women had outstanding traits of personality in the presence of outstanding success as competitors. I must reject the prejudiced view that would deny women the joys and rewards of high level athletic competition. It appears to this investigator that you would have to search the whole world over before you could find twenty women who measure up to these in both personality and natural physical beauty.[18]

Personal fulfillment as expressed by woman in sports and dance experiences must not be manipulated or denied to anyone in the name of archaic cultural roles. They have been binding, limiting and belittling. This is the age of woman in command of her own space and movement. Men will also gain freedom from their role restriction as the process of social change continues.

The argument that "a person is a person is a person" is one to be heeded—and one wishes practiced. However, it seems necessary in this transitional time to name, discuss and research what is practiced so that social roles and systems can be fully understood and exposed. Only when individuals, and more generally the society, become conscious of behavior can that behavior be changed. Until then it's all just so much talk.

[1] J. M. Roberts and B. Sutton-Smith, "Child-Training and Game Involvement," *Ethnology* 1 (1962): 66–185; B. Sutton-Smith, B. G. Rosenberg, and E. F. Morgan, Jr., "Development of Sex Differences in Play Choices During Preadolescence," *Child Development* 34 (1963): 119–26; B. Sutton-Smith, J. M. Roberts, and R. M. Kozelka, "Game Involvement in Adults," *The Journal of Social Psychology* 60 (1963): 15–30.

[2] Sutton-Smith, Roberts, and Kozelka, "Game Involvement in Adults," p. 15.

[3] Karin Winner, "At Night We're Just Like Other Women," *Amateur Athlete* (April 1971): 15.

[4] *Ibid.*, p. 16.

[5] M. Marie Hart, "Factors Influencing College Women's Attitudes Toward Sport and Dance," Master's Thesis, University of Southern California, 1963.

[6] "Still They Fall," *Outing* 67 (November 1912): 253.

[7] "Things Seen and Heard," *Sportsman* 20 (October 1936): 18.

[8] Carl E. Klafs and Daniel D. Arnheim, *Modern Principles of Athletic Training* (St. Louis, Mo.: C. V. Mosby Company, 1969), p. 130.

[9] *Ibid.*, p. 128.

[10] *Ibid.*, p. 128.

[11] Simone de Beauvoir, *The Second Sex* (New York: Bantam Books, 1952).

[12] *Ibid.*, p. 311.

[13] Myrna Blythe, "Girl Athletes: What Makes Them Skate, Fence, Swim, Jump, Run?" *Cosmopolitan* (October 1969): 135.

[14] *Women: A Journal of Liberation* 2 (Fall 1970): 65.

[15] *Ibid.*, p. 65.

[16] Ernst Jokl, *Medical Sociology and Cultural Anthropology of Sport and Physical Education* (Springfield, Ill.: Charles C Thomas, Publisher, 1964), p. 84.

[17] *Ibid.*, pp. 84–85.
[18] Bruce Ogilvie, "The Unanswered Question: Competition, Its Effect Upon Femininity," Address given to the Olympic Development Committee, Santa Barbara, California, June 30, 1967. Here, again, there is the cultural concern and bias toward "feminine" traits and beauty. Conversely, there is full cultural appreciation of excellent male athletes, be they handsome or ugly.

Woman as an Athlete

By Arabella Kenealy, M.D.

In this 1899 article for The Nineteenth Century *Magazine, Dr. Arabella Kenealy, adhering to the accepted medical opinion of her day, suggests that a human being has a fixed amount of energy to expend. Therefore, she warns, if women insist on engaging in physical activity, they will be unable to fulfill their traditional "womanly duties." Kenealy's argument, a common one used by those opposing women's sports, was answered the next month in the same magazine by Mrs. Ormiston Chant, who celebrated female "muscular vigour." Kenealy had the last word, however. In still another issue of the magazine, she responded to Chant and attempted to invalidate her claims by emphasizing that Chant was not a doctor.*

It is wonderful what athletics do for women," a friend observed. "A year ago Clara could not walk more than two miles without tiring; now she can play tennis or hockey, or can bicycle all day without feeling it."

The observation fired a train of evidences and examples which had been accumulating in my mind over a period of years of medical practice.

In what manner have the changes which have recently taken place in the physique and energies of women been effected?

Have reserves of force, impoverished and abeyant under an older-fashioned up-bringing, been called into activity and use by new régimes of thought and training? Were women what they were from lack of opportunity and stress of circumstance? Are women what they are by virtue of circumstance and gift of opportunity? Did man's iron heel indeed and grandmotherly tradition result in the dwarfing and defacement of a sex's powers? Is it faculty heretofore starved and dwindled, but now reclaimed and added to the complement of human energy—this flood of new activity which fills our illustrated papers with portraits of feminine prize-winners, and our sporting journals with female "records"? Is the female Senior Wrangler a bright jewel rescued from the morass of down-trampled wasted capability which has hitherto but littered the path of progress?

These, and other considerations with which I will not weary the reader, I revolved.

Revolving them I came upon an "if" which seemed to be the crux of the situation. If it could be demonstrated that modern woman possesses all her new capacities plus those of her older-fashioned sister, then there could be but one answer to the question.

If Clara from tiring at a two-mile walk had suddenly and simply developed energies which should enable her to bicycle or row or run all day without fatigue, then Clara and the world had plainly benefited—more especially if it should occur to Clara to devote these freshly acquired forces to her fellows' use.

But—and here I stumbled over my crux—if Clara had only acquired these powers at the expense of others, then the case was not at all so clear. If to reclaim abeyant faculties should involve the abeyance of faculties which had previously operated, the question of advantage must rest entirely upon the relative values of the interchanging faculties.

My knowledge of physiology and medicine forbade me to entertain the belief common to the laity that a regimen of habit or diet could result in a material increase of force-production. Change of air, a judicious liver treatment, an efficient blood or nerve tonic will sometimes effect apparent marvels by improving the powers of assimilation and nutrition. But such apparent marvels have their origin in a mere relief of temporary disability, and have nothing to do with so radical a constitutional change as has taken place in Clara and her fellows.

The healthy human body, like a machine, has its fixed standard of force-production, varying according to the individual; and, with trifling variations consequent on temperament and circumstance, every person possesses and finds earlier or later his limitations of energy. According to the powers, and the sensitiveness, any expenditure of force beyond that manufactured by the economy as its daily output is followed by fatigue, irritability or depression and a general sense of not being up to the mark. Further undue demands upon the resources may result in incapacitation, prostration, or actual illness. These results are modified of course by individual recuperative power and the rate whereat force lost to the system is made up.

Speaking generally, it may be said that an individual generates a certain daily fund of energy, which if he exceed one day he must suffer for the next in impoverished vitality, or meet— but this is a larger question and one which does not belong to the subject—by drawing upon and deteriorating his constitutional capital. Personality varies in the degree of force manufactured, but more especially in the manner in which the force is distributed. Infinite variety is obtained by the combination and association of similar qualities in dissimilar quantity. One of muscle, two of mind, three of emotion: three of muscle, one of mind, two of emotion: one-sixteenth of mind, twelve-sixteenths of muscle, three-sixteenths of emotion. And so on *ad infinitum* with the *infinitum* made more endless by still further and more intricate subdivisions of muscular, mental, and emotional attributes. . . .

We come now upon the suggestion that Clara's apparent increase of energy has been an effect merely of altering the relation of her forces in such a manner as to increase the muscle-power at the expense of other qualities—in a word, to destroy a complex, well-planned balance of faculties which had been Nature's scheme when Nature fashioned Clara.

With regard to the value of the newly acquired power I could
(text continued on page 42)

Athletic Foremothers

The women on
these four pages
played sports
during the first
half of the
twentieth century—
in colleges, in
the Olympics,
on teams,
as individuals.
One obstacle
that many of them
faced was
playing in clothing
that seriously
hampered movement.
1: Golfer. 2: A
Cincinnati
tennis player.
3: Basketball game.
4: Softball
pitching, 1945.
5: Philadelphia
Community College
vs. Merion in
field hockey.
6: A U.S. Olympic
track star.
7: Field hockey
squad. 8: Golf team,
ca. 1950.
9: Pole-vaulter
at the University
of Nebraska,
1900. 10: Lacrosse
at St. Albans
College, 1932.
11: Pitcher
for the "Female
Giants," 1913.
12: Volleyball game
at Carnegie
Institute of
Technology, 1925.

not but recognise that muscular force, even in its finest developments of skill and endurance, is the most crude and least highly differentiated of all the human powers. It is one which man shares in common with and possesses in a notably less degree than do the lower animals. For strength, mobility, and sinuous grace he cannot aspire to rival the snake—which indeed is lower than the lower animals. For speed and endurance the horse will far outstrip him. For grip and invincible tenacity he is no match for the bull-dog or the ape.

As a matter of fact, it is not mere muscle-power, but the subordination and application of muscle-power to express idea, emotional, intellectual, or moral, which is man's especial forte. In this he is higher than the highest animals. But this has little or no relation with the muscular vigour which makes "strong men" and navvies. Indeed, the athlete is conspicuously lacking in it. He pleases by agility, by the play and achievement of highly trained members. But it may be said that he portrays muscle rather than man.

To tell the truth, we are somewhat in danger to-day of deifying muscle, muscle being properly a mere means to an end, a system of levers whose chief value lies in the purpose they subtend. The levers must be kept in order by due exercise and use for the means for which they are required. But modern feeling is in the direction of amassing muscles which shall enable their possessor to fell oxen or to beat pedestrian and cycling records.

We waste force surely by keeping in condition muscular systems out of all proportion to the needs; the occasions for felling oxen or for supplanting locomotives being virtually non-existent in civilised communities. One of the advantages indeed of civilisation and one of the means whereby higher faculties are left free to develop is the ability to dispense with such muscular obligations as are indispensable to primitive life—which lives by physical achievement.

It is not wished in any way to discredit the exercise essential to the building up of healthy bodies, and of maintaining the balance mental, emotional, and physical. Only the forced athletics which destroy this balance are condemned. To speak physiologically, the athlete is not a person of fine muscular physique; he is a person whose muscles are hypertrophied, a fact of but little moment were it not a *sine quâ non* that they are hypertrophied at the expense of higher and more valuable factors.

To return, however, to Clara. What are the qualities which Clara and modern woman, of whom she is the prototype, are discarding? And here we come upon a complex question. For the more subtle and fine the essence of human capacity, the more difficult its demonstration. Clara's talents for winning golf matches or for mountain climbing are a power demonstrable and calculable. But Clara's sympathies and Clara's emotionalism and Clara's delicacy and tact, which one can but conclude are the qualities which have gone to feed her augmented sinews, are factors more conspicuous in the breach than in the observance.

Can it be shown then that modern woman is lacking in those which were wont to be considered womanly faculties? Can it be denied? And since the power of a healthy adult can be increased only at the expense of some other power, and since modern woman has inordinately added to her muscle-power, and since muscle-power is the least of human qualities, what is to be deduced but that human capability has lost rather than gained in the exchange?

With Clara at the head of my train of feminine examples, I now set out to determine more exactly what were those qualities she had bartered for a mess of muscle.

That a change indeed had taken place was evident. Clara the athlete was no longer the Clara I remembered two years earlier. She was almost as dissimilar as though she had been another personality. She was as different from herself as their grandmothers were different from the girls of the present day. I drew her portrait as I had first known her. She was then—I had almost written a charming girl—but let me not be betrayed into partisan adjectives, let me portray her as impartially as may be. And to begin with her physical qualifications. She was then—she is now—something more than comely, but her comeliness has altogether changed in character. Where before her beauty was suggestive and elusive, now it is defined. One might have said of her two years since: Her eyes are fine, her features are well modelled, her complexion is sensitive and variable; but, over and beyond these facts, there is a mysterious and nameless something which for the lack of a more definite term I can only describe as "charm;" and it is in this something, which is to her as atmosphere is to landscape, that her chiefest beauty lies.

One would say of her now: Her eyes are fine, her features are well modelled, her complexion is possibly too strong in its contrasting tones, her glance is unwavering and direct; she is a good-looking girl. But the haze, the elusiveness, the subtle suggestion of the face are gone; it is the landscape without atmosphere. Now one could paint her portrait with ease. Formerly only the most ingenious and sympathetic art could have reproduced her subtle and mysterious charm.

There are an added poise and strength about her actions, she inclines to be, and in another year will be, distinctly spare, the mechanism of movement is no longer veiled by a certain mystery of motion which gave her formerly an air of gliding rather than of striding from one place to another. In her evening gown she shows evidence of joints which had been adroitly hidden beneath tissues of soft flesh, and already her modiste has been put to the necessity of puffings and pleatings where Nature had planned the tenderest and most dainty of devices. Her movements are muscular and less womanly. Where they had been quiet and graceful, now they are abrupt and direct. Her voice is louder, her tones are assertive. She says everything—leaves nothing to the imagination.

Exteriorly Clara has distinctly changed. One would suppose that appreciable mental and emotional differences must accompany these marked physical developments. And these, though they cannot so readily be specified, can still be demonstrated.

Curious to relate, Clara's muscle-power has not at all conduced to Clara's usefulness. One might have expected that her new impetus of energy would inspire her to spend it, as had been her wont, in the service of her associates. Strange to tell, the energy but urges her to greater muscular efforts in the pursuit of pleasure, or to her own repute.

In the old days she was one of those invaluable girls who, without being able to point to any very definite achievement at the end of the day, have yet accomplished much. Was there one sick or in trouble, then Clara was the nurse and Clara was the comforter. Had father's ruffled temper to be soothed, or did he need a bright and sympathetic comrade for an expedition; had mother some gift or commission for the great distressed; did brother Tom require assistance in his lessons or a sympathiser with his woes or joys; did Rosy need a ribbon in her hat—Clara's resources had been always at disposal.

Now, however, Clara finds no time for any of these ministrations. Clara is off bicycling upon her own account. "I used to be the idlest person," she will tell you, "finicking all day about the house and getting tired. Now I am splendidly fit. If I feel moped I go for a six-mile spin and come back a new creature!"

When Clara tired with a walk beyond two miles, Clara took flowers and books to her sick or less fortunate friends. Now that she can "manage twenty miles easily," her sick and less fortunate friends miss her. "An out-door life is the only life worth living," Clara announces. "I can't stand knocking about a house—fussing here and fussing there. It's such a shocking waste of time."

And Clara's mother, though she rejoices in her young Amazon's augmented thews and sinews, cannot but sigh for the loss to the home which has resulted from such added vigour as keeps her for ever from it. Still, like her fellows, she misconstrues Clara's muscle capability as evidence of improved health, and, while she sighs for its results, regards it as her maternal duty to be glad.

Now, it is a physiological fact that muscle vigour is no test even of masculine health. A man in training, a man that is at the height of his muscular capacity, is the worst of all subjects for illness. He has little or no resistant power; his recuperative quality is small. Athletes die proverbially young. Lunatics and other diseased persons frequently exhibit muscular strength which seems almost superhuman.

Proofs innumerable might be cited, were it necessary, that

muscular vigour, though inseparable from health, is in itself no warranty whatsoever of constitutional integrity. And this, which is true of the sex whose province it is to be muscular, is essentially more true of the sex whose province it is not. So much is this the case indeed that my experience leads me to regard any extreme of muscle-power in a woman as in itself evidence of disease—measuring human and womanly health by another standard than that of mere *motor* capability. As to its place in the world of human beings, there cannot be two opinions but that it is merely subsidiary. *They also work who do but stand and wait.* The power to stand and wait entails as much expenditure of force as does the power to stir and stride.

Clara sitting sewing flowers in Rosy's hat may be using treble the activities she might be employing on a bicycle. She will be exercising in the first place possibly unselfishness, a quality which requires at least as much nerve output as do the movements of mere muscles. She will be exercising the faculties of skill and taste, she will be educating the obedience of hand to eye and mind; and, still further, she will be exerting the delicate muscular force essential to the movements of placing and sewing.

It is true that were she playing golf or bicycling she would be developing such faculties as calculation, self-control, and fortitude, in addition to developing her muscles. And, inasmuch as these are qualities which are less demanded in the trimming of a hat, let her play golf and bicycle. But let her not do these things to the detriment of other valuable faculties. Do not let her fly off at a tangent with the notion that human activity is a thing merely of muscle. As has been said, the employment of muscle in the achievement of some mental or moral idea is the highest possible expression of muscle. The subordination of muscle to mere muscular achievement holds a very inferior place in the scale of doing. The subordination of muscle to womanhood should ever be kept in mind as being an infinitely higher ideal than can ever be the subordination of womanhood to muscle.

The noblest physical potentiality is by no means the power of swift and agile motion any more than the qualities of

assertiveness and expression are the highest mental potentiality. As the greatest charm of Clara's face—the charm she has
lost in the suspicion of a "bicycle face" (the face of muscular
tension)—was incommunicable, a dainty elusive quality which
could not be put into words nor reproduced on canvas, so the
highest of all attributes are silent, as for example sympathy,
that sweetest quality which, without necessity for speech, lays
the balm distilled in the crucible of one person's emotions for
another's need—lays this balm gently to the wound in that
other's nature.

But the power of sympathy is in the inverse ratio of the
habit of assertiveness. The further one cultivates assertiveness
(that blemish of modern women), the harder the breastplate
wherewith the ego is armoured—the less is retained of the
power to merge the nature into another's for that other's help
and comfort. The more we harden and roughen the hands,
made tender by nature to touch the world's wounds, the less
do they hold of gentleness and smoothness for those wounds.
Use them that they be strong and capable beneath their
gentleness. But do not subordinate their higher qualities to
mere muscular grip. I have known hands which were healing
in their touch—the muscles which moved these moved them
to some purpose indeed! All human action, indeed, has a higher
end than merely action.

It may be objected that these qualities, the lack whereof I
deprecate in Clara, have been well relegated to that morass of
submergence whence woman has laboriously emerged—that
scorned and scoffed at "sphere" of "influence," of unrecognised
and unrewarded labour, that rocking of cradles, that teaching
of children prayers, that weaving of laurel wreaths for masculine victors, that embroidering their deeds in tapestry and
distilling of unguents for their hurts which occupied woman
ere the tide of emancipation set in.

For the reformer has taught her to despise that which, scorn
the term as she will and does, must by the nature of things
remain her "sphere," instead of teaching her to enlarge and
develop and bring to that sphere intelligences which should
lift it for ever and before all men from a position of contempt.
The whole question of evolution turns indeed on the function

of child-bearing. There is no subject occupying the minds of our most eminent politicians, philosophers, or poets, which possesses a tithe of the value belonging to the problem as to the best methods of rearing babies. The philosopher's wisdom is written in sand for every tide to wash away. The Baby is eternal. On his proper nurture devolves the whole question of the race—To be or not to be? Speaking broadly, the tide which made for higher education and more liberty—an undeniable and invaluable impulse when it shall be but rightly directed— was a mere impulse on the part of Nature that the motherhood of her babies should be an intelligent motherhood. It was time instinct should be superseded by intelligence. It was time woman, the mother of men, should be accorded the liberty which belongs to the mothering of freedmen. Nature had no vainglorious ambitions as to a race of female wranglers or golfers; she is not concerned with Amazons, physical or intellectual. She is a one-idea'd, uncompromising old person, and her one idea is the race as embodied in the Baby. . . .

And Nature is groaning for the misinterpretation modern woman is placing upon the slackening of her rein. For Nature knows what are the faculties whence this new muscle-energy is born. She knows it is the birthright of the babies Clara and her sister athletes are squandering. She knows it is the laboriously evolved potentiality of the race they are expending on their muscles.

Nature can but be disgusted with our modern rendering of baby. So sorry a poor creature the baby of this nineteenth century is, indeed, that he cannot assimilate milk. All the resources of the dietist and chemist are taxed to appease the abnormal requirements of his capricious, incompetent stomach. His mother cannot feed him. Those artificial puffings and pads of the modiste are but pitiful insult to his natural needs. And the forces which should have gone to fashion him a stomach capable of digesting the milk of his good wet-nurse Vacca, have been spent in making his mother a muscular system which shall enable her to pay calls or bicycle all day without fatigue.

It is a terrible pity that public opinion sets its face against the discussing of physiological questions in any but medical journals. For physiological questions are of incalculable importance to all persons, seeing that physiology is the science of life. As it is, I dare but hint at a group of important functions, by the physical deterioration and decadence of which the abnormal activities of modern woman are alone possible. Of what consequence, it may be asked, is this to a race which views motherhood with ever-increasing contempt? Of vital consequence, I answer, seeing that, apart absolutely from the incident of motherhood, all the functions of the body—and some in immense degree—influence and modify the mind and character. A woman may be neither wife nor mother, yet is it of immense importance to herself and to the community at large that she retain her womanhood. For womanhood is a beautiful achievement of evolution which it is a crime to deface. With sex are bound up the noblest and fairest aspirations of humanity, and it is at the expense of sex that these abnormal muscle-energies are attained. It is only by approximation to the type masculine—which must be read as a degeneration from the especial excellences Nature planned for the type feminine—that woman is equipping herself with these abnormal sinews.

And it must be understood that such decadence and deterioration show mainly in the loss of the very highest qualities of sex. We do not expect such fine attributes as those of delicacy, tenderness, and virtue from the muscular woman of the brickfields. She can trudge and make bricks all day (as Clara now can bicycle) without undue fatigue, but as such capacity has been attended by a coarsening of body, so the higher evolvements of sex have given place to callousness and lack of modesty. Immodesty is as actual a human degeneration as is indigestion, modesty being, as digestion is, a human function. A brain deteriorated by the rough manual labour of the body to which it belongs loses its more subtle and fine qualities. So an emotional system dwarfed by undue muscular effort loses in its most highly and delicately evolved attributes.

The unsexed female brick-maker may do more than her numerical share in supplying citizens to the State. But of what type are these? It is an unfortunate circumstance that a race may deteriorate pitiably in quality long ere any diminution in quantity occurs.

If Clara were compelled by circumstance to earn her living in a brickfield nobody could question the advantage of such a redistribution of her forces as should enable her to convert higher and more complex—but unremunerative—forces into muscular capability. Belonging to a class, however, which does not live by muscular effort, but, being leisured, is at liberty to develop faculties more complex, such a re-distribution is mere wanton degradation of evolved faculty and a grievous loss to humanity. We might with equal perspicuity uproot the rose bushes and lilies from our gardens and employ them in manuring swede and turnip fields!

The old system for girls of air and exercise inadequate to development and health was wrong, but for my part I am inclined to doubt if it really was so pernicious in its physiological results or so subversive of domestic happiness and the welfare of the race as is the present system which sets our mothers bicycling all day and dancing all night and our grandmothers playing golf.

In her highest development woman is subtle, elusive in that what she suggests is something beyond formulation and fact; a moral and refining influence; as sister, wife, or friend, an inspiration, a comrade and a comforter; as mother, a guardian and guide; as citizen or worker a smoother of life's way, a humaniser, nurse, and teacher.

But none of these her highest attributes are attributes of muscle! And human capability is limited. One cannot possess all the delicately evolved qualities of woman together with the muscular and mental energies of man. And for my part to be a female acrobat or brick-maker appears but a sorry ideal. Modern woman (I speak now of women in the van of the so-called forward movement, and I do not speak of "higher" educated women nor of professional women nor of women trained in any special way, for the wave of "newness" has touched all alike: fashionable woman, fireside woman, all have been splashed by this same wave which, intended to lift them forward in the tide of progress, bids fair to carry them off their feet)—this modern woman, who, instead of serving for a terrible warning, is in danger of proving her sex's example, is restless, is clamorous, is only satisfied when in evidence, is assertive and withal is eminently discontented. She never can get enough, for the reason that the thing she asks is not the thing to satisfy her nature. . . .

In debasing her womanhood, in becoming a neuter, she descends from the standpoint whereat life was interesting. And more and more every year, discarding the duties Nature planned for her employment and delight, she cries out that life is dull and empty.

She no longer preserves and brews. She no longer weaves and fashions. Her children are nursed, fed, clothed, taught, and trained by hirelings; her sick are tended by the professional nurse, her guests are entertained by paid performers. What truly remain which may be called her duties? What is left to her indeed but boredom? Let me not be regarded as merely bringing a grave indictment against the sex with which I have every sympathy by virtue of belonging to it, and least of all let me be understood to deprecate the right of every woman to be educated and self-supporting. All that I urge is that what she does she shall do in a womanly way, striving against all disability to preserve her womanhood as being the best of her possessions. All that I would warn her against is the error into which she has been temporarily led, the error supposing there is any nobler sphere than that of home, that there is any greater work than that of bearing and training fine types of humanity, seeing that this is the sole business wherewith the mightiest forces of the universe and evolution are concerned. But these things to be wholly worthy must be intelligently done. The reign of mere instinctive motherhood is waning. The era of Intelligent Motherhood approaches. And the first care of Intelligent Motherhood will be to see that none of those powers which belong to her highest development and through her to the highest development of the race shall be impoverished, debased, or misapplied. And in that day she will have ceased from regarding muscle as her worthiest possession.

Are Athletics Making Girls Masculine? A Practical Answer to a Question Every Girl Asks

By Dudley A. Sargent, M.D.

*Dr. Dudley Allen Sargent is an important person
in American women's sports history. In the late 1870s,
Harvard University opened its new Hemenway Gymnasium
under Sargent, a move which inspired women's colleges,
anxious to imitate men's, to construct better and larger
gyms. In 1881, Sargent opened his own gymnastic school
and, in 1887, he began admitting women into the
Hemenway's summer sessions. Many of the first professional
female physical educators were trained in one or both
of these programs. Sargent's gymnastics, involving
light props, offered late-nineteenth-century women some of
the most vigorous exercise available.*

*In the twentieth century, Sargent's assessment of female
physical needs broadened to include not only gymnastics,
but many sports. His reasoning, as presented in this 1912
*Ladies' Home Journal *article, was both typical and ahead of
its time. His belief that women's athletics should be
modified versions of men's represented the growing
consensus of physical educators and other professionals. But
his claim that the sexes shared a common physiology and
athletic potential was distinctly avant-garde. While this
view hinted at the fuller cultural acceptance of female
athleticism that would come in the 1920s, it was strongly
resisted by many of his colleagues. Just six months after this
article appeared, *Harper's Bazar *featured an article by
Dr. Angenette Parry who ignored Sargent but cited "many of
our most distinguished physicians" to argue that because
the sexes were physiologically different, competitive
athletics impeded childbearing.*

That there is a change taking place in our American girls
and women is unquestioned. And it is so elusive, so baffling

of description that it is proving the most attractive of subjects for discussion in the newspaper and magazine. Every journalistic wind that blows either moans or shrieks, according to its source, of feminine activities, and we are forced to listen whether we will or not. Much of the reading matter put forth in certain somewhat sensational papers so utterly disregards truth and reason that we are in danger of half believing that womankind has already become a distorted Amazon creation, to be talked about and wondered at, but no longer to be loved and admired.

What It Is Believed Athletics Are Doing for Girls. There is really nothing in the present state of women's development, either mental or physical, which calls for the pen of a Jeremiah. As a nation we are probably deteriorating physically, and in enlarging upon this topic the alarmist might find much material to his liking. But this statement applies no more to women than to men, and perhaps not as much. Heretofore women have been more creatures of the kitchen and fireside than of the great outdoors, and the present generation of young women who will become the mothers of the next generation have more muscle and more lung capacity than their own mothers. The growth of athletics for girls is largely responsible for this. Colleges for women have more or less grudgingly made room in their curricula for gymnastics and athletics, and the noncollegiate world has followed suit and made athletic sports accessible to women.

Any one who practices gymnastics or engages in athletics with regularity must find a change in certain organs and muscles of the body: the waist-line is enlarged, the chest expansion is increased, the muscles of the back are strengthened. These are some of the results in both men and women. They are not regarded as alarming in men, but when we mention them in connection with our young women we are interpreted as claiming that our girls are becoming masculine.

Many persons honestly believe that athletics are making girls bold, masculine and overassertive; that they are destroying the beautiful lines and curves of her figure, and are robbing her of that charm and elusiveness that has so long characterized the female sex. Others, including many physicians, incline to the belief that athletics are injurious to the health. This double charge, of course, gives a serious aspect to the whole question, and it should be met.

What Athletics Really Are. Now, what are athletics and how are women affected by them? An athlete is one who contends against another for a victory; athletics are the events in which one contends. A gymnasium is a place for the performance of athletic exercises; a gymnast is a person who trains athletes, and gymnastics are the exercises practiced in the gymnasium for the purpose of putting one's self in proper condition for competing in the athletic contests. In our times the terms athletics, gymnastics and physical training are often used synonymously, while actually they are not alike and may bring about very different results.

If a schoolgirl practices jumping a bar with other girls, as one of the physical exercises prescribed for general development, she is engaging in gymnastics. If, however, the bar is jumped with the purpose of finding out which girl can clear the bar at the greatest height the performance becomes an athletic one. In the first instance the exercise would be undertaken as a means of physical improvement for its own sake. In the second instance, if the spirit of emulation ran high the girls would be engaging in a course of special physical training, not primarily to benefit themselves physically, but for the set purpose of improving their jumping powers so as to vanquish their nearest competitor.

This distinction, that gymnastics are pursued as a means to an end, and athletics as an end in themselves, would apply equally well to such forms of exercise as walking, running, vaulting, swimming and skating, which may be measured in time or space and thus be made competitive. The element of competition and "sport" must, therefore, enter into what we now term athletics.

Athletics for Men and Athletics for Women. All the highly specialized athletic sports and games have been developed to meet the requirements of men, but many of our girls and women have entered into them, and hence the query: "Are our women becoming masculine?" From the biologist's point of view, men and women, like the males and females of most animals, show by their organization that they have been evolved from a type in which both sexes were combined in the same individual. The separation of the sexes did not destroy this dual nature, as is demonstrated by the development of secondary male characteristics in women in extreme age and of feminine characteristics in aged men. This contention may also be supported by the structure of the body's tissue cells, the nuclei of which are made up of paternal and maternal parts.

It is in consequence of this dual structure that secondary sexual characters are latent in both males and females, which may make their appearance in abnormal individuals or under certain conditions of habit and surroundings. In the early history of mankind men and women led more nearly the same life, and were therefore more nearly alike physically and mentally than in the subsequent centuries of civilization. This divergence of the sexes is a marked characteristic among highly civilized races. Co-education and participation in occupations and recreations of certain kinds may have a tendency to make the ideals and habits of women approximate those of men in these highly civilized races. But such approximation would not belong to the progressive stages of the evolution of mankind.

Do Women Need As Much Exercise As Men? Such changes would be convergences in structure and character, and while they might lead to what we should now consider an advancement this condition would not in any way alter the fact that the tendency would be for women to become virile and men to become effeminate, and both sexes would approximate each other, which would mean the retrogressive period of the evolution of the sexes. These biological theories, although usually considered in connection with the evils of co-education, are equally applicable to the consideration of the evils which have followed the entrance of women into commercial life, and must follow them into competitive athletics which are regulated according to men's rules and standards.

From a physiological point of view woman needs physical

exercise as much as man. She has the same kind of brain, heart, lungs, stomach and tissues, and these organs in her are just as responsive to exercise as in men. Fundamentally both sexes have the same bones and muscles. They are much larger, however, in the average male than in the average female.

The average male weighs about one hundred and thirty-five pounds without clothes and is about five feet seven inches in height, while the female weighs about one hundred and fifteen pounds and is about five feet two inches in height. The male has broad, square shoulders, the female narrow, sloping ones. The male has a large, muscular chest, broad waist, narrow hips and long and muscular legs, while the female has little muscle in the chest, a constricted waist, broad hips, short legs and thighs frequently weighted with adipose tissue. The ankles, waist, feet and hands in the male are much larger than those in the female. In point of strength the female is only about one-half as strong as the male; and the average lung capacity of the male is two hundred and forty cubic inches, of the female one hundred and sixty cubic inches. To these average conditions there are, of course, many exceptions.

Acrobats Not Always What They Seem. In speaking of the mental or physical qualities of a man or woman we should bear in mind that each is the product of two factors, male and female. According to the law of chance a son may inherit from one-tenth to nine-tenths of his characteristics through his mother's side, and a daughter may inherit from one-tenth to nine-tenths of hers through her father's side, the inheritance from remote ancestry not being taken into consideration. Twenty-five per cent, of men and women, however, will inherit about equally from their fathers and mothers.

It is an interesting fact that most of the famous athletes whom I have examined attributed their great power largely to the fine physiques of their mothers. The mother of Louis Cyr, the strongest man in the world, could readily shoulder a barrel of flour and carry it up several flights of stairs. I have seen one of the scrubwomen who clean the Hemenway Gymnasium at Harvard University put a hundred-pound dumbbell above her head with each hand. Great feats of strength, skill and endurance are frequently performed by women at the circus and the vaudeville theater, and it is well known in the profession that some of the best gymnasts performing in public are women disguised as men. In justice to my sex I should mention the obvious corollary to this fact that many of the best acrobats are men attired as women.

No Athletic Sport Prohibitive to Women. I have no hesitation in saying that there is no athletic sport or game in which some women cannot enter, not only without fear of injury but also with great prospects of success. In nearly every instance, however, it will be found that the women who are able to excel in the rougher and more masculine sports have either inherited or acquired masculine characteristics. This must necessarily be so, since it is only by taking on masculine attributes that success in certain forms of athletics can be won. For instance, a woman could not hope to be successful in the practice of heavy gymnastics where she has to handle her own weight without reducing the girth of her hips and thighs and increasing the development of her arms, chest and upper back. She could not hope to succeed in rowing or in handling heavy weights without broadening the waist and shoulders and strengthening the muscles of the back and abdomen. Her relatively short legs and heavy hips and thighs would handicap her severely in all running, jumping and vaulting contests, and render it practically impossible for her to make records in these events comparable to those made by men.

These athletic limitations do not apply only to women as women, but also to men who have women's physical characteristics. Nor do the limitations which I have mentioned apply to young girls from ten to fifteen years of age, who, if properly trained, will often surpass boys of the same age in any kind of game or athletic performance. But it is at these ages that girls have neat, trim and boyish figures. If girls received the same kind of physical training as boys throughout their growing and developing period they could make a much more creditable showing as athletes when they become adult women. The interesting question is: Would such girls become more womanly women, and the boys more manly men?

The Best Sports for Girls. The athletics in which girls most frequently indulge are lawn tennis, running, jumping, hurdling, swimming, skating, field hockey, cricket, basket-ball, rowing, canoeing, fencing, archery, bowling, vaulting and certain forms of heavy gymnastics. Some girls also play ice hockey, lacrosse, baseball, polo and association football, while others box and wrestle and play Rugby football just as their brothers do. There is really no such thing as sex in sport, any more than there is sex in education. All sports are indulged in by most men, and most sports are enjoyed by some women.

There are no sports that tend to make women masculine in an objectionable sense except boxing, baseball, wrestling, basket-ball, ice hockey, water polo and Rugby football. These sports are thought better adapted to men than to women, because they are so rough and strenuous. They afford opportunity for violent personal encounter, which is distasteful to many men as well as to most women. That is the real objection to all antagonistic sports, and that is the reason why it is so difficult for a lady or a gentleman to indulge in them. But we must bear in mind that all athletic sports are of the nature of a contest, and in this very fact lies much of their physical, mental and moral value.

These Make Women More Masculine. Physically all forms of athletic sports and most physical exercises tend to make women's figures more masculine, inasmuch as they tend to broaden the shoulders, deepen the chest, narrow the hips, and develop the muscles of the arms, back and legs, which are masculine characteristics. Some exercises, like bowling, tennis, fencing, hurdling and swimming, tend to broaden the hips, which is a feminine characteristic. But archery, skating and canoeing, which are thought to be especially adapted to women, tend to develop respectively broad shoulders, long feet and deep muscular chests, which are essentially masculine; while rowing, which is thought to be the most masculine of all exercises, tends to broaden the hips, narrow the waist, develop the large front and back thighs and give many of the lines of the feminine figure.

Just how all-round athletics tend to modify woman's form

may be judged by comparing the conventional with the athletic type of woman. The conventional woman has a narrow waist, broad and massive hips and large thighs. In the athletic type of woman sex characteristics are less accentuated, and there is a suggestion of reserve power in both trunk and limbs. Even the mental and moral qualities that accompany the development of such a figure are largely masculine, but this is because women have not yet had as many opportunities to exercise them.

Sports Should Be Adapted to Women. Some of the specific mental and physical qualities which are developed by athletics are increased powers of attention, will, concentration, accuracy, alertness, quickness of perception, perseverance, reason, judgment, forbearance, patience, obedience, self-control, loyalty to leaders, self-denial, submergence of self, grace, poise, suppleness, courage, strength and endurance. These qualities are as valuable to women as to men. While there is some danger that women who try to excel in men's sports may take on more marked masculine characteristics . . . this danger is greatly lessened if the sports are modified so as to meet their peculiar qualifications as to strength, height, weight, etc. Inasmuch as the average woman is inferior to the average man in nearly all physical qualifications, all the apparatus used and the weights lifted, as well as the height and distance to be attained in running, jumping, etc., should be modified to meet her limitations. Considering also the peculiar constitution of her nervous system and the great emotional disturbances to which she is subjected, changes should be made in many of the rules and regulations governing the sports and games for men, to adapt them to the requirements of women.

Modify Men's Athletics for Women. Any one who has had much experience in teaching or training women must have observed these facts in regard to them: Women as a class cannot stand a prolonged mental or physical strain as well as men. Exact it of them and they will try to do the work, but they will do it at a fearful cost to themselves and eventually to their children. Give women frequent intervals of rest and relaxation and they will often accomplish as much in twenty-four hours as men accomplish. So firmly have I become convinced of this fact that I have arranged the schedule of work at both the winter and summer Normal Schools at Cambridge so that periods of mental and physical activity follow each other alternately, and both are interspersed with frequent intervals of rest.

The modifications that I would suggest in men's athletics so as to adapt them to women are as follows: Reduce the time of playing in all games and lengthen the periods of rest between the halves. Reduce the heights of high and low hurdles and lessen the distance between them. Lessen the weight of the shot and hammer and all other heavy-weight appliances. In heavy gymnastics have bars, horses, swings, ladders, etc., adjustable so that they may be easily adapted to the requirements of women. In basket-ball, a favorite game with women and girls, divide the field of play into three equal parts by lines, and insist upon the players confining themselves to the space prescribed for them. This insures that every one shall be in the game, and prevents some players from exhausting themselves. If the field of play is large enough seven or nine players on a side are preferable to the five required by the men's rules. As the game is played today by men, with only five on a side and without lines, it brings a harder strain on the heart, lungs and nervous system than the game of football does.

I am often asked: "Are girls overdoing athletics at school and college?" I have no hesitation in saying that in many of the schools where basket-ball is being played according to rules for boys many girls are injuring themselves in playing this game. The numerous reports of these girls breaking down with heart trouble or a nervous collapse are mostly too well founded. Other instances are recorded where schoolgirls have broken down in training for tennis tournaments, or for running, jumping and swimming contests. These instances generally occur in schools or colleges where efforts are made to arouse interest in athletics by arranging matches between rival teams, clubs and institutions, and appealing to school pride, loyalty, etc., to furnish the driving power. Under the sway of these powerful impulses the individual is not only forced to do her best, but to do even better than her best, though she breaks down in her efforts to surpass her previous records.

There will be little honor or glory in winning a race, playing a game, or doing a "stunt" which every other girl could do. It is in the attempt to win distinction by doing something that others cannot do that the girl who is over-zealous or too ambitious is likely to do herself an injury. For this reason girls who are ambitious to enter athletic contests should be carefully examined and selected by a physician or trained woman expert, and the usual method of trying out unprepared candidates by actual contests in order to determine "the survival of the fittest" should not be allowed.

To Handle a Girl in Athletics. By slow and careful preparation a girl who is organically sound may be trained to participate safely in almost any form of athletics. But inasmuch as the heart, lungs and other important organs do not attain their full power and development until a girl is about eighteen to twenty years of age no girl should be pushed to her limit in physical or mental effort before that time, if ever.

It is during the youthful period of from ten to fifteen years of age that girls are most susceptible of improvement if judiciously looked after; it is during the same period that they are most likely to be injured if they are not wisely cared for. For this reason every girls' school where athletics are encouraged should have a special teacher to look after the physical condition of the girls, who should not be left to become victims of their own zeal and the unbridled enthusiasm of a partisan school community.

Parents should insist upon the supervision of the physical as well as the mental training of their girls, especially if the girls are encouraged, through school politics, to engage in athletic contests. Most of the colleges for women have directors of physical training and instructors in athletics and gymnastics whose duty it is to look after the physical condition of the girls and to supervise their athletic sports and games as well as their gymnastic exercises.

It is largely on account of the intelligent supervision of the physical work in the women's colleges that athletics are less likely to be overdone than in many of the schools for girls where there is little or no supervision, though it is much more necessary than in the colleges.

Cause of Good Health of College Girls. College girls as a class are more matured in judgment and discretion and know better what is best for them than other girls. Most of them have had gymnastics or athletics of some kind in the preparatory schools, which, in addition to vigorous mental and social training, have made habits of right living and obedience to the ordinary laws of hygiene quite necessary to enable the girls to withstand the test of fitting for college.

The good health of college girls as a class is not due so much to their studious life and regular habits of living, as has often been stated, as to their fine physique and good constitutional vigor. In a way they represent the natural correlation between a sound mind and a sound body, and they are the survival of a type from which the weaklings have been weeded out in the elementary and secondary schools. Sometimes these naturally strong and vigorous girls think they can go on working indefinitely with their brains without recreation or physical exercise. They make the fatal mistake of drawing too heavily on their inherited constitutional vigor, without doing anything to add to their capital stock. Sooner or later these girls break down and are out of the race for further honors and preferment. These are the girls whose vital resources the college should try to conserve, for they are going to do the work for which the college stands as soon as they have been graduated.

Women Athletes

By Paul Weiss

Paul Weiss is a professor at Yale University and author of nearly two dozen books. Although he is one of America's most respected philosophers, when writing about women

and sport he is surprisingly imprecise. In this selection,
taken from his 1969 work, Sport: A Philosophical Inquiry, *he*
equates social conditioning with biological behavior. His
view, that "young men's energies overflow to an extent that
the energies of women of the same age do not," has
traditionally been used to limit women's participation
in sports. However, the results of scientific studies and the
achievements of women athletes do not support Weiss's
contentions, and have long made the validity of his
perspective questionable.

Are women athletes to be viewed as radically and incomparably different from men or as comparable with them, both as amateurs and as professionals? . . .

At the Olympic level, women are not permitted to lift heavy weights or to throw the hammer. They are, however, permitted to put the shot, hurl the discus, and throw the javelin. Similarly, they are barred from the pole vault, the high jump, the high hurdles, and the longer foot races, but they are permitted to compete in the long jump, the low hurdles, and the shorter races. They are also barred from the more strenuous team games, but in 1964 they were permitted to compete in the milder game of volleyball—the only team game in which there is no possibility of direct body contact between opponents. . . .[1]

At the international level, some forms of competition appear to be categorically unacceptable, as indicated by the fact that women are excluded from Olympic Competition in . . . wrestling, judo, boxing, weight lifting, hammer throw, pole vault, the longer foot races, high hurdles, and all forms of team games, with the recent exception of volleyball. These forms appear to be characterized by one or more of the following principles: an attempt to physically subdue the opponent by bodily contact; direct application of bodily force to some heavy object; attempt to project the body into or through space over long distances; cooperative face-to-face opposition in situations in which body contact may occur.[2]

Some forms of individual competition are generally acceptable to the college women of the United States . . . swimming, diving, skiing, and figure skating . . . golf, archery, and bowling . . . characterized by one or more of the following principles: attempts to project the body into or through space in aesthetically pleasing patterns; utilization of a manufactured device to facilitate bodily movement; application of force through a light implement; overcoming the resistance of a light object. . . . Some forms of face-to-face competition are also generally acceptable . . . fencing . . . squash, badminton, tennis.[3]

There is considerable justification for these decisions in the results of tests and studies which have been made on women by themselves and in comparison with men. Women have comparatively less muscular strength and lighter arms, do not use their muscles as rapidly, have a longer reaction time, faster heart rates, and achieve a smaller arm strength in relation to their weight than men do. Their bones ossify sooner, they have a narrower and more flexible shoulder girdle, smaller chest girth, and smaller bones and thighs. They also have wider and more stable knee joints, a heavier and more tilted pelvis, longer index fingers, and a greater finger dexterity. They have shorter thumbs, legs, feet, and arm length, a smaller thoracic cavity, smaller lungs, smaller hearts, lower stroke volumes, a smaller average height, lower blood pressure, fatigue more readily, and are more prone to injury. Their bodies are less dense and contain more fat; they have less bone mass, and throw differently.

Some women are outstanding athletes and have better records than most of the men involved in the sport. Some women have made better records in the Olympic Games than were previously made by men. But it is also true that when women compete in the same years with men, the women's records are not better than the men's. Marjorie Jackson won the 100 meter race in 1952 at eleven and one-half seconds, but the best time made in 1896 by a man was twelve seconds. In 1896 the best time for the men's 100 meter free style swimming race was one minute and twenty-two seconds, but in 1932 Helene Madison made the distance in one minute and six-tenths second. More spectacular advances are reported of Russian women in the shot-put and discus. That these and other women can more than match the records made by men in other years is understandable when we take account of the fact that women begin their athletic careers at an earlier age than they once did, that they are willing to practice for considerable periods, that they are benefiting from improved training methods, that they are using better equipment than they had previously, and that more of them are participating in contests and sports.

Women are unable to compete successfully with the best of men, except in sports which emphasize accuracy, skill, or grace—shooting, fancy skating, diving, and the like. Their bones, contours, musculature, growth rate, size, proportion, and reaction times do not allow them to do as well as men in sports which put a premium on speed or strength.

It is part of our cultural heritage to make an effort to avoid having women maimed, disfigured, or hurt. That is one reason why they do not usually engage in and are not officially allowed to compete in such contact sports as boxing, wrestling, football, and rugby, with inexplicable exceptions being made for karate and lacrosse. . . .

One way of dealing with these disparities between the athletic promise and achievements of men and women is to view women as truncated males. As such they could be permitted to engage in the same sports that men do (except where these still invite unusual dangers for them), but in foreshortened versions. That approach may have dictated the different rules which men and women follow in basketball, fencing, and field hockey. Where men have five players on a basketball team, women have six, and are not permitted to run up and down the court. . . . Women's field hockey, a most popular team sport, is played in two thirty-minute halves whereas the men play in two thirty-five minute halves.[4] The illustrations can be multiplied. But enough have been given to make the point that in a number of cases the performances of males can be treated as a norm, with the women given handicaps in the shape of smaller and sometimes less dangerous or difficult tasks.

Men and women can be significantly contrasted on the average and on the championship level as stronger and weaker, faster and slower. So far as the excellence of a performance depends mainly on the kind of muscles, bones, size, strength, that one has, women can be dealt with as fractional men. This approach has considerable appeal. It not only allows us to compare men and women, but to acknowledge that some women will be outstanding, and, given their handicaps, surpass the men. But we will then fail to do justice to the fact that there are men who are more like most women in relevant factors than they are like most men, and that there are women who are more like most men in these respects than they are like most women.

Simply scaling women in relation to men in terms only of their physical features and capacities, can lull us into passing over a number of important questions. Are women and men motivated in the same way? Do they have the same objectives? Is the team play of women comparable to that of men's? Negative answers to these questions need not blur the truth that men and women are of the same species, and that what is of the essence of human kind is therefore present in both. If it is of the nature of man to seek to become self-complete, both male and female will express this fact, but not necessarily in the same way. They may still face different problems and go along different routes. The very same prospects may be realized by both of them, but in diverse ways. Their characteristic desires give different expressions to a common drive; similar activities do not have the same import for both of them.

Comparatively few women make athletics a career, even for a short time, and fewer still devote themselves to it to a degree that men do. Many reasons for this fact have been offered. Social custom, until very recently, has not encouraged them to be athletes. Fear of losing their femininity plays some role. Also, the appeal of a social life quickly crowds out a desire to practice and train, particularly where this forces them to be alone and without much hope of being signally successful. Swimmers, champions at thirteen and fourteen, seem bored with competitive swimming as they move toward the twenties. But more important than any of these reasons seems to be the fact that a young woman's body does not challenge her in the way in which a young man's body challenges him. She does not have to face it as something to be conquered, since she has already conquered it in the course of her coming of age. Where a young man spends his time redirecting his mind and disciplining his body, she has only the problem of making it function more gracefully and harmoniously than it natively can and does.

Men are able to live in their bodies only if they are taught and trained to turn their minds into bodily vectors. And they can become excellent in and through their bodies, only if they learn to identify themselves with their bodies and what these do. Normal women do not have this problem, at least not in the acute form that it presents to the men. A woman's biological growth is part of a larger process in which, without training or deliberation, she progressively becomes one with her body. What a man might accomplish through will and practice after he has entered on his last period of biological growth, she achieves through a process of bodily maturation. By the time she passes adolescence she is able to live her body somewhat the way in which a male athlete lives his.

A woman starts with an advantage over the man in that she masters her body more effortlessly and surely than he does his. . . .

A woman is less abstract than a man because her mind is persistently ordered toward bodily problems. Emotions, which are the mind and body interwoven intimately, are easily aroused in her as a consequence. There are times when she will give herself wholeheartedly to intellectual pursuits, and may then distinguish herself in competition with men. But easily, and not too reluctantly, she slips quite soon into a period when her mind functions on behalf of her body in somewhat the way in which a trained athlete's mind functions on behalf of his. A woman, therefore, will typically interest herself in sport only when she sees that it will enable her to polish what she had previously acquired without thought or effort. . . .

This account raises some hard questions. Why do not more women become athletes? Is it because they find that the advantage that they have in their comparatively easy and satisfying union with their bodies, makes athletic exertion and competition of not much interest? Is that why women athletes are often so young and stop their careers so soon? Why are not men, who have become one with their bodies, content with the result? Why do they go on to use that body, to identify themselves with equipment, to test themselves in contests, and to make themselves into representatives in games? Do they think of their attractiveness as too adventitious and episodic to be able to give them the kind of satisfaction they need? Why is not a good physique enough for all men or even for a good number of those who embark on an athletic career?

An almost opposite set of questions arises when we assume that biologic urge and social pressure tend to make men use an impersonal and women a personal measure of the success they achieve as embodied humans. Why do some men avoid all athletics? Why is it that some women follow an athletic career? It is too easy an answer, and one not apparently supported by the facts, to say that neither is normal. Many a man appears well adjusted, healthy, happy, and admired, despite the fact that he participates in no sport. Many women athletes are attractive; some are married; some have children. We beg our question when we assume that women athletes are men *manqué*, females without femininity, a fact supposedly evidenced by their devotion to an athletic career; we beg it, too, when we assume that nonathletic men are emasculated males, a fact supposedly evidenced by their unconcern with athletic matters.

If perfection can be achieved through the use of a perfected body, one should expect that women would want to compete with their peers. The fact that most do not, cannot be altogether ascribed to the social demands that are made on their bodies and their time. They are not biologic and social puppets. If they were, must we not also say that men are puppets as well, and that they do not devote themselves, as women do, to the task of making themselves attractive, because this is not a socially respectable goal for them? And what should we say then of those who withstand the pressures? Do they alone have a free will enabling them to counter what the others are driven to do? But a free will is not an adventitious feature, like hair, or bow legs, or a snub nose, resident in only some humans; if some women and men have will enough to withstand natural forces, surely all the others have it too, and might be expected to exercise it.

It is sometimes said that women feel challenged by men and yet know that they are not strong enough to overcome them through force. Their best recourse is to try a different route. This is an old story, told again and again in song, play, and novel, and for that reason alone should give us pause. From this perspective, the woman athlete is seen to be at a disadvantage in comparison with men, and must try to become equal or to prove herself superior to them by deception or flattery, or by disorienting them or taking advantage of their weaknesses. But she can also be taken to suppose that she is suffering from an unfair disadvantage, and must strive first to put herself in the position where her biological and social status is on a footing with his. The first of these alternatives sees women as inescapably inferior beings who compensate through wiles for what they cannot obtain through open competition; the second takes her to be disadvantaged and the disadvantages are to be overcome by discipline and determination. Neither alternative is satisfactory; neither takes adequate account of the joy, the devotion, the dedication, and the independence of spirit exhibited by many women athletes, their concentration on their own game, and their indifference to what the men are doing. . . .

A woman must train and practice if she is to become an athlete. This demands that she make an effort to stand away from her body. The result she obtained through biological maturation she must for a while defy.

Most women do not make the effort to train or to participate because they are not subject to the tensions that young men suffer—tensions resulting from the discrepancy in the ways in which their minds and bodies tend to be disposed; the women have already achieved a satisfying integration of mind and body. Nevertheless, women can improve the functioning of their bodies. This is best done through exercise. And it can be helped through a vital participation in games.

A woman who wants to be an athlete must, for the time being, stand away from her body in preparation for the achievement of a different kind of union than that which she naturally acquired, and then must work at reaching the stage at which a man normally is. He starts with a separated mind and body; she must produce this before she can enter on an athletic career. She has to make a sacrifice of a natural union before she begins her athletic career, while he must for a while sacrifice only the pursuit of merely intellectual matters.

A man, of course, has achieved some union of mind and body, but it is not as thorough as a woman's normally is; she, of course, has had her intellectual moments and has found them desirable, but they do not last as long nor come as frequently as his do. Embarked on their athletic careers, both must make similar sacrifices of time and interest in other tempting activities. But some of them—security, a family, and a home—appeal to the woman more strongly and at an earlier age than they appeal to the man, and as a consequence she is prone to end her athletic career sooner than he.

Comparatively few women interest themselves in sport, and when they do they rarely exhibit the absorption and concern that is characteristic of large numbers of men. They do not have as strong a need as men to see just what it is that bodies can do, in part because they are more firmly established in their roles as social beings, wives, and mothers, than the men are in their roles as workers, business men, husbands and fathers, or even as thinkers, leaders, and public figures.

The number of people who give themselves wholeheartedly to an athletic career is not large. More men do so than women, but not enough to make the women who do have the shape of aberrational beings who are to be accounted for by means of a distinct set of principles. Both women and men seek to be perfected. But a woman finds that her acceptance of her matured body, promoted by her carrying out biological and social functions, offers a readily available and promising route by which the perfection can be reached.

Team play does not have much of an appeal to most women. The contests women enter are usually those in which they function as individuals alongside one another. Women are evidently more individualistic in temper, more self-contained than men. They live their own bodies while men spend their time and energy on projects, some of which demand team work. . . .

There are, of course, exceptions. Women make good partners in tennis, and good members of teams in field hockey, basketball, and lacrosse. These exceptions do not belie a general tendency of women to perform as individuals. That tendency is supported by the fact that team sports invite undesirable injuries, and the fact that a woman's acceptance of her body, gradually intensified as she develops, encourages an individualistic outlook. This persists even when she makes a strong effort to abstract from her natural bodily condition and tries to identify herself with her body in the way male athletes identify with theirs. . . .

Once women have decided to engage in athletic activities they must, like men, train and practice; otherwise they cannot hope to do well. Their training follows the same general procedures followed by men, with account, of course, being taken of their difference in musculature, strength, and attitudes toward exhaustion, injury, and public display. Since they do differ from men in these regards, there should be sports designed just for them, enabling them to make maximal use of their distinctive bodies. Thought should be given to the woman's lower center of gravity, her greater flexibility in the shoulders, girdle, and fingers, to her greater stability in the knee joints, and to her greater heat resistance, if we are to give her opportunities for attaining a degree of excellence comparable to that attained by men, and this without taking her to be a fractional male. Though basketball was not designed to take advantage of neglected muscles or organs, but merely to provide an opportunity for men to play in summer and winter, with a minimum amount of easily available equipment, etc., it testifies to the truth that a sport can be a fresh creation, made to satisfy definite purposes. Other new sports could be created; some of these should be built around the use of a woman's body. The rules that govern women's games, particularly those involving teams, today often pay attention to what women can do and what they wish to avoid. Still further rules could be introduced which promote the perfecting of women, by making it possible for them to use their distinctive bodies in distinctive ways.

The sports we have today are heterogeneous. They do not

explore every side of the human body; they are not grounded in an understanding of the main bodily types. More often than not, they are accidental products of history, slowly modified to take advantage of various innovations and to avoid discovered limitations. It is not likely that they are now in the best possible form for men; foreshortened versions cannot be expected to be altogether appropriate to women.

Apart from softball and what is called women's lacrosse, thinking about women's athletics has tended to emphasize gracefulness, accuracy, and coordination, particularly in those sports where some attempt is made to avoid imitating the men. There is an inclination to treat their sports as developments and extensions of the dance. Part of the reason for this, undoubtedly, is our socially inherited view of women's capacity and function; another part is traceable to the fact that women have come into educational institutions and public activities in only comparatively recent times; a third reason is the firm conviction that women should be graceful rather than strong or swift. It is also true that thinking about women's athletics has been characterized by a singular lack of imagination, inventiveness, and concern.

Little choice has been given to women to do more than dance or to adapt the sports which men pursue. Rarely has there been an attempt made to observe and objectively measure what they do. Even in those educational institutions reserved for them, the needs of women are not given the attention they deserve. . . .

One of the aims of a good athletic program is the development and intensification of good character. With the growth of professionalism in the schools, it has been cynically remarked that character building is the most that coaches of losing teams can produce. Were that true it would be enough. Character building justifies an emphasis on athletics in the high schools and colleges. And it is no less needed by women than it is by men. They, too, can profitably learn how to meet crises, how to withstand fear, and where to draw the line between self-indulgence and excessive restraint. And they can learn these things effectively, as men now do, in the gymnasium and on the field. Because the building of character is one of the tasks of education, both women and men should be given the opportunity to prepare themselves for vigorous participation in relevant sports.

Character is built by engaging in limited, well-controlled acts. By imitating what had been splendidly done in the large, the young are helped to grow. We then teach them how to make a proper estimate of who they are and what they can do, by promoting their correct assessment of when and where they are to advance and retreat. Like other virtues, assessment is a habit; like all habits, it is strengthened through repetition. A game allows for its manifestation and provides additional opportunities to entrench it further.

The adoration of the crowds, of the young, and of girls, can make a male athlete misconstrue just what he has achieved, what he is yet to achieve, who he is, and what he might become. The virtues which he painfully acquired in practice are then muted and sometimes distorted; he begins to lose focus and to misunderstand the nature of sport. Women are fortunate in that few of their games come to the attention of the public; they are thereby enabled to avoid most of the misconstructions which beset male athletes. But it is also true that men have in their games a unique opportunity to show what they can do under well-specified, controlled, yet trying circumstances. Men are normally put to tests much more difficult than women face, and as a consequence are able to attain heights denied to them.

The comparative neglect of team sports by women entails that they have fewer opportunities to see themselves as needing to work on behalf of the rest, to make sacrifices for others with whom they share a common objective, and to function in coordinated roles. Because they have fewer occasions when they can carry out difficult tasks together with other players, they do not have the opportunity to master specialized skills, or to know the kind of bodily mastery which others have achieved and of which they make effective use.

Women need to be disciplined and self-disciplined, trained and self-trained, both as individuals and as members of groups. They should have the right and the privilege of contributing in judgment, skill, and imagination to the making of a distinguished game. They, too, have need for and deserve to be suffused with the pleasure that comes from a game well played. They, too, can gain by belonging to something bigger than themselves, such as a tradition-bound sport.

Even when women have little aptitude or interest, they can profit from athletic activity. Physical fitness and bodily tone are thereby usually improved. The women most likely will become healthier, perhaps more graceful, and gain some sense of the fair play that proper playing demands. They might thereby become better adjusted to themselves and to others.

Maladjustment is a form of illness. He who is inharmonious is not well. The movement from the state of being ill to that of being well is therapy or cure. Athletics, because it enables one to move from a poor to a better state of being, can be viewed as a branch of medicine, but one which fortunately finds room for the expression of spontaneity, ingenuity, and judgment. Sport is, of course, not to be treated as primarily an agency for promoting health—or anything else for that matter—regardless of how important this is. Sport is an end in itself. One can become perfected by engaging in it, but it does not have even that perfection as its aim. Perfection is an inevitable consequence of sport only when this is properly pursued in an enclosed arena where men and women find out what man can bodily be. If health is also achieved, so much the better.

Athletes run the risk of overexerting themselves. They expose themselves to strain and the possibility of injury, with a consequent lessened tolerance to disease. Appetites are developed in training which continue to be insistent later, making an accumulation of fat more likely, and, therefore, shorter breath and conceivably a shorter life expectancy. There is a proneness to accidents, particularly when challenging and unpredictable situations have to be faced with quick decisions and appropriate action. An error can scar a life, psychologically and emotionally as well as physically. No one likes to see women subjected to these risks. Still, a risk is not yet a failure. Women need to risk more; only if they do, can they hope to gain all that is possible for them.

A well-trained athlete can rightly expect to engage in sport throughout his life, providing that he so alters his interests, intentions, and efforts that he can keep abreast of changes in his age and physical condition. There is no reason why a woman should not be able to continue in a similar way, and maintain a trim, firm body, suffused with a desirable tone, for an indefinite period. If her athletic potentialities are taken with as much seriousness as a man's, it will become more evident than it now is that sport concerns not only males but mankind, and deserves to be viewed as a basic enterprise, devoted to the production of the excellent in and through the body.

General discourse of this sort deals with idealized types of men and women, and is rooted in speculations for which there is little empirical warrant. Its primary justification is that it opens up possibilities for investigation and may help one focus on issues otherwise slurred over. To some degree it rests on the observation that young men's energies overflow to an extent that the energies of women of the same age do not. Young men are restless and exuberant; vigorous action seems natural to them, while women are content to move smoothly, using their energies to improve the union of body and mind that is natural to them.

Sport is a young person's most promising opening into excellence. Unfortunately, no one has a clear and well-substantiated knowledge as to what a career devoted to sport exactly imports for either men or women. Most of what is claimed for it today is the product of rapid empirical summaries, not a little prejudice and hope, and some limited experiments. We would be on surer ground if we knew how to compare what was done in one sport with what was done in another, and how the various sports were related to one another, for we would then be able to place them all before us and see what they, severally and together, might mean for all, professionals as well as amateurs, women as well as men.

[1] Eleanor Metheny, *Connotations of Movement in Sport and Dance* (Dubuque, Iowa, 1965), p. 53.
[2] *Ibid.*, p. 49.
[3] *Ibid.*, p. 50.
[4] On these see Frank G. Menke, *Encyclopedia of Sports* (New York, 1963), and Parke Cummings, ed. *The Dictionary of Sports* (New York, 1949).

TWO:
Sportswomen

Reflections on Their Lives

FOR SOME WOMEN, sport has been an important part of their lives. This section focuses on a number of these individuals— athletes who have made sports their career as well as women for whom sports fill leisure time. They are black and white

women who come from rural, urban, and suburban areas. Although most of the sportswomen here were active in the last three decades, one was a champion of the 1920s and another lived in the nineteenth century. Despite the diversity, however, the selections about these women are all concerned, in one way or another, with the issue of femininity. Some of the athletes in these selections accept the fact that they must "prove" their femininity since they have chosen a traditionally masculine occupation. Track and field star Willye B. White says, "There is a stigma attached to being a female athlete." To compensate, White likes to "wear short dresses and lots of

makeup" when she is not playing sports. She points out that
"a female athlete is always two different people. A male athlete
can be the same all the time."

Other women in these selections—Frances Willard and Ann
Geracimos—gave up athletic activity when they reached puberty because it was time to "act like a lady." Willard recalls,
"The conventions of life had cut me off from what . . . had
been one of life's sweetest joys." In contrast to Willard and
Geracimos, Althea Gibson did not give up athletics when she
became an adolescent. But she, too, remembers the pressure
to be more feminine, and writes, "It used to hurt me real bad
to hear the girls talking about me. 'Look at her throwin' that
ball just like a man,' they would say, and they looked at me
like I was a freak."

For those, like Gibson, who continued to play sports, the
choice of which sport is closely related to the stereotyped
views of appropriate feminine behavior. Significantly, not one
of the women in this section plays a team sport. This reflects
the fact that contact team sports have generally been considered
less desirable for women than noncontact individual sports
such as swimming, tennis, track and field. As Ann Geracimos
ironically remarks, "Swimming is a clean sport, well-suited to
the classically long-limbed bodies and clean minds of young
American girls." In his selection on Gertrude Ederle, Paul
Gallico suggests that, in the 1920s, the appeal of seeing women
in revealing swim suits was related to the acceptability of that
sport for women. Louise Bernikow chooses *the* acceptable
athletic endeavor for women—cheerleading. Although physically strenuous and requiring practice, cheerleading fits nicely
into traditional notions of feminine behavior, with the women
who cheer supporting the men who play. In fact, the athletic
aspect of cheerleading is usually glossed over, with the emphasis placed on the social nature of the activity.

If these selections indicate that women who participate in
sports have to overcome negative social attitudes, they also
illustrate the satisfactions women find in athletics. Sport offers
the women in these pages the same kind of joy that it has
traditionally offered men. For some, like Willye B. White, it is
a way of getting out of the house, out from under strict
supervision. Many of the women speak of the physical exhil-

aration of sport. In long-distance running, Francie Kraker "discovered the joy of letting go. . . . She became conscious of the small pleasures of being fit—the harmony of mind and body." But, like male athletes, female athletes also experience satisfaction in winning. When Ann Geracimos describes the physical pleasure of swimming, she candidly admits how difficult it is to separate that joy from the joy of winning. Althea Gibson also speaks frankly about the sweetness of victory.

Through their victories, some of the sportswomen in this section have gained wide recognition—often they have delighted in such attention. Althea Gibson "always wanted to be somebody"; for her, and for others, sport is a way out of a tough neighborhood, a way to "make good." Willye B. White's athletic achievements also brought her fame. When she returned to her formerly segregated hometown in Mississippi, White, a black woman, was honored by blacks and whites who had proclaimed a state-wide "Willye B. White Day." In 1926, Gertrude Ederle's English Channel swim was celebrated with a ticker tape parade so large that it broke all previous records.

For many of the women in this section, an athletic life has not been an easy life. But it has offered its share of satisfactions. Althea Gibson writes: "If I've made it, it's half because I was game to take a wicked amount of punishment along the way and half because there were an awful lot of people who cared enough to help me. It has been a bewildering, challenging, exhausting experience, often more painful than pleasurable, more sad than happy. But I wouldn't have missed it for the world."

Sweet Home: Willye B. White

By Pat Jordan

Willye B. White is a five-time Olympian whose competitive track and field career lasted from the mid-1950s to the mid-1970s. White has recently served on the President's Commission on Olympic Sports. This selection, by former

baseball player Pat Jordan, was originally published in
Sports Illustrated in 1975. It is included in Broken Patterns
(1977), a book of Jordan's articles on athletic women.
In it, Jordan follows White "home" to Greenwood,
Mississippi, and, often letting White speak for herself, he
explores her life and thoughts.

P ull over here," she says. There is a sign by the side of the
road—MONEY, MISSISSIPPI. Across the highway, pointing
down a dirt lane, is another sign—SWEET HOME PLANTATION.
Up ahead on a sagging, unpainted, wood-frame building are
the hand-lettered words GROCERY STORE. Farther on is a mobile
home propped on cinder blocks. POST OFFICE. And finally, at
the edge of Money, the tallest building, THE COTTON MILL.

A railroad track runs alongside the highway, and beyond are
rows of green bushy plants flecked with white. A morning mist
hovers over the plants. "I was born out there," she says,
pointing out the car window toward the cotton fields. "On the
plantation. We lived way down in the fields. Now they build
the houses closer to the road, but in those days, before anyone
had an automobile, they built them in the middle of the fields.
My first memory is of my uncle leaving home. My mother
stood in the yard and watched him walk through the fields.
You could see the top of his head moving between the rows.
When he reached the road and turned left, my mother said,
'Well, your uncle's leaving home.' He lives in Oakland now.

"I started chopping cotton when I was 10. We used a long
hoe called 'the ignorant stick.' At five in the morning the
plants were cold and wet and they soaked your clothes as you
moved down the rows. It was a terrible kind of chill. But by
late morning the sun would be hot. Lord, it was hot! You could
see the heat waves shimmering behind you. 'Hurry up,' someone would shout. 'Hurry up, the monkey's coming!' And then
others would pick up the shout, 'The monkey's coming, the
monkey's coming!' Lord, those rows were long! You could
chop for a whole week and never finish a row. I got paid $2.50
a day for 12 hours. I never understood why my father made me
chop until now. He wanted me to be independent, and it
worked. I call him my father, but he was really my grandfather.

I was born with red hair, gray-green eyes, and skin so pale you could see my veins. My real father looked at me and told my mother I was not his child. Three days later he took a boat across the Tallahatchie River from Racetrack Plantation, picked me from my mother's arms and carried me 15 miles to my grandparents'. They raised me. I hold no animosity toward my father. It was just ignorance. Later on he realized that I *was* his child.

"We can go now."

It is nine in the morning and the temperature is 92° as the car heads south to Greenwood. Inside, however, the only sound is the hum of the air-conditioner. The road runs through fields of cotton. Occasionally, there is a shack alongside the highway.

"They painted sharecropper homes all one color, according to the plantation," she says. The ones along here are a faded red. "Plantation life was not bad, really. Every holiday there would be a picnic. They would dig a hole in the ground and start a fire, then throw a fence over the top and roast a pig on it. The owners supplied the food. Each plantation would have its own baseball team and the men would play against each other. If someone died on the plantation everyone would stock that person's house with chickens and greens and stuff, and if it was a woman who was left, they would come and pick her crops for her. It was a warm relationship. The hardest adjustment to make when I moved to the city was learning I could not be friendly, that you did not sit down beside someone on a bus and talk.

"This was a dirt road when I was a child. There were always people walking up and down, usually couples holding hands. They walked from Money to Greenwood and back, a distance of over 20 miles. They were courting. Now that is heavy courting. Then people got automobiles and the Ku Klux Klan started riding again. Right over there is where Emmett Till was lynched. You remember Emmett Till, in the '50s? He was the 14-year-old black boy from Chicago who supposedly whistled at a white woman in a grocery store. That night they dragged him from his uncle's home, tortured and shot him and dumped his body in the Tallahatchie. I remember once my cousin came to visit, and she got off the bus at the wrong stop.

It was already dark so she started to walk. Two white men drove by. They turned around and came back toward her. She knew what was going to happen so she ran into the cotton fields and lay down. They searched for her for hours but couldn't find her. She heard them thrashing up and down the rows. It was the most frightening experience in her life, she said. I imagine it was. I never had any experiences like that. I try not to put myself in that kind of position."

The car crosses the Tallahatchie River into Greenwood's city limits. A tree-lined esplanade divides the main thorough-fare, Grand Boulevard. On both sides are massive mansions, aging and untended. From the second-floor balcony of one hangs a Confederate flag.

"They raised me well," she says. "My grandparents, I mean. It was not the same as having parents, of course. They were not affectionate. I never remember any warmth, any feeling that they really cared, but I never wanted for necessities. And they were strict. Very strict. Why, they would not even let me receive company until I was 16. Whenever a boy called the house and asked to speak to Miss White, my mother—my grandmother—would answer the phone and say, 'I'm the only lady in this house who receives company, and I am sure you are not calling me because I am a married woman.' And they would hang up quick. I appreciate that kind of thing now. It taught me self-respect. But then I just wanted to get out of the house. That was why I turned to sports. It was the only way I could stay out past five o'clock. And I was good at it, too.

"When I was in the fifth grade I played on the high school's varsity basketball team, and when I was 16 I was running track for Tennessee State. Sports was another kind of escape, too. As a child I was an outcast. Blacks were prejudiced against me because I was so light-complexioned. Parents would not let their kids play with me. They said horrible things about me. In school, whenever there was a play or a dance, the instructors would choose the black girls with wavy black hair, starched dresses and patent leather shoes. It did not matter that I could sing and dance better. I was too light and I had this funky red hair, and I was always running around in overalls with a dirty face and no shoes. The only way I could get any recognition was through sports. Now those same parents want me to stop

by their house to visit a spell whenever I return to Greenwood.
I can't do it. I feel funny. I remember things. Lord, I had a
miserable childhood. But I survived. Baby . . . I . . . have . . .
survived."

The car passes over another river, the Yazoo, which is the
color of mud. It smells of mud. It barely flows. A twig floats
without moving. Greenwood (pop. 22,500) lies at the confluence
of the Yazoo and Tallahatchie in the green heart of the
Mississippi Delta. The city still bills itself as "The Cotton
Capital of the World" and is building on the outskirts of town
a replica of a pre-Civil War plantation. Downtown, the city's
streets and sidewalks are littered with balls of cotton that have
spilled out of trucks and warehouses. Although cotton is no
longer the only crop harvested here (soybeans and rice are
increasingly popular), it remains a dominant force in the area,
and the attitudes of the Old South endure.

The townspeople have retained the disquieting habit of
narrowing their eyes at the sight of anyone, white or black,
who is not a native. That narrowed glance, however, is less
threatening than it once was—and still is in nearby Carroll
County. Greenwood blacks have a saying, "It takes a certain
kind of black to live in Carroll County." They do not drive
through Carroll County unless absolutely necessary.

In Greenwood blacks cross the railroad tracks that divide
the black and white communities in order to shop, and they
can dine and dance without incident at the Ramada Inn out on
U.S. 82 and Park Avenue. Still, there are plenty of white-owned
restaurants and bars where blacks do not venture. Greenwood
may not be Carroll County, but neither is it the North, which
is why it is so noteworthy that three years ago the city, not to
mention the entire state, declared March 12, 1972, "Willye B.
White Day" in honor of a 32-year-old black woman who had
passed her youth on a nearby plantation pulling "the ignorant
stick."

On that day the city was festooned with banners and bunting
and larger-than-life photographs of Miss White. There was a
motorcade. Miss White rode in a shiny Buick and waved to the
townspeople lining the streets and shouting her name. The
mayor gave a speech in which he claimed that the city of
Greenwood was proud to have once been the home of Miss

White. She was ushered into the town library, the same library for which her grandfather had once been the gardener and where she could never have gone years before. Inside, the walls were papered with her photograph.

Willye had warranted such an occasion because of her athletic achievements—she has been one of this country's premier competitors in track and field for 20 years. She first won notice in 1956, when as a 16-year-old she surprised the experts by winning a silver medal in the long jump at the Melbourne Olympics. Her mark of 19'11¾" was bettered only by Elzbieta Krzesinska of Poland. This would be her best Olympic showing, but she has made every Olympic team since, finishing 12th at Rome, 12th at Tokyo, 11th at Mexico City. At Munich she was eliminated in the qualifying round. In 1964 she won a silver medal at the Tokyo Games as a member of the 400-meter relay team. In that same year she broke Wilma Rudolph's indoor 60-yard-dash record of 6.8 seconds with a 6.7. It was not until she was 28 that she gave up sprinting. She won four medals in the 1959, 1963 and 1967 Pan-American Games, and has 17 national indoor and outdoor track titles to her credit. Her 17th and last U.S. title came in 1972 when she won the long jump with a leap of 20'6¼".

She is jumping considerably farther today, but so is the competition that she will be facing if she qualifies for her sixth Olympic Games. Last summer she jumped 22'9¾", which, she thinks, is almost two feet longer than she will need to make the Montreal Olympic team, and is only 4½ inches short of the women's world record. She feels she is one of the four best long jumpers in this country today (the others are Martha Watson, Kathy McMillan and Sherron Walker).

In more candid moments Willye White will admit doubt that she can win medals anymore, that she hopes, rather, to inspire younger women to fulfill their talents. "The Olympics are not as much fun anymore," she says. "Now, society says if you don't win five or six gold medals, why bother to go? I go because I like to travel, and because I'm good competition for the younger girls, and because I still feel I am world-record material."

Willye's fame lies less with any single achievement, record or medal than it does with the longevity of her career. The mere fact of having competed all those years is overwhelming. Willye says of herself, "I am the grand old lady of track." On April 30, 1971, a story in *The New York Times* suggested that "women's track and field began with Willye B. White."

She has traveled around the world twice and has competed in scores of foreign countries. She has been better remembered as a goodwill ambassador to these countries than as a victorious athlete. In the People's Republic of China she was a favorite of both its athletes and citizens, and in Moscow she taught the male Russian athletes how to rock 'n' roll. She has dated an Italian nobleman, whom she almost married, and American movie actors like Bernie Casey, who was once a professional football star. Among her good friends were some of the Israeli Olympians murdered in Munich. In 1966 she was cited for "fair play" by UNESCO and, along with other athletes, received her award in Paris amid much pomp and circumstance. The ceremony took place at UNESCO headquarters. A UNESCO official said, "Her poise and charm made her the star of the ceremony." She has been elected to the Black Hall of Fame in Las Vegas and currently serves on the President's Commission on Olympic Sports.

For the last 15 years Willye White has lived in an apartment on the South Side of Chicago instead of Greenwood. She holds a position as a health administrator with the city and trains twice daily. She leads the cosmopolitan yet subdued life of an attractive, independent bachelor woman. She says, "I can go anywhere, talk about anything. My whole personality has been affected by my travels. My travels have broadened me. When you're confined to one area you think the whole world is the same."

She is 35 years old now as she prepares for her sixth Olympics. She has the smooth skin of a younger woman. She has thick brows and a modest Afro hairdo. Her hair is a pale, translucent orange, which, when caught by the sunlight, dissolves into an orange halo. It is one of her most striking features, along with a wide mouth that breaks easily into a smile.

That smile is disarming; it obliterates defenses before they can be properly constructed. At times, it is a conscious weapon, and at other times it is merely a natural emanation from within. Concealed by the softness of that smile and her appearance (everything about her—skin, eyes, hair—is soft, pale, translucent) is a woman of resilient toughness, but not hardness. She takes a firm initiative in setting the tone of relationships with people of whom she is unsure. She has consciously cultivated this quality as a necessity for survival on her terms, but it is not a trait she finds particularly admirable. "When I first came to Chicago," she says, "I applied for a job. I was interviewed by a black man. I asked him if he had anything I might be able to do. He said, 'How about a job as a maid?' I told him that was not really what I was looking for. 'Then say what you want, girl!' he snapped. 'Don't give people that "I'll-take-whatever-you'll-give-me approach." ' He taught me a lot. Being black, I have to be on my toes, to state what I want in a positive way. Whites respect intelligence, authority. I do not like this approach, but society does not allow me to be any different. I would much rather have society make offers than for me to make demands."

Once she has set the tone for a relationship, she flashes that smile, and thereafter appears ingenuous and open. Hers is the kind of candor one first mistakes for confession, for the seeking of approval, but which one soon realizes is nothing more than the frankness of the self-assured.

Unlike many blacks, Willye White does not speak an elitist jargon. She uses no code words. Confronted by such jargon once, she said, "Excuse me, but could you please speak English?" She says of black lingo, "Maybe some people need that kind of thing for identity, but I don't." She speaks perfectly enunciated formal English prose, the prose of an essay. It is not, however, too consciously stylized or devoid of modernisms. But she speaks like a woman from another time, a lady. These days the term "lady" is often used in derision, although once it was prized, as it still is in some places, particularly the South.

The woman Willye White has become is both vastly different from, and inexplicably similar to, the kind of woman she might have become had she never left Mississippi.

Miss Willye B., wearing cut-off jeans and a loose-fitting white blouse, sits on a straight-backed chair on the front porch of her grandparents' home and sips from a can of Tab. She had come to Greenwood thinking it might be for good. She was prepared to surrender her apartment in Chicago, quit her job, abandon her ambition of competing in another Olympics, give up sports, give up her life-style in order to nurse back to health the 83-year-old grandfather who had raised her and who was dying in a small house on East Percy Street. She raises a hand to adjust the kerchief around her head. Her hair has been corn-rowed. She stares at the street and says, "Whenever I would talk to him I would say, 'Now Daddy, don't you die while I'm gone, you hear.' These old people, you know, they're like children. He had lost the will to live. I had to come back to give him the will. He had been in the hospital and had not moved for days. He had a 105° fever. I stayed up all night washing him with cold towels to bring down the fever. The next day he was sitting up, smiling, laughing with me."

She sips from the can, staring blankly at the street. There is only a dirt curb for a sidewalk. The houses are set close together and close to the road, some of them separated by picket fences, and are alike—long, narrow, some unpainted, some sagging this way and that like the deserted barracks of an army. Their fronts are dominated by porches, often screened. Now, in the afternoon of a scorchingly hot day, almost every porch is occupied, mostly by older men and women with dark skin and steely white hair. They stare at the street as if expecting, at any moment, an event. A passing car. Children returning from school. A dump truck delivering dirt.

Parked in front of the house where Miss Willye B. sits are a late-model Buick and a Cadillac, both with California license plates. They belong to her uncles, the Buick to the uncle she had seen leave home when she was two years old and whom she'd seen only once since. He is sitting beside her on the porch. He is a husky man with a gold tooth. Hanging on the wall between them is a flyswatter. Inside the house there is the slapping of backless slippers against a linoleum floor. There is the sound of women's voices, hushed, and then the dialing of a telephone, and now a man's voice inquiring about a tombstone.

"He was a man's man," says Miss Willye B. "In the South, you know, when older blacks are talking to whites they have a habit of taking off their hats. They shuffle their feet a lot and look down or off to the side, but never at a white man's eyes. My father, now—my *grand*father, I mean—he never took off his hat and he always looked white people in the eye. When I realized what he did—I was only a child—I began to practice it in front of a mirror. We didn't get along then. He was a stubborn man, but as I got older I realized how similar we were. When he got sick I started commuting between Chicago and Greenwood.

"I could live in Greenwood, you know. Yes I could. It is not the same as it was during the freedom marches. You don't fear personal injury anymore. And the other kind of thing I can handle. For example, when my grandfather passed I went to the doctor's office to find out the exact cause of death. The receptionist there was hostile. Finally, I said to her, 'Now listen, Miss, I think we have a misunderstanding here and we had best straighten it out.' We did.

"I *would* have come back to live here. I feel I am what I am today because of my grandparents. If I could give them some happiness by coming home, I was willing to do it. I have roots. It does not matter how far I have traveled and where I live. Sometimes I envy the younger athletes. They just take off anytime they want. They never worry about returning home. I would like to be like that sometimes, and then other times I am thankful I do have roots."

She flicks at a fly with her hand and her silver bracelets jingle. Her fingers are long and thin and adorned with sparkling rings, metals and precious stones of various hues. Her nails are frosted pink. Around her neck she wears assorted gold and silver chains and pendants.

"God has it all planned," she says. "He does not give you burdens you cannot bear. I was only home a few days when my grandfather passed. And then my brother came home and had a seizure right on the kitchen floor. He would have died, too, if it had not been for me. And I said, 'Oh Father! Oh Father! what have you in store for me next!' All I could think of was getting out on the track again and running and running and running and letting the tears come."

Ah . . . Willye . . . runs . . . leaps . . . hangs . . . lands in a spray of sand. She sits in the sand like a child, legs outstretched.

Behind her, Rosetta Brown, dark, plump, wearing slacks and a jersey, gets down laboriously on all fours and begins to measure the jump with a tape.

Two blacks in their late teens watch from the cinder track that surrounds the football field and long-jump pit at Greenwood High School. Home of the Bulldogs. One of the youths is muscular, athletic-looking, the other is thin, knowing, wearing purple shades. The athletic-looking youth says, "I heard Miss Willye B. was back so I come to watch."

Willye takes off her track shoes and stands up. She is 5'4", 130 pounds. The muscles in the front of her thighs are so developed they partially obscure her kneecaps. Her stomach is flat. She is wearing a kerchief, a Pan-American Games T shirt that has been cut off just below the bust, exposing her navel, and tight-fitting track shorts. Her toenails are painted pink. The youth with the purple shades stares as she dusts the sand off her rump and the backs of her thighs. He says, "My main interest is Miss Willye B., too."

Whenever Willye works out, she is watched by boys. They follow her to the weight room, where she can squat upward of 380 pounds; then to the football field, where she sprints from goalpost to goalpost, her thick thighs writhing and her knees rising almost to her chin; then to the track where she takes each of the 10 hurdles with an effortless leap and a rhythmic crunch of her feet; and finally to the long-jump pit where she concludes her workout. After she leaves a segment of her workout, a few boys remain behind to imitate her just-completed feats. They try to heft the weights she had mastered, or leap the hurdles she had cleared, and when their feet get tangled and they tumble to the cinders they are jeered and hooted at by friends. They laugh at themselves, too, when they fall, because in their mimicry of Miss Willye B. there is no desire to equal or surpass her efforts. They are merely trying to show how inadequate they are by comparison.

Willye resumed training shortly after the death of her grandfather. Since she promised her grandmother, a gaunt woman with quivering hands, that she would not leave Greenwood until a tombstone had been arranged for, she is conducting her workouts at Greenwood High. She could never have used its facilities years ago. But the school has been integrated, and

now as she works she can see on the practice field the Bulldogs'
integrated football team going through its paces under the
watchful eyes of black assistant coaches and a white head
coach, heavy men. The head coach, dressed in shorts, is only
too happy to make available the school's facilities for Miss
Willye B. He seems to have little choice in the matter. Willye
approaches him during a coaches' meeting and says, "Coach,
I want to use the weight room now."

"Sure thing, Miss Willye."

Walking toward the weight room with the coach, Willye
smiles and says with only a hint of a drawl, "Say, Coach, didn't
you play at Mississippi College?"

The coach lowers his head and says, "Yes, I did, Miss
Willye."

"I heard you were *some* kind of football player."

Watching from a distance, Rosetta Brown laughs. "That
Red, she's somethin' else. She gonna have him all over her in
another minute."

Willye's workouts are conducted during the hottest part of
the afternoon, and when she is in Greenwood, Rosetta, her
childhood friend, always comes along. Rosetta sets up the
hurdles on the track, spacing them just so at Willye's instruction, and then Rosetta rakes and hoes the sand in the long-
jump pit as Willye prepares her jump. Finally, at Willye's
urging, Rosetta may begin to train, too. Not for any international competition, but merely to lose weight. She begins to
jog. While Willye lopes gracefully over the hurdles, Rosetta
huffs and puffs around the field with tiny steps. Passing Willye,
Rosetta calls out in a high voice, "Oh, Red! I'm gonna be a
traffic stopper again!" and plows on. Willye smiles.

Their lives, once concentric, have long since branched off
on different tangents. Willye pursued sports, traveled, became
famous, while Rosetta remained at home, married, had five
children, saw her husband leave, and took a job as a supervisor
in the cafeteria at Mississippi Valley State University. Once
Willye invited her to Chicago. Rosetta stayed only a few days
and returned to Greenwood. "I didn't like the city," she says.

"Rosetta has never traveled," says Willye. "I've experienced
things in my life she would never see in her world. Whenever
I get the chance I like her to share in some of those things.

They are not big things, but they are experiences she can talk about for the rest of her life."

Although Willye's life may have been a succession of victories, Rosetta's has not been entirely devoid of them. She has raised her children, and has participated in civil-rights protests in Greenwood. "She was a freedom marcher," says Willye. "On one occasion she was attacked by police dogs.

"I look at Rosetta sometimes and think, that could have been me. Sports gave me an escape. My mother—my grandmother—was against my being in sports. But it kept me off the street. The time I spent at practice wore me out. If I needed 20 hours of sleep to compete successfully then I got it. And I learned early that to survive in sport I had to be a thinker. I was better organized than most girls my age. I knew what was best for myself. That is one reason why I turned from sprinting to the long jump. It is very technical. It requires thinking, strategy, not just power. The other reason was that I saw for every 500 sprinters there were only two long jumpers. I played the odds. It was easier. Long-jumping is something I could do successfully when I became older. When I was younger I had the talent, the determination, the hard work—and no coaching. I have learned more in the last few years than I did in the previous 25. That is why I am still competing. But nothing is forever. I do not expect to jump forever.

"The hardest thing for me to do when I quit will be to find some way to fill the hours between 4 and 7 p.m. Those are the workout hours. But I will be able to quit when the time comes. Some people say I am afraid, that time has passed me by and I am still hanging on. I see athletes I once competed with and they say, 'Willye, when you gonna quit? You're too old.' And I say, 'You are the same age as me, why did you quit?' And they say, 'Well, I got married and I had kids.' 'Well, I am not married,' I tell them, 'and I don't have kids and I am not 50 pounds overweight like you are.' I know my body and its capabilities. I am going to sacrifice this year so I can compete in my sixth Olympic Games and win a medal. It is my Last Hurrah. They say it cannot be done. That I am too old. But I love challenges. It will mean more to me now than ever just because society says I am too old. I have been old for a very long time."

When Willye completes her final workout before returning
to Chicago, she walks over to the football coach to thank him
for his kindness. The coach is standing among uniformed
players. He is shouting instructions to the part of the squad
that is scrimmaging. A few parents, all white, are standing on
the sidelines. Willye, wearing shorts and her cut-off T shirt,
slips between the players, is dwarfed by them and their
grotesque shoulder pads. She taps the coach on the back; he
whirls around and seeing her there smiles. She says something,
shakes his hand firmly and gives him that dazzling smile. She
slips out from between the players and walks toward the car.
The eyes of everyone, players, coaches, parents, are on her.
When she reaches the car, she says, "Personality, Baby. That
is all I got."

The platinum blonde is still beautiful, standing there in the
one-room Greenwood airport staring out the window at a
runway partly covered with weeds. She taps a foot impatiently.
She is wearing a pink chiffon dress and white spikes. Beneath
the gauzy dress one can see the delicate lace of a slip. Her hair
is stiff and flipped in a style favored by Miss America beauty
contestants. She has the bold, perfect features of a beauty
queen, although they are much too heavily made up. Her face
is orangey, her brows too sharply penciled, her lips too thickly
smeared. She is the kind of woman who prepares prematurely
for a loss others have not yet noticed.

It is eight in the morning and Willye White and her
companion are the only other persons in the airport. Willye is
sitting with her back to the window. "I am glad to be getting
back to Chicago," she says. "I miss my boyfriend. He is a
policeman. I do not date athletes anymore. It is a waste of
time. Athletes expect you to idolize them and since I am an
athlete, too, I do not think they are a big deal. All female
athletes have the same problem. We are too independent for
male athletes. And then there is the femininity thing. As an
athlete you take on certain masculine qualities on the field.
Off the field you have to be feminine. It is not a natural
transition. You have to work very hard at it. There is a stigma
attached to being a female athlete. If you wear your hair too
short and you are always in jeans, the fellows say you are

funny. That is why I like to wear short dresses and lots of makeup."

Willye no longer looks like the woman sitting on the porch of her grandparents' home. She is wearing a halter top that bares her midriff. Her eyelids are dusted with makeup and her cheeks have a gloss. She has discarded her kerchief and fluffed her hair.

"A female athlete is always two different people," she continues. "A male athlete can be the same all the time. He doesn't have to defend his masculinity. On the track I walk very stiffly but on the street I make sure that everything is moving."

There is the sound of a single-engine airplane. The blonde woman smooths the sides of her dress with her palms and walks outside toward the runway. She waits while the plane taxis up beside her. Its whirling propeller blows back her hair and flattens her dress against her body. The hatchway opens and stairs drop down. A man's hand grasps her hand and helps her inside. The door closes, the plane taxis onto the runway and is gone.

"There is nothing in this world like the Southern Belle," Willye says. "She has never worked, never done anything, and yet Miss Belle is a proud woman. That one, she was not a Greenwood girl. Maybe she was from Greenwood once, but she has gone to the city. She has gotten herself a sponsor. When I was 16 I had a sponsor, a kindly old white man. When he died, he left me well. That is why I have been able to pursue my track career. This past week when word got out that Miss Willye B. might be returning to Greenwood I had three offers. A sponsor will bid for you, just like at an auction. If you are going to listen you better make sure that the house and the furniture and the car are in your name. You don't want to be sleeping some night and have him come and drive off with your Cadillac."

The door opens. An old black man, wearing a cowboy hat and carrying suitcases, enters. He is followed by his wife, his daughter and her two children. "Good morning," he says to Willye. "How are you this morning, Miss?"

"Fine," says Willye. "Good morning to you, too." In quick succession, his wife, his daughter and her children, all say, "Good morning." Then they sit and wait. The daughter, who

is dressed in a pants suit, sits back and crosses her legs. The
children are big-eyed, silent. The old man and his wife are
white-haired. They sit on the edge of their seats. The old
woman is rocking, and the old man is hunched over, fingering
the brim of his hat.

"They are so friendly in the South," says Willye. "In Chicago
I always make sure I've got protection. Eventually, I will come
back to Greenwood. I can see myself as an old lady living on
East Percy Street. I will get up at five o'clock in the morning
and go stand on the porch to watch for the garbage truck.
Maybe I will go out to my garden and sprinkle dust on the
beans and then go inside to prepare breakfast, lunch and dinner,
all at the same time. Then I will go back outside to take care
of everybody's business on the street. I will sit on a straight-
backed chair on the porch and nod. My head will nod down to
my chest until I am asleep. That is it. My life."

Her hands rest one on top of the other in her lap. She looks
suddenly very slight, fragile. And then she begins to smile,
that same dazzling smile, only somehow different, her mouth
pulling down slightly into her jaw.

She is still smiling moments later when, in a flat, cold voice
completely devoid of inflection, she says, "Life is a bitch, ain't
it, Baby?"

See Jane Run

By Lucinda Franks

*Lucinda Franks has covered foreign and national affairs for
United Press International (UPI) and the* New York
Times. *Her investigative series on radical Diana Oughton
and the Weather Underground earned her a Pulitzer
Prize in 1971. She is the author of* Waiting Out a War: The
Exile of Private John Picciano *(1974) and is currently
writing a novel.*

In this 1973 Ms. Magazine *article, Franks profiles
Olympic runner Francie Kraker to illustrate the obstacles*

*faced by female Olympians at the 1972 games. Although
women's status continues to improve with each Olympiad,
most of the problems described here still exist, including
the Barr Sex Test. And even in the 1980 Olympics, women
will be included in only sixteen of the thirty-seven
competitions.*

The Olympic stadium was packed with 80,000 blurred heads. Francie Kraker thought she heard voices emerging from the roar ("C'mon, Francie, you can do it!"), or maybe they were inside her head. She was going all out to keep contact with the leaders of the 1,500-meter race; their arms were pumping back and forth like piston rods. Earlier, they had walked single file in silence through a narrow corridor onto the field, their spiked track shoes clicking on the concrete. A sensation of panic came to her then. A fear of falling, being spiked in the face—of running last. But now she was up with the front-runners, and it seemed too easy. She felt light, almost giddy.

The whole race felt different from any she had ever run. Until this time, she had always been afraid of the starting gun. In the seconds before it went off, her feet seemed to want to run backward instead of forward. She would be stretched taut like a bow on the starting block, in danger of snapping back at any moment, wanting to yell out, "Wait, wait just a minute. I'm not ready!" This time, though, she was ready.

The 800-meter mark was called out in three languages— English last—and she suddenly realized how slow the pace had been. They had all been saving up and the real speed would come now, in the third lap. She took off with the others, holding back nothing: 600 meters to go, 500, 400, 300. She had never run so fast in her life. Even in the last 200, when she realized her leg speed was just not good enough, and she would be left behind.

The corners of her mouth were white by the time she crossed the finish line. Not knowing what to expect (once before, she had turned blue and thought she was dying), she sat down and took off her shoes to keep her mind off her body. The results of the semifinals flashed onto the electronic board. No. 7—Francie Kraker. Next to last. She had been eliminated.

Her legs were heavy and tired as she left the stadium, but she was not sick. In fact, she felt rather good. She had run 4: 12.8, 2.4 seconds better than ever before, and that took the edge off her disappointment at not making the finals. But it was more than that. She felt unusually good. Loose, free, in harmony. A harmony that could never be achieved from running "like a lady," knees knocked, elbows locked—an apologetic waddle that somehow got to be considered decorous.

Francie was one of 900 women athletes competing in the Munich games. Although they represented only a small percentage of the total entries, it was a long struggle to get into the Olympics at all.

In 776 B.C. the ancient Greeks, who had definite ideas about the function of the female body (bearing children, servicing men, and pleasing the eye), barred women from their Olympic games. Any female caught near the stadium was condemned to death and hurled from a cliff.

Things hadn't changed much by 1896, when the first modern Olympics were held. But women slowly began chipping away at the concept of athletics as exclusively a man's domain. By 1928 women were competing in swimming and a few select track events, and this year female competitors were an integral part of the festival instead of just a grudging afterthought.

The women's Olympic Village at Munich was bustling with new world-record breakers, individualists, and political activists: U.S. discus thrower Olga Connolly, a recent refugee from Czechoslovakia, who mobilized Olympians to send anti-war telegrams to President Nixon (she was chosen to carry the U.S. flag at the opening ceremony, an honor traditionally given to a man); Australian swimmer Shane Gould, who got almost as many medals and as much publicity as Mark Spitz; and Russia's Ludmila Bragina, who broke the women's 1,500-meter world record by so wide a margin that people were going around for days saying, "No woman can run as fast as that." But it was Mary Peters, 33, Britain's gold medalist in the pentathlon, who perhaps did most to convince skeptics that sportswomen should be taken seriously. She brought home to anguished Northern Ireland perhaps its only moment of glory. Asked what worried her most about training amid bombs and bullets, she said, "You'd think, as a woman, I'd fear getting my face cut. But I've always thought, Not my legs; I'll be all right if my legs don't get hurt."

The Olympic women found that they had more to fight for than medals during the three weeks of excitement, frustration, and profound tragedy. Protests were launched over women's exclusion from sports they commonly competed in outside the Olympics—basketball, rowing, cycling, among others—and in the end the International Olympic Committee did yield to the persistence of European sculling champion Ingrid Dusseldorp, and scheduled women's rowing for the 1976 games.

The U.S. women's team criticized the fact that its large medical staff did not include a single woman, or even a single doctor who showed any great knowledge of the special problems of female athletes. The younger athletes (some of the swimmers were barely 15) could not gather the courage to consult men about gynecological problems, and the older ones who did were often dismissed as having overactive imaginations. Two sprinters who had contracted yeast infections were given ointment for insect bites. The doctors were equally vague when track competitors came in worried about the effect of premenstrual stress on their performances. Although medical consultants at the pre-Olympic training camp had advised them to take birth-control pills to prevent their periods coinciding with their competitions, the U.S. Olympic doctors advised against it—all of which created unnecessary last-minute panic and confusion.

Another persistent complaint was that the women always seemed to be getting half of what the men got, from equipment to visitors' permits to their living quarters. Passes for the men's village were in good supply, but the adjoining women's village, fortified by a tall wire fence and several checkpoints, was as hard to penetrate as Buckingham Palace. In the end, only "husbands" of female athletes were permitted entry. Forged passes for the women's village started cropping up by the dozens, and shadowy figures were scaling the fence at night.

The sex tests, required of all female entrants to determine hormone levels, were humiliating—as well as painful. One American swimmer described the testing room as "full of these bug-eyed doctors looking you up and down as though they

were dying to say, 'Flat-chested, eh? Well, we'll see. . . .' "
Bona fide womanhood was established by pulling out a strand
of hair (which often took more than one yank to get) and
examining the cells in the root. (Women athletes are tested
because their strength doesn't conform to the "feminine"
stereotype. According to this logic, men capable of getting to
the Olympics cannot be suspect; they're never tested at all.)

But these complaints were minor compared to the discrim-
inatory practices which began long before the 1972 Olympic
torch was lit. Months before the track and field trials, former
U.S. medalists who expected to qualify for Munich caught wind
of a plan by the Olympic Committee to locate the women's
pre-Olympic training camp at Champaign, Illinois, while the
men trained in Maine, where the climate was similar to
Munich. They wrote letters urging that a cooler, drier site be
chosen, to which the U.S. Olympic Committee replied with
the curt suggestion that the women concentrate on making
the team before making demands. To Olga Connolly, this was
an example of how the committee treated men as "human
beings capable of decisions" and women like "trained seals."
The humidity in Illinois turned out to be unbearable—a long
road run meant two days of dehydration.

The committee officials appeared particularly eager to see
that the women were in shape for the games. While attendance
at the training camp was made optional for men, women were
scratched from the team if they didn't show up. But the same
officials lost their interest in practice sessions when the
women, backed by the Amateur Athletic Union, lobbied for a
warm-up meet with the international track stars like the one
the committee had arranged for the men in Europe a month
before the Olympics. The best the committee could come up
with was a brief meet in Indianapolis with a Canadian squad.
The women's track and field team claims that, as a result, it
went into the games at a double disadvantage: the women had
missed the opportunity to learn just what kind of international
competition they would be up against (it turned out to be
much fiercer than they expected), and they had been forced to
race against one another at a time when it was most important
to build up team unity.

Francie Kraker had none of this in mind 11 years ago when she ran her first 100-yard dash in Ann Arbor, Michigan. It was sheer desperation that started 17-year-old Francie running. She had shot up into adolescence in misery—all elbows, knees, long skinny hands, and a head higher than the tallest boy in her class. To make matters worse, she could run faster than any of the boys. As a social misfit, so different from the petite and popular girls—who led the cheers or sat on the sidelines in pleated skirts—Francie began to look to track as a means of winning some kind of respect.

Like many female athletes, Francie owes her entry into serious athletics to a dedicated gym instructor who offered to train her for the Olympics and set up an Amateur Athletic Union club totally outside the school. The AAU club depended on the good will of sympathetic people for the use of a track, taking their chances that a bathroom, let alone a locker room, would be left unlocked for them. In her first eight years of competition, Francie never remembers being able to shower and change after a meet.

The AAU did little to help improve conditions. They ran the women's section more or less like a Sunday school. Scholarships and promotion money usually went to the men, and if the women did receive money from promoters for a competition abroad, they had to bear the added expense of taking along a chaperone—a rule that did not apply to men. Pressure on women to appear "neat and standard" once put Francie into a rage at a West Coast meet: AAU officials complained that her hair was too long and sloppy, handed her a headband (which she detested), and said she could not compete without it.

In spite of poor facilities, stuffy officials, and other hardships, Francie kept running, spending every spare moment on the track. Each time she won a race, it doubled her passion to win again—but the applause, the ribbons and medals never totally eradicated the desire to flee when she was called to the starting line to perform at something so offbeat for her sex. Although she never quite felt she was giving herself completely to her running, she was becoming strong and independent.

By 1968, Francie had reached Olympic caliber, and she ran the 800 meters in Mexico City. Soon after, American coaches who had been training women cautiously, uncertain how much their bodies could take, discovered that females could run long distances. The 1,500 meters was introduced in women's events, and coaches began to give distance—jogging, road runs—as well as speed training. It was then that Francie's attitude toward her sport began to change. From the day of her first race, running had been simply a means of avoiding anonymity. Winning was the only important thing, and the means to that end, the training itself, offered no source of pleasure. Running intervals—repeats of some distance over and over with short rests in between—was boring and left one with a painful oxygen debt.

With jogging, she discovered the joy of letting go, of taking off barefoot down a country road or across a field. She became conscious of the small pleasures of being fit—the harmony of mind and body, the ability to bound up stairs with ease, to sleep well and wake with a feeling of anticipation. In the morning, she would crave a cross-country run and she wondered why no one had ever told her about the intense pleasure of flying through the woods, watching the trees and ground merge with her motion. At those times, she never doubted who she was. Winning diminished in importance when she realized she had already won most of what she wanted.

The United States Women's Olympic Team made a poor showing in Munich, particularly in track and field (down from 3 gold medals in 1968 to 0). As the rest of the world bagged medal after medal, leaving American track stars far behind, it became obvious that U.S. training methods were pallidly inferior. The Polish women, for instance, trained steadily for four years, the Olympic goal taking precedence over home and family. The East Germans underwent even more stringent programs, and they had an added incentive. Not only were they paid to train full time (U.S. competitors get no such subsidy and usually work out in between holding down jobs or homes), but they were guaranteed $6,000 for every gold medal they won. The U.S. coaches babied their athletes in comparison with the spartan methods of training employed by the Japanese: volleyball coach Koji Kojima's favorite technique was to throw the ball in a team member's face when she wasn't looking, thereby making her angry enough to whop it harder. If that didn't work, he would twist her nose.

The fundamental reason behind the failure of the U.S. women's track team in Munich is that there are just not enough qualified coaches in America who are willing to bother with "ladies." Female coaches are rare, and few men are willing to take lower pay and less prestige for the sake of training women.

"Americans just haven't gotten around to recognizing that women can sweat and strain and achieve, on a smaller scale, as much as men," remarked Jim Bush, a UCLA coach who has trained many former Olympians. "Even now, when I try to schedule a couple of women's events in a men's track meet, I get all sorts of criticism. It's a vicious circle—women get poor training and then never have a chance to improve through competition because promoters don't want to enter athletes who have been improperly trained. It destroys spectator interest, and they lose money."

Perhaps someday there will be equality of opportunity. Equality of performance between men and women in traditional sports probably will never be—a possibility feminists have found hard to accept. The best woman doctor, lawyer, writer might be as good as or better than the best man, but the best male athlete may always be better than the best woman—at least in existing sports, which have been designed by and for male musculature anyway.

It is true that the gap between world records for men and women is narrowing, especially in swimming, but this is primarily because women, who came into sports so late, are improving that much more rapidly. The reason they are breaking men's records of fifty years ago is largely due to the vast improvement in coaching techniques, equipment, and diet since then.

This does not mean, however, that women do not have qualities all their own which give them advantages in certain sports. Their high degree of balance and flexibility, for instance, makes their performances in gymnastics and, often, diving closer to aesthetic perfection than men's. In equestrian sports, women have shown they possess a greater sensitivity in handling the reins and manipulating the horse—British horsewoman Alison Dawes, for example, was the only one who could control a horse called Maverick after several men had failed. In tennis, women may use less brute force, but this often causes them to develop a strategy and skill that men do not, and may make women's tennis more interesting to watch.

In spite of the differences in their capabilities, women improve as much in training as men. Their performances begin at a lower level and reach a maximum below that of men, but the range is the same. Moreover, it is only the *best* male athletes who can sometimes better women. A trained woman athlete of superior skill can react, run, jump, and throw faster than an untrained man or one of mediocre talent. That alone seems a good enough reason to end sex divisions in many sports and to integrate men and women in teams on the basis of skill, size, and weight. In the Olympics, men and women compete in shooting and equestrian events, and there is talk of future mixed relay teams in swimming and track.

Suggestions of sports integration, however, have been met with furious responses from male athletic officials in the United States. The first woman jockey, Kathy Kusner, a member of the U.S. Olympic equestrian team, had to go to court to get her license. Cases are still being fought by women who want to be baseball umpires, little league players, football coaches. Even the comparatively tame world of golf responded with panic to the threat of female penetration. The U.S. Golf Association still won't hear of men competing against women, and point to a rule that the men hurriedly rushed through in an emergency meeting back in 1948 when the late Babe Didrikson Zaharias—perhaps the greatest woman athlete of all—announced her intention of entering the U.S. Open.

Such frantic reactions on the part of male athletes are too complex to be dismissed as *machismo*. Even fear of being beaten by an "inferior" is too simple an explanation. It seems unlikely that men would go to such lengths to keep women away from their competitions if competing against one another didn't in itself hold some special importance. The mere presence of women is enough to devalue these sacred male ceremonies.

One woman athlete living in New York notices a distinct difference in the reactions of a man when he's playing squash against another man and when he's playing against a woman just as good: "There's something missing when the woman comes in. It's hard to put your finger on, but men seem to get a certain thrill competing against each other ... it's a whole emotional thing, sweating with each other, showing off their bodies. It's almost a kind of repressed homosexuality."

No one has ever noticed quite the same thing going back and forth between women competitors. But then women can touch, cry, hug, and otherwise relate to each other on an emotional level, for that is within the bounds of their sex role. Perhaps sports offers men a vital and coveted medium through which they can express to each other indirectly what society has forbidden them to express outright, and perhaps they fear the consequences of letting the "outside" into their club. If so, it is ironic because it is a similar desire to contravene the limitations of sex roles and express themselves in a natural way that has led women to sports. Francie Kraker felt that fulfillment as she raced in the Olympics:

"The most important thing that's happened to me over the years is that I've learned to define myself only in terms of myself. I consider myself lucky when I see certain girls with their fleshy bodies done up in cute clothes for the benefit of their men. I feel sorry for them because I know they don't have any idea of what it's like to get out there and move and feel the way most guys do sometime in their life."

How I Learned
to Ride the Bicycle

By Frances E. Willard

Frances E. Willard, best known as the leader of the Woman's Christian Temperance Union from the late 1870s to the late 1890s, has been called one of the ablest women of the nineteenth century. A skillful speaker, indefatigable

organizer, and committed reformer, she made the WCTU the
largest and most ambitious women's organization in
the United States. Besides temperance, its numerous causes
included women's suffrage, physical culture and hygiene,
prison and education reform, and home health care. She
coined its motto: "Do Everything."

Willard's enthusiasm for the bicycle in the 1890s
was therefore in keeping with her larger interests and
characteristic of her approach toward life. Though she was
one of an estimated 30,000 women who owned and rode
bicycles in that decade, she was the only one to write
an entire book about it. In A Wheel Within a Wheel; How I
Learned to Ride the Bicycle *(1895), she equated mastery*
of the bicycle with mastery of the self. This selection is
excerpted from that book.

From my earliest recollections, and up to the ripe age of
fifty-three, I had been an active and diligent worker in the
world. This sounds absurd; but having almost no toys except
such as I could manufacture, my first plays were but the
outdoor work of active men and women on a small scale. Born
with an inveterate opposition to staying in the house, I very
early learned to use a carpenter's kit and a gardener's tools,
and followed in my mimic way the occupations of the poulterer
and the farmer, working my little field with a wooden plow of
my own making, and felling saplings with an ax rigged up
from the old iron of the wagon-shop. Living in the country, far
from the artificial restraints and conventions by which most
girls are hedged from the activities that would develop a good
physique, and endowed with the companionship of a mother
who let me have my own sweet will, I "ran wild" until my
sixteenth birthday, when the hampering long skirts were
brought, with their accompanying corset and high heels; my
hair was clubbed up with pins, and I remember writing in my
journal, in the first heartbreak of a young human colt taken
from its pleasant pasture, "Altogether, I recognize that my
occupation is gone."

From that time on I always realized and was obedient to the
limitations thus imposed, though in my heart of hearts I felt
their unwisdom even more than their injustice. My work then

changed from my beloved and breezy outdoor world to the indoor realm of study, teaching, writing, speaking, and went on almost without a break or pain until my fifty-third year, when the loss of my mother accentuated the strain of this long period in which mental and physical life were out of balance, and I fell into a mild form of what is called nerve-wear by the patient and nervous prostration by the lookers-on. Thus ruthlessly thrown out of the usual lines of reaction on my environment, and sighing for new worlds to conquer, I determined that I would learn the bicycle. . . .

As a temperance reformer I always felt a strong attraction toward the bicycle, because it is the vehicle of so much harmless pleasure, and because the skill required in handling it obliges those who mount to keep clear heads and steady hands. Nor could I see a reason in the world why a woman should not ride the silent steed so swift and blithesome. I knew perfectly well that when, some ten or fifteen years ago, Miss Bertha von Hillern, a young German artist in America, took it into her head to give exhibitions of her skill in riding the bicycle she was thought by some to be a sort of semi-monster; and liberal as our people are in their views of what a woman may undertake, I should certainly have felt compromised, at that remote and benighted period, by going to see her ride, not because there was any harm in it, but solely because of what we call in homely phrase "the speech of people." But behold! It was long ago conceded that women might ride the tricycle—indeed, one had been presented to me by my friend Colonel Pope, of Boston, a famous manufacturer of these swift roadsters, as far back as 1886; and I had swung around the garden-paths upon its saddle a few minutes every evening when work was over at my Rest Cottage home. I had even hoped to give an impetus among conservative women to this new line of physical development and outdoor happiness. . . .

Not a single friend encouraged me to learn the bicycle except an active-minded young school-teacher, Miss Luther, of my hometown, Evanston, who came several times with her wheel and gave me lessons. I also took a few lessons in a stuffy, semi-subterranean gallery in Chicago. But at fifty-three I was at more disadvantage than most people, for not only had I the impedimenta that result from the unnatural style of dress, but I also suffered from the sedentary habits of a lifetime. And then that small world (which is our real one) of those who loved me best, and who considered themselves largely responsible for my every-day methods of life, did not encourage me ... in their affectionate solicitude—and with abundant reason— that I should "break my bones" and "spoil my future." It must be said, however, to their everlasting praise, that they opposed no objection when they saw that my will was firmly set to do this thing; on the contrary, they put me in the way of carrying out my purpose, and lent to my laborious lessons the light of their countenances reconciled. . . .

The order of evolution was something like this: First, three young Englishmen, all strong-armed and accomplished bicyclers, held the machine in place while I climbed timidly into the saddle. Second, two well-disposed young women put in all the power they had, until they grew red in the face, offsetting each other's pressure on the cross-bar and thus maintaining the equipoise to which I was unequal. Third, one walked beside me, steadying the ark as best she could by holding the center of the deadly cross-bar, to let go whose handles meant chaos and collapse. After this I was able to hold my own if I had the moral support of my kind trainers, and it passed into a proverb among them, the short emphatic word of command I gave them at every few turns of the wheel: "Let go, but stand by." Still later everything was learned—how to sit, how to pedal, how to turn, how to dismount; but alas! how to vault into the saddle I found not; that was the coveted power that lingered long and would not yield itself.

That which caused the many failures I had in learning the bicycle had caused me failures in life; namely, a certain fearful looking for of judgment; a too vivid realization of the uncertainty of everything about me; an underlying doubt—at once, however (and this is all that saved me), matched and overcome by the determination not to give in to it. . . .

Another thing I found is that we carry in the mind a picture of the road; and if it is bumpy by reason of pebbles, even if we steer clear of them, we can by no means skim along as happily as when its smoothness facilitates the pleasing impression on the retina; indeed, the whole science and practice of the bicycle is "in your eye" and in your will; the rest is mere manipulation.

As I have said, in many curious particulars the bicycle is like the world. When it had thrown me painfully once . . . and more especially when it threw one of my dearest friends, hurting her knee so that it was painful for a month, then for a time Gladys [the bicycle] had gladsome ways for me no longer, but seemed the embodiment of misfortune and dread. Even so the world has often seemed in hours of darkness and despondency; its iron mechanism, its pitiless grind, its swift, silent, on-rolling gait have oppressed to pathos, if not to melancholy. Good health and plenty of oxygenated air have promptly restored the equilibrium. . . .

Gradually, item by item, I learned the location of every screw and spring, spoke and tire, and every beam and bearing that went to make up Gladys. This was not the lesson of a day, but of many days and weeks, and it had to be learned before we could get on well together. To my mind the infelicities of which we see so much in life grow out of lack of time and patience thus to study and adjust the natures that have agreed in the sight of God and man to stand by one another to the last. They will not take the pains, they have not enough specific gravity, to balance themselves in their new environment. Indeed, I found a whole philosophy of life in the wooing and the winning of my bicycle.

Just as a strong and skilful [sic] swimmer takes the waves, so the bicycler must learn to take such waves of mental impression as the passing of a gigantic hay-wagon, the sudden obtrusion of black cattle with wide-branching horns, the rattling pace of high-stepping steeds, or even the swift transit of a railway-train. At first she will be upset by the apparition of the smallest poodle, and not until she has attained a wide experience will she hold herself steady in presence of the critical eyes of a coach-and-four. But all this is a part of that equilibration of thought and action by which we conquer the universe in conquering ourselves.

I finally concluded that all failure was from a wobbling will rather than a wobbling wheel. I felt that indeed the will is the wheel of the mind—its perpetual motion having been learned

when the morning stars sang together. When the wheel of the
mind went well then the rubber wheel hummed merrily; but
specters of the mind there are as well as of the wheel. In the
aggregate of perception concerning which we have reflected
and from which we have deduced our generalizations upon the
world without, within, above, there are so many ghastly and
fantastical images that they must obtrude themselves at certain
intervals, like filmy bits of glass in the turn of the kaleidoscope.
Probably every accident of which I had heard or read in my
half-century tinged the uncertainty that by the correlation of
forces passed over into the tremor that I felt when we began
to round the terminus bend of the broad Priory walk. And who
shall say by what inherited energy the mind forced itself at
once from the contemplation of disaster and thrust into the
very movement of the foot on the pedal a concept of vigor,
safety, and success? I began to feel that myself plus the bicycle
equaled myself plus the world, upon whose spinning-wheel we
must all learn to ride, or fall into the sluice-ways of oblivion
and despair. That which made me succeed with the bicycle
was precisely what had gained me a measure of success in
life—it was the hardihood of spirit that led me to begin, the
persistence of will that held me to my task, and the patience
that was willing to begin again when the last stroke had failed.
And so I found high moral uses in the bicycle and can commend
it as a teacher without pulpit or creed. He who succeeds, or,
to be more exact in handing over my experience, she who
succeeds in gaining the mastery of such an animal as Gladys,
will gain the mastery of life, and by exactly the same methods
and characteristics. . . .

Once, when I grew somewhat discouraged and said that I
had made no progress for a day or two, my teacher told me
that it was just so when she learned: there were growing days
and stationary days, and she had always noticed that just after
one of these last dull, depressing, and dubious intervals she
seemed to get an uplift and went ahead better than ever. It was
like a spurt in rowing. This seems to be the law of progress in
everything we do; it moves along a spiral rather than a
perpendicular; we seem to be actually going out of the way,
and yet it turns out that we were really moving upward. . . .

I studied my various kind teachers with much care. One was so helpful that but for my protest she would fairly have carried me in her arms, and the bicycle to boot, the whole distance. . . . Another was too timorous; the very twitter of her face, swiftly communicated to her arm and imparted to the quaking cross-bar, convulsed me with an inward fear. . . . Another . . . was herself so capable, not to say adventurous, and withal so solicitous for my best good, that she elicited my admiration by her ingenious mixture of cheering me on and holding me back; the latter, however, predominated, for she never really relinquished her strong grasp on the cross-bar. . . .

We rejoiced together greatly in perceiving the impetus that this uncompromising but fascinating and illimitably capable machine would give to that blessed "woman question" to which we were both devoted; for we had earned our own bread many a year, and she, although more than twenty years my junior, had accumulated an amount of experience well-nigh as great, because she had lived in the world's heart. . . . We saw that the physical development of humanity's mother-half would be wonderfully advanced by that universal introduction of the bicycle sure to come about within the next few years, because it is for the interest of great commercial monopolies that this should be so, since if women patronize the wheel the number of buyers will be twice as large. If women ride they must, when riding, dress more rationally than they have been wont to do. If they do this many prejudices as to what they may be allowed to wear will melt away. Reason will gain upon precedent, and ere long the comfortable, sensible, and artistic wardrobe of the rider will make the conventional style of woman's dress absurd to the eye and unendurable to the understanding. A reform often advances most rapidly by in-direction. An ounce of practice is worth a ton of theory; and the graceful and becoming costume of woman on the bicycle will convince the world that has brushed aside the theories, no matter how well constructed, and the arguments, no matter how logical, of dress-reformers.

A woman with bands hanging on her hips, and dress snug about the waist and chokingly tight at the throat, with heavily trimmed skirts dragging down the back and numerous folds

heating the lower part of the spine, and with tight shoes, ought
to be in agony. She ought to be as miserable as a stalwart man
would be in the same plight. And the fact that she can coolly
and complacently assert that her clothing is perfectly easy, and
that she does not want anything more comfortable or con-
venient, is the most conclusive proof that she is altogether
abnormal bodily, and not a little so in mind.

We saw with satisfaction the great advantage in good
fellowship and mutual understanding between men and women
who take the road together, sharing its hardships and rejoicing
in the poetry of motion through landscapes breathing nature's
inexhaustible charm and skyscapes lifting the heart from what
is to what shall be hereafter. We discoursed on the advantage
to masculine character of comradeship with women who were
as skilled and ingenious in the manipulation of the swift steed
as they themselves. We contended that whatever diminishes
the sense of superiority in men makes them more manly,
brotherly, and pleasant to have about; we felt sure that the
bluff, the swagger, the bravado of young England in his teens
would not outlive the complete mastery of the outdoor arts in
which his sister is now successfully engaged. The old fables,
myths, and follies associated with the idea of woman's incom-
petence to handle bat and oar, bridle and rein, and at last the
cross-bar of the bicycle, are passing into contempt in presence
of the nimbleness, agility, and skill of "that boy's sister";
indeed, we felt that if she continued to improve after the
fashion of the last decade her physical achievements will be
such that it will become the pride of many a ruddy youth to
be known as "that girl's brother." . . .

My last teacher was—as ought to be the case on the principle
of climax—my best. . . . No. 12 had the wit and wisdom to
retire to the rear of the saucy steed, that I might form the habit
of seeing no sign of aid or comfort from any source except my
own reaction on the treadles according to law; yet cunningly
contrived, by laying a skilled hand upon the saddle without
my observation, knowledge, or consent, to aid me in my
balancing. She diminished the weight thus set to my account
as rapidly as my own increasing courage and skill rendered
this possible. . . .

But at last (which means in two months or thereabouts, at ten or twenty minutes' practice off and on daily) I reached the goal, and could mount the bicycle without the slightest foreign interference or even the moral support of a sympathetic onlooker. . . .

And now comes the question "What do the doctors say?" Here follow several testimonies:

"The question now of great interest to girls is in regard to the healthfulness of the wheel. Many are prophesying dire results from this fascinating exercise, and fond parents are refusing to allow their daughters to ride because they are girls. It will be a delight to girls to learn that the fact of their sex is, in itself, not a bar to riding a wheel. If the girl is normally constituted and is dressed hygienically, and if she will use judgment and not overtax herself in learning to ride, and in measuring the length of rides after she has learned, she is in no more danger from riding a wheel than is the young man. But if she persists in riding in a tight dress, and uses no judgment in deciding the amount of exercise she is capable of safely taking, it will be quite possible for her to injure herself, and then it is she, and not the wheel, that is to blame. Many physicians are now coming to regard the 'wheel' as beneficial to the health of women as well as of men."

Dr. Seneca Egbert says: "As an exercise bicycling is superior to most, if not all, others at our command. It takes one into the outdoor air; it is entirely under control; can be made gentle or vigorous as one desires; is active and not passive; takes the rider outside of himself and the thoughts and cares of his daily work; develops his will, his attention, his courage and independence, and makes pleasant what is otherwise most irksome. Moreover, the exercise is well and equally distributed over almost the whole body, and, as Parker says, when all the muscles are exercised no muscle is likely to be over-exercised."

He advocates cycling as a remedy for dyspepsia, torpid liver, incipient consumption, nervous exhaustion, rheumatism, and melancholia. In regard to the exercise for women he says: "It gets them out of doors, gives them a form of exercise adapted to their needs, that they may enjoy in company with others or alone, and one that goes to the root of their nervous troubles."

He instances two cases, of girls fourteen and eighteen years of age, where a decided increase in height could be fairly attributed to cycling. The question is often asked if riding a wheel is not the same as running a sewing-machine. Let the same doctor answer: "Not at all. Women, at least, sit erect on a wheel, and consequently the thighs never make even a right angle with the trunk, and there is no stasis of blood in the lower limbs and genitalia. Moreover, the work itself makes the rider breathe in oceans of fresh air; while the woman at the sewing-machine works indoors, stoops over her work, contracting the chest and almost completely checking the flow of blood to and from the lower half of her body, where at the same time she is increasing the demand for it, finally aggravating the whole trouble by the pressure of the lower edge of the corset against the abdomen, so that the customary congestions and displacements have good cause for their existence. . . ."

Let me remark to any young woman who reads this page that for her to tumble off her bike is inexcusable. The lightsome elasticity of every muscle, the quickness of the eye, the agility of motion, ought to preserve her from such a catastrophe. I have had [only one] fall. . . . I have proceeded on a basis of the utmost caution, and aside from . . . one pitiful performance the bicycle has cost me hardly a single bruise.

They that know nothing fear nothing. Away back in 1886 my alert young friend, Miss Anna Gordon, and my ingenious young niece, Miss Katherine Willard, took to the tricycle as naturally as ducks take to water. . . . Remembering my country bringing-up and various exploits in running, climbing, horseback-riding, to say nothing of my tame heifer that I trained for a Bucephalus, I said to myself, "If those girls can ride without learning so can I!" Taking out my watch I timed them as they, at my suggestion, set out to make a record in going round the square. Two and a half minutes was the result. I then started with all my forces well in hand, and flew around in two and a quarter minutes. Not contented with this, but puffed up with foolish vanity, I declared that I would go around in two minutes; and, encouraged by their cheers, away I went without a fear till the third turning-post was reached, when the left hand played me false, and turning at an acute angle, away I went sidelong, machine and all, into the gutter, falling on my right elbow, which felt like a glassful of chopped ice, and I knew that for the first time in a life full of vicissitudes I had been really hurt. Anna Gordon's white face as she ran toward me caused me to wave my uninjured hand and call out, "Never mind!" and with her help I rose and walked into the house, wishing above all things to go straight to my own room and lie on my own bed, and thinking as I did so how pathetic is that instinct that makes "the stricken deer go weep," the harmed hare seek the covert.

Two physicians were soon at my side, and my mother, then over eighty years of age, came in with much controlled agitation and seated herself beside my bed, taking my hand and saying, "O Frank! you were always too adventurous."

If I am asked to explain why I learned the bicycle I should say I did it as an act of grace, if not of actual religion. The cardinal doctrine laid down by my physician was, "Live out of doors and take congenial exercise"; but from the day when, at sixteen years of age, I was enwrapped in the long skirts that impeded every footstep, I have detested walking and felt with a certain noble disdain that the conventions of life had cut me off from what in the freedom of my prairie home had been one of life's sweetest joys. Driving is not real exercise; it does not renovate the river of blood that flows so sluggishly in the veins of those who from any cause have lost the natural adjustment of brain to brawn. Horseback-riding, which does promise vigorous exercise, is expensive. The bicycle meets all the conditions and will ere long come within the reach of all. Therefore, in obedience to the laws of health, I learned to ride. I also wanted to help women to a wider world, for I hold that the more interests women and men can have in common, in thought, word, and deed, the happier will it be for the home. Besides, there was a special value to women in the conquest of the bicycle by a woman in her fifty-third year, and one who had so many comrades in the white-ribbon army that her action would be widely influential. . . .

It is needless to say that a bicycling costume was a prerequisite. This consisted of a skirt and blouse of tweed, with belt, rolling collar, and loose cravat, the skirt three inches from the ground; a round straw hat, and walking-shoes with gaiters. It was a simple, modest suit, to which no person of common sense could take exception.

As nearly as I can make out, reducing the problem to actual figures, it took me about three months, with an average of fifteen minutes' practice daily, to learn, first, to pedal; second, to turn; third, to dismount; and fourth, to mount independently this most mysterious animal. January 20th will always be a red-letter bicycle day, because although I had already mounted several times with no hand on the rudder, some good friend had always stood by to lend moral support; but summoning all my force, and, most forcible of all, what Sir Benjamin Ward Richardson declares to be the two essential elements—decision and precision—I mounted and started off alone. From that hour the spell was broken; Gladys was no more a mystery: I had learned all her kinks, had put a bridle in her teeth, and touched her smartly with the whip of victory. Consider, ye who are of a considerable chronology: in about thirteen hundred minutes, or, to put it more mildly, in twenty-two hours, or, to put it most mildly of all, in less than a single day as the almanac reckons time—but practically in two days of actual practice— amid the delightful surroundings of the great outdoors, and inspired by the bird-songs, the color and fragrance of an English posy-garden, in the company of devoted and pleasant comrades, I had made myself master of the most remarkable, ingenious, and inspiring motor ever yet devised upon this planet.

Moral: *Go thou and do likewise!*

Memoirs of a Would-Be Swim Champ

By Ann Geracimos

Ann Geracimos is a free-lance writer and lecturer who won the 1974 Penney-Missouri Magazine Award for this womenSports *article. In it she recreates the pleasure she*

*experienced in swimming competitively at summer
camp. But camp was not the "real world," and Geracimos,
like countless other women, felt compelled to give
up competitive athletics for more conventional feminine
pursuits when she reached adolescence.*

Once when I was very young I nearly drowned. I remember going under in a shallow lake bottom, curling up helplessly and sinking before being rescued by my frightened mother. Doubtless the incident sent off shock waves in my subconscious, but it was not until much later that I connected water with life's momentous events and understood that, inevitably, in swimming as in other measures of performance, one faces them alone.

Perhaps more than anything this explains my fascination with the sport, my complete identification with it from an early age. Of course, it also counts that a great-uncle, the man who helped raise me, was an athletics "professor" and owner of a prestigious New Hampshire boys' camp, whose sister institution, Interlaken, some 60 miles away, agreed to take me in. I was a "scholarship case," determined to prove my worth. At camp, at the age of ten, I was destined to learn about the territorial imperatives of the great outdoors, about the even greater imperatives of the body. I was scared to death.

It is a shock coming from the sneaky doldrums of a Lancaster, Pennsylvania school where there is no swimming pool and sport activities consist of all-girl hockey games and tumbles on a gym mat tittering about the boys at play on the other side of the curtain. Camp is sun-washed log cabins bordering leafy paths, a whole lake to play in, empty mountains to hike around on, the smells of pine, the sight of white birch, the sound of crickets, loons, frogs.

The cabin where I am to spend the preliminary days is a cool dark space, a square box with a pointed roof made of plain wood set on raised supports over a pine needle ground cover. At night the branches of the trees sweep against the cabin walls, and in the distance I hear frogs mingled with the sound of waves lapping on the lake shore. Such solitude is strange, but I do not confess this to anyone, even to myself. It is the solitude of the water, too, that both attracts and repels me.

I am uncertain, not knowing the water's depths, not yet
able to swim. The bottom is cold, dark, and full of mud
between the stones. But the texture, when I gain courage
enough to slide into the beginners' section between plank dock
supports, is wonderfully smooth. Slowly I immerse myself up
to my neck, paddling chaotically with my arms, raising my
feet up from the bottom. Cautiously at first, until I can control
myself, I am suspended this way in liquid, free of gravity's
pull, for minutes at a time, feeling freer than I have been
before. All sense of time is lost, as are all notions of guilt. Tiny
fish dart between my legs, treading in place with their tails. I
follow them through shafts of sunlight and gradually, by
lowering my face more deeply, holding my breath, I learn to
submerge, pulling in my arms and legs until I am a floating
fetus.

The bugle blows at 7 a.m. each morning, making the air
sing. We are in swim suits and towels, lined up for "body
exercises" before the mist has cleared the lake. The soft green
shoreline a mile away is barely visible. In the foreground, like
a glinting stage, are floating wooden buoys on ropes, red
markers on white turning boards, the depths of green-black
water shot through with the morning sun. There are blood-
suckers in the depths. I look at the lake through sleepy eyes.

Shrieking, we wet our toes to test the temperature and wade
in slowly for the risks of immersion. More advanced swimmers—among them a distant cousin of mine—walk by to the
far section with a bare nod in passing and fling themselves out
boldly across the water. I return to the lake each morning
determined to do as well or better than my cousin. It is the
start of an ambition I do not call by name. It isn't a word that
anyone, apart from our coach, the "swim director," (he spends
his winters at the Harvard University athletic department)
ever uses.

Nevertheless, camp is an aggressive, competitive place. We
are divided into two tribes—Mohegan and Iroquois—and work
two months each year racking up points, medals, skills. It is
the best way to learn, we are told; dutifully, we obey—although
the object lesson never is spelled out.

Swim sessions are strenuous. Our bodies become machines
in which liquid substances blend with the sun that turns into

soluble material and back into flesh again. Happily, greedily, I steal time from other sports to be able to spend time in the lake—a fluid charging object counting turns.

Swimming is a clean sport, well-suited to the classically long-limbed bodies and clean minds of young American girls. It is a very singular occupation. All that sleekness and sublimated aggression made respectable for a few hours under a "sporting" sky. Forgetfulness, team spirit, sensuality, monotony, absurdity—and utter sexlessness. It suits us perfectly. Novitiates of ascetic religious orders don't undergo the ritual chastisement by water that we budding swimmers do, kicking one and two miles a day, routinely doing laps, arms flailing, neck twisting. Like chasing your tail and being chased by it at the same time.

Do we work for the feel of working, or for the sake of winning? We understand—we are told over and over—how it is not who wins but how each girl plays. But when, each year, the camp enters the New England Swimming and Diving Championships (for girls' camps only), our team carries home a spread of trophies.

How we worship the inexorable spin of the silent seconds that pace the swimmer's journey! Our eyes are fixed on the circular silver mechanism resting in the palm of the referee's hand like a silver dollar of rare vintage caught in the gleam of a collector's eye on auction day. All of the weak sun's rays this day seem drawn to the spot. Light gathers there as though fixed by gravity.

There will be two events for me, plus diving. A full program; exhausting in view of the pressure.

My hands are hot, my feet cold. An intermittent drizzle has wet down the dock. I shift the towel from one hand to the other. Different parts of my body keep changing temperature. I stand as firmly, as confidently, as possible. Silence in the bleachers. The crowd likes the tension, appreciates the drama. They are waiting for familiar chaos to break through the order.

A sudden burst of sun sends streaks of color across the lake's dark surface. Boats outline the competition area, anchored haphazardly. Surprisingly, the bleachers are filled; who would bother to come see a group of campers exercise? The judges are

(text continued on page 122)

Sweet Victory

An athletic life,
though not
always easy,
has offered the
women on
these four pages
real satisfactions—
the thrill of
competition, the
physical
exhileration of
sport, the
joy of winning.
1: Wilma Rudolph,
Olympic champion,
1960, signing
autographs.
2: High school
cheerleader.
3: Althea Gibson in
a tournament.
4: Frances Willard
learning to
ride the bicycle,
ca. 1890.
5: Gold-medal-
winning Olympic
relay team,
1960. **6:** Gertrude
Ederle in
training. **7:** Lizzie
Murphy, base-
ball player.
8: Willye B. White
winning 100-
yard event, 1961.
9, 10: Willye
B. White in
long jump events.
11: Althea
Gibson with first-
place trophy,
1956. **12:** Gertrude
Ederle with
mayor of New York.

3

6

9

10

11

120

in place; the starter waits. I take off the itchy green wool bathrobe and step up to the starting block.

I shake my fingers loose, a cool flutter like a swan shaking its feathers. Deep breaths of air, hyper-extension, more shakes of the fingers. The race belongs to me, what is there to worry about? My pulse charges. Six contestants in this heat, a medley event. Our lanes are covered with oil slicks, just enough to taste bad if a swimmer accidentally gets a swallow.

I push breath into my lungs and throw my chest forward, keeping my shoulders level. If someone had come up to me then and asked what I was preparing myself for, I could have answered: Childbirth or murder.

Real control is in the pelvis, slung low and back, ready to force the plunge. The downward pull is in the fingers. My neck, however, responds first when I hear the shot. I spring. Cool slippery wet embraces me.

Too late for escape, I am aware only of flight.

A thousand different thoughts hang in the sky overhead—in the instant before hitting the water I see a split-second silhouette of a bird. "I am that bird." I think. "I sing without sound, fly without wings. . . ."

The ropes on either side are like wet rough snakes. I swerve on landing to avoid them, losing half a second, cursing as I dig in deep from the shoulders, arms taut, fingers groping, grasping for the turn ahead. The water unfolds like soft silk; a boat in the distance floats towards my mouth. I breathe in the Horizon as I raise my head. The shoreline falls away; I breathe again. Water dissolves against me. My breath is the wave, I am the sea, I am floating, my eyes are my fingers, my feet are the sky . . . breathe, relax, every muscle awake, ready to work. Spring and soar, take possession of space: that is what this sport is about. The head leads with a minimum of direction, arms forward, ready for the plunge, eyes open on recovery, staring hard. . . .

Below, churning the water, the swimmer's body adjusts to the pull of weight underneath while keeping enough balance to stay in touch with the air. The motion is a constant bending and yielding flight through water, the reflexes tuned to subtle changes of sight and sound, pressure and temperature. Swimming is a way of freeing the mind; only by preoccupying the body so completely does the mind come alive. Weightless, nearly nude, out of physical touch with all other human beings, the swimmer is an elemental force. The sureness of the limbs as they cut through the water in regular rhythm is comforting. The muscles are smooth and lean, their action directly related to their function. The course—a few feet wide by fifty feet long—is a universe of several dimensions within which the swimmer maneuvers as fast as possible towards a destination, simultaneously keeping watch on either side. Thus vulnerable and exposed, she takes her chances.

The turn. Into a backstroke now. Two lengths to go.

What is that speck on the horizon, between the trees? Birds? A balloon? Are the spectators cheering; what do they do when all of us are knocking our hearts out in this crib? Do they sit on their hands or what? What are the other swimmers up to, bunched up in towels and robes, their skin gone to goosebumps, little prickly fingertips and all?

There is some cheering, a smattering of applause. I hit the turn again, faster than I expected, catching the slime below the waterline, then around and out again with the sound of a gun to signal the last lap.

The clouds are gaining; they seem to be advancing with jagged edges, snaking overhead under the gray cover. What is the girl in the lane next to me doing now? No time to look. I grab the water voraciously. My body is weak—a moment of danger. Heavy arms, short breath, nervous legs. Shoulders up and around. The final push. Where is the girl on the far side?

Then cheers, yells, no time to check out anybody, head down for a long breath and twenty last strokes. Quick down the middle, a touch of the hand at the end of the course (another shotgun blast, more cheers), I am home.

The last night of my last year the whole camp gathers for award ceremonies in the dining room, dressed in identical blue and orange sleeveless pullovers and blue shorts, regulation equipment like the smiles, the songs, the speeches. It is a well-lacquered, clean, bright room. Previous campers' names are written in black on pinewood boards against the rough pine walls. We have tradition, excitement, fellowship. When the Best Camper Trophy is handed out, I am chosen over my cousin, who seemed to me to be so superior long ago. My tribe wins the most points for the season; as chieftain I collect the prize. Our swim team has had an unbroken string of victories; the team members stand up with their coach. Afterwards he tells me that I should think about training seriously for Olympic tryouts four, eight, years away.

But there is a conflict: Camp is a play world that has nothing to do with the rigorous dedication of a "serious life." This is, after all, a girls' camp where we were being trained up carefully to be "young ladies." Most of us eventually will take our rightful place at the head of the family dining room tables across America like our executive director. Summer is for fun and games; no one really expects the experience to relate directly to decisions in the "real world." It is a period of life in which I feel I lead two lives. Whatever happens in one seems to bear no relation to the other.

This was a double bind: Camp wasn't "real," yet the evidence of my senses told me otherwise. For about the age of puberty, every girl in America learns that to survive she must compete, that to compete she must be strong. And, as always, there are rules.

Such rules, of course, depend on the status quo, which said that competition for the sake of character was good; but competition for its own sake, as a game or sport to be played without a moral imperative, was not. It wasn't ladylike. . . . Real rules had to do with etiquette, with knowing how to please others, with being a "good girl."

Back home in Lancaster, I join the Middle Atlantic YWCA Swim League. I swim the 15 meets per season with growing awareness of my abilities.

Our coach's nickname is Angel, a booming rush of sound surrounding a mass of curly black hair and rippling muscles on a tall broad frame. Angel is a philosopher: he would like to be able to move water by words. Sometimes his words exceed the limits imposed on them by the dictionary. He talks about our "corporate welfare." Other times he does not bother with a dictionary. His dual nature keeps us in thrall; his body and mind seem to be at odds with one another. (Years later, I am not surprised to discover that Angel has become a business entrepreneur operating a chain of swimming pools and the "Y" has appointed a woman in his place.)

"Hey you guys, whatsa matter in there? Whatda ya think this is, some picnic or something?"

Angel stands just outside the lockerroom door leading to the pool, hesitating. He has been inside just once, when he wanted to congratulate us on winning a home game with a rival team. He was excited then and forgot the rules; the newspaper had just taken a team photograph.

Generous and unpredictable in his speech, he is never boring. The orders ring out like tremors on a seismograph. It is the prelude to his weekly pep talk, half jokes and half teasing. We file out in high spirits. He puts his arm around the shoulders of one of the girls, so her soft skin brushes his chest. She giggles; a tiny blush spreads over her face. Then he releases her with a hearty slap on the back and the noise reverberates against the ceiling. We work in an echo chamber. He stands on the perimeter and gives orders:

"Go on in there, get'em. Don't be shy. Show your stuff. PUSH that water."

We push it. The water's agitation actually creates sound waves against the walls; the pungent chlorine smell burns our nostrils. No one stops to rest in the first round—six lanes, six girls following six others, ten laps, slow-slow, quick-quick. Angel watches, cheering us on.

The rituals of our sport demand instant response. We strip souls and bodies alike for each fresh assault on the man-made pond; we follow our instincts without thinking and are rewarded with the sense of continuity in time. Possibly it is the most absurd activity in the world, confining oneself to an airless cement chamber full of the nasty smells of human sweat and toxic chemicals, throwing oneself headlong willy-nilly upon a quivering body of water no more than 25 yards long and 10 yards wide and eight feet deep at the far end. Make a flip turn in the shallow section and your hand is likely to develop a rough patch on top like a newly-mown hay field. To do this over and over and pretend it's fruitful, constructive, mind-expanding, demands mindless diligence and a total absorption in the spirit of the occasion.

Next we practice turns and racing starts, forward dives and backward plunges. Ten each. Then ten with the starter's whistle. It is no wonder that at least one girl will drop out of the team because she is ashamed of appearing in a swim suit. Her chest muscles have expanded unnaturally; her breasts have grown "too big." The rest of us have "Angel wings," as we call them—stretched shoulders. Strong, powerful, all-American shoulders on long limbs, a chorus of blue nylon virgins, one hundred pound imitation Esther Williamses lined up under the bright lights in the basement of the converted Georgian-styled, white-trimmed, red-brick mansion next door to Snyder's Funeral Parlor, opposite the Central Presbyterian Church.

We are all innocent abandon, unself-conscious achievers full of meat, tea, peas, toast, breathing exercises and lots of sleep. Or pretending to be. I mention one day to Angel that I expect to go on to liberal arts college. He is puzzled, not being accustomed to hearing women talk in terms of "college and career," and asks if I am going to study painting.

To his credit, Angel treats us like members of a family. "Persevere," he says. "You gotta build endurance. The more time you spend in the water the more natural it becomes." He talks about Amateur Athletic Union meets, assaults on local, regional, national levels, ignoring the fact that most of the team by then will be either pregnant or married or both.

I swim the required lengths, concentrating simultaneously on arms and legs like a bug awash in a dishpan, the state of doing instead of being. Forget to do your homework one day and it becomes that much harder the next. Muscles have to be forced one-tenth of a second faster each time.

My lungs are filled with the steamy air. Hypertension exercises stretch my tank suit to capacity. I step up to the edge of the pool in a crouch, poised like a cat on a tree limb eyeing a bird on the branch: taut, mindless, determined. Angel's commands echo like cannon shots. I fling arms and shoulders forward into a giant arch, dropping my head in anticipation of the splash, the welcoming sting—the signal for life to begin. Gravity's rainbow is within reach as I spring. A single swallow of air lasts a full length. I don't hear it when Angel calls out my time.

Lengths completed, I move to the diving board. I'm ambidextrous: Angel's words. Swimming and diving. You never know when they will come in handy: My uncle's words. The bug has found its way out of the tub and become a bee in a tailspin, dipping into a flower. I bend my knees and grab with my toes for balance, feeling for the right stance. Instinctively, almost magically, the toes know their job, holding the body upright, intact, tense, primed for the fall.

Five or ten times warm-up on the approach, then a jack-knife into the pool. Five, ten jack-knifes. Then somersaults, forward and backward. Back jack-knife, back dive, forward one and one-half twists. I climb out for a towel. It smells of ammonia. We take turns; each girl watching the others carefully, measuring the performance against her own.

It's a short board, and the water beneath is comparatively shallow. We have to hold out our hands each time on entry to protect our heads from hitting the bottom. For some reason during the next round I miss.

My mouth bangs down hard on cement. My hands come forward. Too late.

On top of the water, my fingers cupped to my mouth in fright, I grab for the towel and press it against my face. My tongue feels bloated. Angel pulls me aside for inspection. I see red on the towel. A jagged piece is missing from the side of an upper front tooth, a diagonal break, one-eighth of an inch at the bottom. I poke a finger into the gap. "Just a baby break," says Angel. "You can hardly see a thing."

But the accident, I feel, has destroyed my privacy. I have been singled out for punishment by the fates, with whom I previously felt on equal terms.

"Back in the pool, kids. Nothing happening on the side." Angel waves his arm grandly, a call for order. Black curls fall down the center of his forehead as he leans over with an arm on my shoulder:

"Do it again."

"I'm scared." I'm shaking.

"Never mind, it'll go away."

"No."

"Yes.

"*Now.*"

I have no choice; disobeying him scares me more. Wiping the last bit of blood off my chin, I mount the board. Wet feet have made the rough matting slippery. One, two, three steps, feet together in the air. Think! No, don't think. Act, don't react; don't anticipate, don't imagine the dark. The body is resilient. Now breathe in, relax. Another breath. Tighten the brain, the muscles. Forward with eyes down and out, taking possession of space. Spring, soar, fold in the neck and roll with arms clasped around knees bent to the chest; turn around and kick the feet out as the arms move forward on entry in a perpendicular pose, eyes open on recovery, staring hard.

"Okay, that's better. C'mon here a minute."

I drag myself slowly out of the pool, Angel offering a hand.

"Can you get a little higher?" he asks. "Your feet weren't together on that last entry. Try it again."

That night at dinner I keep feeling my tooth, saying how peculiar the accident was. I feel peculiar. My uncle scoffs. Attributing my condition to shock, mother cautions me not to chew too hard, to rest after dinner.

I undress for bed early. Taking off my underpants, I notice a brownish-red stain. Connecting it somehow with the accident (had they brushed next to the towel?) I drop them into the clothes hamper and climb into bed. Mother comes in soon afterwards, awkwardly holding out to me a bundle of bulky cotton pads and a book called, "Baby and Me."

She tells me not to be alarmed, that I have reached "a very significant stage" in life. Has she been looking into the hamper nightly? For how many years? She says I should read the book carefully and ask her questions later.

My innocence about the human body could be explained by my years, being barely at the stage where I understand that women function differently from men; that it is a difference in the number and function of holes. But how many holes and which one for what. I am not sure about it in spite of information passed between lavatory stalls at school. I expect the book will tell me, but it does not; the minds of young girls do not easily accommodate news from sources other than their own. Discovering that the body makes its own decisions has a religious dimension, to be sure, but it is never news passed out in Sunday School. I have a mirror and examine my choice. The hole for blood is one of three. The center one seems logical; I aim for that. I take the pads and place them between my legs according to directions and never mention the subject to my mother.

Next day I am up early preparing a surprise for my English class—painting bright red letters on a poster in honor of Mephistopheles, the Devil, Satan. All the names that represent the figure of evil I write on the sign. Our class is studying Macbeth's dark deeds. I am moved by the spectacle of power in Macbeth's mind and wish to reproduce it in color. I carry the poster to school and carefully unfold it for the teacher to examine. Pleased by my initiative, she comments on my "ingenuity" and fastens it to the outside of the classroom door to the accompaniment of giggles: "SATAN LIVES." Red marks, printed boldly in scraggly letters, lick the edge of the paper like flames of the inferno. I feel proud and the rest of the morning am unable to concentrate on any part of Shakespeare, who, if not exactly a stranger to us, is not known either as a close friend.

My exaltation is short-lived. The school principal sees the sign, which has caused a commotion in the hall. He notifies our teacher on the intercom system to take down the decoration immediately and henceforth be more diligent in her duties. This is a Christian school, he reminds her; Devil-worship is banned. The teacher, a fragile dark-haired young woman with painted red fingernails, turns the poster over to me gingerly, one adult to another. She thanks me for my effort and, covering her embarrassment, encourages me to continue my interest in art.

My notions of the Devil's power are confirmed: The world, the flesh, and the devil are one. I am a sinner, a sufferer; good deeds alone will clear my name.

Too alarmed to confess my confusion, I go home that night and thank mother for her book, reassuring her that, yes, I feel fine. No pain, no discomfort: only tiredness and wonder. My body has become A Responsibility. But if the body has a mind of its own, how is one ever to become fully acquainted with it? I have already glimpsed the truth. We float with the current—an accident here, an operation there—worrying about our sexual capacities, trying to shed the fat. The real world has come home to me. I am a fully-conditioned woman.

Friends of my uncle mention a swimming scholarship that might be available for me at a private girls school in the state. Nobody in my family pushes the opportunity. I hold back, claiming pride in the "democratic principle"—a glib phrase stolen from my history class—and say, no thank you, I'll stick to public school. I enter a single AAU meet and then withdraw from further competition. It is a slow turning off; the mysteries of life and the mysteries of the body are irretrievably mixed up in my mind. I have learned my lessons well: To glory in sport is vain and unladylike.

Today at the ocean's edge, I feel an immediate predictable threat. My compulsion is to run and at the same time to move closer. The rhythm of the waves is a release, but one that seems to doom me. I stand paralyzed, thinking I will drown for sure if I continue to wait. Admitting the fear offers some relief. Still, I wonder whether had I pursued the course of ambition when I was younger would I feel such a cowardly emotion; whether had I been able to take my chosen sport seriously, would I be standing there at all?

I Always Wanted to Be Somebody

By Althea Gibson

In 1950, Althea Gibson broke the color barrier in American tennis. When the United States Lawn Tennis Association (USLTA) ruled against Gibson's participation in the Forest Hills play-offs because she was black, a controversy erupted. Champion player Alice Marble, who was white, took up Gibson's cause, and the USLTA finally reversed its ruling. Gibson won the finals and emerged as the first black athlete to receive national recognition in tennis. There had been other great black female tennis players before Gibson. Ora Washington, who had held the all-black American Tennis Association's women's title for twelve years between 1924 and 1936, had even challenged USLTA champion Helen Wills (who declined) to a match. But Washington and her successors had been ignored by the white press and remain virtually unknown today.

Gibson's championship tennis career continued through 1958. In 1957 and 1958, she won both the British

*(Wimbledon) and American (Forest Hills) titles. In 1957, she
was given a ticker tape parade in New York and became the
first black person to win the Associated Press's annual
Woman Athlete of the Year Award. Gibson's tennis career
was followed by one in professional golf and by some public
relations work. She has served as New Jersey State Athletic
Commissioner since 1975. In the following passage,
excerpted from Gibson's 1958 autobiography, she describes
her Harlem childhood and explains how tennis—by giving
her self-discipline and purpose—changed her life.*

I always wanted to be somebody. I guess that's why I kept
running away from home when I was a kid even though I
took some terrible whippings for it. It's why I took to tennis
right away and kept working at it, even though I was the
wildest tomboy you ever saw and my strong likings were a
mile away from what the tennis people wanted me to do. It's
why I've been willing to live like a gypsy all these years, always
being a guest in other people's houses and doing things the
way they said, even though what I've always craved is to live
the way I want to in a place of my own with nobody to answer
to but myself. It's why, ever since I was a wild, arrogant girl
in my teens, playing stickball and basketball and baseball and
paddle tennis and even football in the streets in the daytime
and hanging around bowling alleys half the night, I've wor-
shipped Sugar Ray Robinson. It wasn't just because he was a
wonderful fellow, and good to me when there was no special
reason for him to be; it was because he was somebody, and I
was determined that I was going to be somebody, too—if it
killed me.

If I've made it, it's half because I was game to take a wicked
amount of punishment along the way and half because there
were an awful lot of people who cared enough to help me. It
has been a bewildering, challenging, exhausting experience,
often more painful than pleasurable, more sad than happy. But
I wouldn't have missed it for the world. . . .

They tell me I was born on August 25, 1927, in a small
town in South Carolina called Silver. I don't remember anything
about Carolina; all I remember is New York. But my daddy
talks about it a lot. He describes it as a three-store town,

meaning that it wasn't as small as towns that only have one store for all the people. But it wasn't very big, either. My father, Daniel, and my mother, Annie, both lived in Silver. . . .

After they got married, my mother and father lived in a little cabin on a cotton farm. Daddy was helping one of my uncles sharecrop cotton and corn, and there was plenty of hard work to go around. Daddy is a powerfully built man—he looks a lot like Roy Campanella, the famous Dodger catcher—and Mom is a strong woman; they had no trouble meeting the requirements. Mom is the first one to say that she was no delicate flower in those days. She used to love to ride, and because there wasn't much chance of her going to a riding stable, she used to ride not only horses but cows, hogs and everything. "Sure," she told me once, "I'd jump on that cow or that hog just like it was a horse. I believe I really could do some of that right now." I believe she could, too. She looks ten years younger than she is, and she's in shape. . . .

It's too bad I wasn't big enough to be of some help on the farm. They could have used me. Daddy and my uncle only had five acres of land and they never had a chance of making out. Even if things had gone well, they couldn't have put anything by. But when bad weather ruined the crops three years in a row, they were in bad shape. "I worked three years for nothin'," Daddy says. "That third year, all I got out of it was a bale and a half of cotton. Cotton was sellin' for fifty dollars a bale then, so I made seventy-five dollars for the year's work. I had to get out of there, and when Mom's sister, Sally Washington, came down from New York for their sister Blanche's funeral, I made up my mind it was time."

What Daddy did was agree to let Aunt Sally take me back to New York with her on the understanding that he would come up a couple of months later and get a job, and then, as soon as he could, send for Mom. He came as soon as he got the cash for his bale and a half of cotton. . . .

We all lived together in Aunt Sally's apartment for quite a while before Daddy and Mom got an apartment of their own. I was only three years old when Aunt Sally first brought me up with her, and I don't remember very much about what it was like at her place. . . .

I didn't start getting into real trouble until the Gibson family settled into a place of its own, the apartment on West 143rd Street in which my mother and father, my sisters, Millie and Annie and Lillian, and my brother Daniel, still live. I was a traveling girl, and I hated to go to school. What's more, I didn't like people telling me what to do. Take it from me, you can get in a lot of hot water thinking like that.

The only thing I really liked to do was play ball. Basketball was my favorite but any kind of ball would do. I guess the main reason why I hated to go to school was because I couldn't see any point in wasting all that time that I could be spending shooting baskets in the playground. "She was always the outdoor type," Daddy told a reporter once. "That's why she can beat that tennis ball like nobody's business." If I had gone to school once in a while like I was supposed to, Daddy wouldn't have minded my being a tomboy at all. In fact, I'm convinced that he was disappointed when I was born that I wasn't a boy. He wanted a son. So he always treated me like one, right from when I was a little tot in Carolina and we used to shoot marbles in the dirt road with acorns for marbles. He claims I used to beat him all the time, but seeing that I was only three years old then, I think he's exaggerating a little bit. One thing he isn't exaggerating about, though, is when he says he wanted me to be a prize fighter. He really did. It was when I was in junior high school, like maybe twelve or thirteen years old, and he'd been reading a lot about professional bouts between women boxers, sort of like the women's wrestling they have in some parts of the country today. (Women's boxing is illegal now but in those days it used to draw some pretty good small-club gates.) Daddy wanted to put me in for it. "It would have been big," he says. "You would have been the champion of the world. You were big and strong, and you could hit."

I know it sounds indelicate, coming from a girl, but I could fight, too. Daddy taught me the moves, and I had the right temperament for it. I was tough, I wasn't afraid of anybody, not even him. He says himself that when he would whip me, I would never cry, not if it killed me. I would just sit there and look at him. I wouldn't sass him back or anything but neither would I give him the satisfaction of crying. He would be doing all the hitting and all the talking, and I guess after a while it must have seemed like a terrible waste of time. He liked our boxing lessons better. He would say, "Put up your dukes," and I had to get ready to defend myself or I would take an even worse beating. He would box with me for an hour at a time, showing me how to punch, how to jab, how to block punches, and how to use footwork. . . .

Of course, once he got the idea of me boxing professionally out of his head, all Daddy was trying to do, aside from teach me right from wrong, was to make sure I would be able to protect myself. Harlem is a mean place to grow up in; there's always somebody to gall you no matter how much you want to mind your own business. If Daddy hadn't shown me how to look out for myself, I would have got into a lot of fights that I would have lost, and I would have been pretty badly beaten up a lot of times. . . .

Sometimes, in a tough neighborhood, where there is no way for a kid to prove himself except by playing games and fighting, you've got to establish a record for being able to look out for yourself before they will leave you alone. If they think you're an easy mark, they will all look to build up their own reputations by beating up on you. I learned always to get in the first punch. . . .

It wasn't only girls that I fought, either. I had one terrible fight with a boy, on account of my uncle Junie. . . . There was a tough gang on the block called the Sabres. The leader of the gang and I used to pal around together a lot; we played stickball and basketball and everything. No loving up, though. I wasn't his girl. We were what we called boon-coons, which in Harlem means block buddies, good friends. Well, this one day I'd been up visiting Aunt Sally, and on my way out, just as I turned around the last landing, I saw Uncle Junie lolling on the stairs, slightly intoxicated, and this Sabre leader was standing over him going through his pockets. "What you doin'?" I hollered down at him. "That's my uncle! Go bother somebody else if you got to steal, but don't bother him!" I ran down and lifted Uncle Junie up. . . . Then I looked back over my shoulder to see if the kid was leaving, and I was just in time to see him take a sharpened screw driver out of his pocket and throw it at me. I stuck my hand out to protect myself and got a gash just above my thumb that still shows a scar as plain as day. Well, . . . we had a fight that they still talk about on 144th Street. We fought all over the block, and first he was down and then I was down, but neither of us would stay down if we died for it. He didn't even think of me as a girl, I can assure you. He fought me with his fists and his elbows and his knees and even his teeth. We were both pretty bloody and bruised when some big people finally stopped it, and I guess you would have to say it was a draw. But at least those Sabres respected me from then on. None of them ever tried to use me for a dartboard again. . . .

Except for the fights I got into, and playing hooky all the time, I didn't get into much serious trouble when I was a kid or do anything very bad. . . . We were just mischievous. I think one good thing was that I never joined any of those so-called social clubs that they've always had in Harlem. None of my girl friends did, either. We didn't care for that stuff, all the drinking and narcotics and sex that they went in for in those clubs—and we didn't care for the stickups that they turned to sooner or later in order to get money for the things they were doing. I didn't like to go to school but I had no interest in going to jail, either. Mostly my best girl friend, Alma Irving, and I liked to play hooky and spend the day in the movies, especially Friday, when they had a big stage show at the Apollo Theatre on 125th Street. Alma liked to play basketball, too, almost as much as I did. She was a good basket shooter, and we'd spend hours in the park shooting for Cokes or hot dogs. At night we used to go to the school gymnasium and challenge anybody, boy or girl, man or woman, to play us in what we used to call two-on-two. We'd use just one basket and see which team could score the most baskets on the other. We played hard, and when we got finished we'd go to a cheap restaurant and get a plate of collard greens and rice, or maybe, if we were a little flush, a hamburger steak or fried chicken and French fried potatoes. In those days, of course, you could get a big plate of food like that for only thirty-five cents. . . .

Now I realize how poor we were in those days, and how little
we had. But it didn't seem so bad then. How could you feel
sorry for yourself when soda was a nickel a quart?

I think my worst troubles started when I graduated from junior
high school in 1941. How I ever managed to graduate, I don't
know, but I guess I was there just often enough to find out a
little bit about what was going on. . . . I didn't like the idea of
going to the Yorkville Trade School, which was where I'd been
transferred to. . . . I guess I went pretty regularly for the first
year, mostly because I was interested in the sewing classes. I
got to be pretty good on the sewing machine. . . . But after a
while I got tired of the whole thing, and from then on school
and I had nothing in common at all. . . .

I must have worked at a dozen jobs in the next few years,
maybe more. I was restless and I never stayed in any one place
very long. If it wasn't to my liking, I quit. I was a counter girl
at the Chambers Street branch of the Chock Full O' Nuts
restaurant chain. I was a messenger for a blueprinting company.
I worked in a button factory and a dress factory and a department
store. I ran an elevator in the Dixie Hotel, and I even had a job
cleaning chickens in a butcher shop. . . . Out of all of them, I
only had one job that I really liked, and I lost that one for being
honest. . . .

For a while I didn't exactly knock myself out looking for
another job. I suppose you could say I was sulking. Anyway,
I just stayed away from home and bummed around the streets.
It wasn't long before a couple of women from the Welfare
Department picked me up and laid down the law. If I wouldn't
live home, and I wouldn't go to school, I would have to let
them find me a place to stay with a good, respectable family
and report to them every week so they could keep a check on
me. . . . So they got me a furnished room in a private home, and
even gave me an allowance. . . . It was during this time, when
I was living in a never-never land through the courtesy of the
City of New York, that I was introduced to tennis. My whole
life was changed, just like that, and I never even knew it was
happening.

The 143rd Street block my mother and father lived on was
a Police Athletic League play street, which means that the

policemen put up wooden barricades at the ends of the street during the daytime and closed it to traffic so we could use it for a playground. One of the big games on the street was paddle tennis, and I was the champion of the block. In fact, I even won some medals representing 143rd Street in competition with other Harlem play streets. . . .

There was a musician fellow, Buddy Walker, who's known now as "Harlem's Society Orchestra Leader," but who in those days didn't get much work in the summer months and filled in by working for the city as a play leader. . . . Buddy took me to the Harlem River Tennis Courts at 150th Street and Seventh Avenue and had me play a couple of sets with one of his friends. He always has insisted that the way I played that day was phenomenal for a young girl with no experience, and I remember that a lot of the other players on the courts stopped their games to watch me. It was very exciting; it was a competitive sport and I am a competitive sort of person. When one of the men who saw me play that first time, a Negro schoolteacher, Juan Serrell, suggested to Buddy that he would like to try to work out some way for me to play at the Cosmopolitan Tennis Club, which he belonged to, I was more than willing. The Cosmopolitan is gone now, but in those days it was *the* ritzy tennis club in Harlem. . . .

Those days, I probably would have been more at home training in Stillman's Gym than at the Cosmopolitan Club. I really wasn't the tennis type. But the polite manners of the game, that seemed so silly to me at first, gradually began to appeal to me. So did the pretty white clothes. I had trouble as a competitor because I kept wanting to fight the other player every time I started to lose a match. . . . After a while I began to understand that you could walk out on the court like a lady, all dressed up in immaculate white, be polite to everybody, and still play like a tiger and beat the liver and lights out of the ball. I remember thinking to myself that it was kind of like a matador going into the bull ring, beautifully dressed, bowing in all directions, following the fancy rules to the letter, and all the time having nothing in mind except sticking that sword into the bull's guts and killing him as dead as hell. I probably picked up that notion from some movie I saw. . . .

The Cosmopolitan members were the highest class of Harlem people and they had rigid ideas about what was socially acceptable behavior. They were undoubtedly more strict than white people of similar position, for the obvious reason that they felt they had to be doubly careful in order to overcome the prejudiced attitude that all Negroes lived eight to a room in dirty houses and drank gin all day and settled all their arguments with knives. I'm ashamed to say I was still living pretty wild. I was supposed to be looking for a job but . . . the hardest work I did, aside from practicing tennis, was to report to the Welfare ladies once a week, tell them how I was getting along, and pick up my allowance. . . . I guess it would have been too much to expect me to change completely right away. Actually, I realize now that every day I played tennis and got more interested in the game, I was changing a little bit. I just wasn't aware of it. . . .

One of the days I remember best at the Cosmopolitan Club was the day Alice Marble played an exhibition match there. I can still remember saying to myself, boy, would I like to be able to play tennis like that! She was the only woman tennis player I'd ever seen that I felt exactly that way about. Until I saw her I'd always had eyes only for the good men players. But her effectiveness of strike, and the power that she had, impressed me terrifically. Basically, of course, it was the aggressiveness behind her game that I liked. Watching her smack that effortless serve, and then follow it into the net and put the ball away with an overhead as good as any man's, I saw possibilities in the game of tennis that I had never seen before. . . . I had no way of knowing then that when the time came for me to be up for an invitation to play at Forest Hills, my biggest supporter aside from a handful of my own people would be this same Alice Marble. . . .

The American Tennis Association, which is almost all Negro, was putting on a New York State Open Championship at the Cosmopolitan Club. . . . It was the first tournament I had ever played in, and I won it. . . . By this time I was accustomed to winning games. I think what mostly made me feel good was that the girl I beat in the finals, Nina Irwin, was a white girl. I can't deny that that made the victory all the sweeter to me.

It proved to my own satisfaction that I was not only as good as she was, I was better. . . .

Being eighteen, I was able to play in the A.T.A. national women's singles in 1946; I was out of the girls' class. . . . [I lost] But I had played well enough, anyway, to attract the attention of two tennis playing doctors, Dr. Hubert A. Eaton of Wilmington, North Carolina, and Dr. Robert W. Johnson of Lynchburg, Virginia, who were getting ready to change my whole life. . . .

It was their idea that what I ought to do first was go to college, where I could get an education and improve my tennis at the same time. . . . I suppose . . . they already were hoping that I might just possibly turn out to be the Negro player they had been looking for to break into the major league of tennis and play in the white tournaments. . . . The plan they finally came up with was for me to leave New York City and go to Wilmington to live with Dr. Eaton during the school year, go to high school there, and practice with him on his private backyard tennis court. In the summer I would live with Dr. Johnson in Lynchburg and I would travel with him in his car to play the tournament circuit. . . .

Not that it was an easy decision for me to make. I was a city kid and I like city ways. How did I know what it would be like for me in a small town, especially in the South? I'd heard enough stories to worry me. Up north, the law may not exactly be on your side, but at least it isn't always against you. . . . I would have to go into this strange country, where, according to what I'd heard, terrible things were done to Negroes . . . and nobody was ever punished for them. . . . Harlem wasn't heaven but at least I knew I could take care of myself there. . . . In the end I decided . . . I was coming. That was in August, 1946. . . .

The first big problem was where I would fit into the school. . . . they gave me an aptitude test, and . . . said they would assign me to the sophomore class and give me a chance to stick there if I could. That meant I would be able to earn my diploma in three years, and I was determined to do it. I buckled down to my schoolwork like nobody's business. . . . I really hit those books.

Gradually, living in Dr. Eaton's house as one of the family, I learned how to obey rules and get along with people. It was the first real family life I had ever known. Nobody stayed out all night in that house, or decided to eat lunch in a dog wagon downtown instead of coming home for lunch with the family. And the rules that applied to the Eatons' own children applied to me, too. . . .

I worked hard on both my schoolwork and my tennis. I think the doctor was proud of what I did with both. . . . He loved to see me beat the men he matched me against. His court was a gathering place for all the Negro tennis players of the district, as it had to be, because there wasn't any place else for them to play. There were a number of public courts in Wilmington, but no Negro could play on them. . . .

The local segregation setup wasn't quite as bad as I had feared it might be, but it was plenty bad enough. I'll never forget my first bus ride into the downtown shopping area. The first thing I saw when I got on the bus and paid my fare was the sign, "White in front, Colored in rear." I was burned up that I had to conform to such an ignorant law, and I picked out a seat as near to the front as I thought I could possibly get away with. It disgusted me, and it made me feel ashamed in a way I'd never been ashamed back in New York.

It was even worse when I went to the movies. The ushers practically knocked us colored down making sure we got up to the back balcony. . . .

Of course, it was nothing more than I'd expected and, like I said, it wasn't a Ku Klux Klan nightmare like I'd been afraid it might be. I managed to conform to whatever the program was wherever I went. But I hated every minute of it. I made up my mind once and for all that I was never going to live any place in the South, at least not as long as those laws were in existence. My daddy thinks I'm wrong. He says he would like nothing better than to go back to Silver, South Carolina. . . . When I say something about the Jim Crow, he points to the slum tenements in Harlem with the plaster falling down and the plumbing stopped up and the kids getting killed in the streets, and he says, Is this better? It makes you wonder what's right. But I still say I'll take Harlem, or worse, before I'll live somewhere where all the talent or brains or success in the world won't get you treated like anything except an untouchable if your skin happens to be dark. You can have my share of the South—if you want it. . . .

The other big problem I had in Wilmington was the girls in school. Most of them didn't like me at all. . . . I wasn't much for dressing up. . . . I still wore slacks and a T-shirt every chance I got, and because I loved to play basketball and baseball and football with the boys, all the girls thought I was the worst tomboy they'd ever seen. I was the star of the girls' basketball team, and later on they elected me the captain of it, but that wasn't enough athletic action to keep me happy, so I used to go out to the field during football and baseball practice and play with the varsity boys. It used to hurt me real bad to hear the girls talking about me when they saw me doing that. "Look at her throwin' that ball just like a man," they would say, and they looked at me like I was a freak. I hated them for it. I felt as though they ought to see that I didn't do the things they did because I didn't know how to, and that I showed off on the football field because throwing passes better than the varsity quarterback was a way for me to express myself, to show that there was something I was good at. . . .

Somewhat to my own surprise, because I'd had so little to do with books before I went to Wilmington, I finished up my high school course in three years, just as I had hoped I might be able to, and was graduated, in June, 1949, tenth in my class if you please. I was happy about it. I was twenty-one years old and I felt it was time I set out on my own. Partly I was ready to break loose and have a little fun, but partly I was dead serious about making something out of my life. . . .

My last month in Wilmington I wrote letters to a number of Negro colleges, asking what chance I might have of getting a scholarship. As the two-time winner of the national Negro women's tennis championship, I had a pretty good claim. One of the schools that encouraged me was Florida A. and M., at Tallahassee. In fact, they did more than encourage me. Even before I got my high school diploma they wrote and said I was welcome to a scholarship at A. and M., and that I should come down as soon as I got out of high school and spend the summer playing tennis down there. I had my bags packed two days after graduation, and I was gone. I'm afraid the Eatons were a little bit hurt about the speed with which I left, but I couldn't help being eager to get started on my own. Nobody could have been more grateful than I was to both the doctors for everything they had done for me in those three years, but it was good to feel a little bit independent again. It's a feeling I've always been partial to.

Gertrude Ederle

by Paul Gallico

Gertrude Ederle was the first woman to swim the English Channel successfully. Since she failed the attempt once in April 1926, her success in August of that same year took the international public by surprise. Certain that Ederle would fail again, a London newspaper had no time to withdraw a preset front-page editorial arguing that Ederle's failure demonstrated the futility of competitive athletics for women, due to their hopeless physical inferiority. Today, women hold the fastest records for crossing the English Channel. Women's lower center of gravity and greater percentage of body fat than men's are both advantages in long-distance swimming.

Paul Gallico, one of this century's leading sportswriters, wrote this piece in 1964 for his book, The Golden People. *Like many sports journalists who write about female athletes, he comments excessively on physical appearance, and even suggests that Ederle's "lack of beauty had something to do with her choice of ordeals."*

If you will look today into a modern almanac or record book, you will find under the heading of Channel Swimmers some two columns of names of men and women who have conquered this treacherous body of water under their own steam. Why they bothered to do so and still do, is anybody's guess. Even recently that much abused strait has been trampled and

threshed by individuals determinedly trying to eke out firsts
from its cross-currents, heavy tides, and choppy waters, including children and graybeards looking to be the youngest or
the oldest or the fastest. Others have been attempting to swim
it both ways in one gulp.

But up to the year 1926 there were only five who had made
it; Matthew Webb of Britain, 1875; Thomas Burgess of Britain,
who crossed in 1911; Henry F. Sullivan of the United States
who, along with Enrique Tiraboschi of Argentina and Charles
Toth, another American, swam it in 1923. Of these five the
fastest time recorded was that of the Argentine, who swam
from France to England in sixteen hours and thirty-three
minutes. Many more had tried and failed, and those who
succeeded were well-larded giants.

Women had attempted it in vain. The test of that particular
body of water was thought to be too severe for the so-called
weaker sex. This situation was corrected on August 6, 1926,
when another name was added to this brief list. It was that of
an eighteen-year-old girl, an American. She hustled from Cap
Gris Nez to Dover in fourteen hours and thirty-one minutes,
not only breaking the time record of the fastest man by two
whole hours, but achieving the only first that really mattered
from then on. Her name was Gertrude Ederle and she was the
pioneer of her sex to succeed in this arduous passage.

Females have been making the crossing ever since but the
trips are meaningless. Everest had been climbed, so to speak.
It was Gertrude Ederle who once and for all had softened the
English Channel for women and showed that it could be done.

That was thirty-nine years ago and nothing remains today
but that single line in the record books and the memory of the
great din unloosed in New York Harbor the day of her return
from abroad, when the whistle-cord of every steamship within
range was tied down. Sirens brayed and hooted as airplanes
buzzed and thundered overhead, pelting her with flowers as
she stood upon the deck of the city tug *Macom,* surrounded by
municipal dignitaries in plug hats and frock coats, who were
escorting her up the Bay.

In my ears still rings that great rolling roar which followed
her triumphant motorcade up Lower Broadway, swelling from
block to block as the crowd, packed from sidewalk to sidewalk,

caught its first glimpse of the young, brown-haired girl standing in the back of an open car, her arms extended as though to embrace them all. In my mind's eye I can see this mass, so dense that motorcycle police had to thrust open a lane for her passage as the wildly enthusiastic welcomers rushed and fought for the privilege of touching the car in which she rode. She progressed through the canyons of the skyscrapers beneath the bizarre August snowfall of ticker tape, torn up telephone books, shredded newspapers, broker's sheets and toilet rolls descending upon her from every window.

For this paper blizzard was something new in the line of welcomes to returning heroes, which had developed since the war, along with the incumbency as official City Greeter of the late Grover Whalen, appointed to that stately office by New York's Broadway playboy mayor, Jimmy Walker. Mr. Whalen was a gorgeous piece of man, born to the top hat, striped trousers, frock coat, and gardenia in the buttonhole which was his uniform when he went down the Bay to receive an incoming celebrity. With his pink face and black, toothbrush mustache, he was as much a part of the municipal scene as Battery Park, the Aquarium, and the downtown skyscrapers.

A routine had evolved in which the *Macom* chuffed down to Quarantine, the arriving v.i.p. was received officially by Mr. Whalen, transferred from the liner to the tug, and decanted at The Battery, where a cavalcade of open motorcars awaited. Then followed the ride up from Lower Broadway to City Hall, where his Honor the Mayor was enthroned to climax the reception.

Office workers in the tall buildings lining both sides of America's most famous street, having been alerted, waited like excited children with their home made storm. When the motorcade came past, they unloaded from the heights and the paper, fluttering down, was one of the prettiest sights you ever saw and strangely moving as well.

Spectators usually lined the sidewalks to watch the procession go by, but for Ederle the largest crowd ever turned out, spilling from the curbs and jamming the thoroughfare. Never before in the history of the city had there been such a demonstration for a sports hero; never before had the Department of Sanitation been called upon to sweep up so many tons of Broadway confetti. Not until the following year, when Lindbergh came back from France, were the decibels of cheers, tonnage of shredded paper, and hysterical warmth of welcome equaled or surpassed.

And all this for a simple, unassuming girl, the daughter of a German-American family who owned a small delicatessen store on upper Amsterdam Avenue in New York City.

This was the kind of welcome one would expect to be reserved for conquering admirals and generals, or crowned heads. But it was in this era that America produced a new royalty, the kings and queens of sport, as a vivid and thrilling demonstration of the workings of this unique democracy, where the poorest and the humblest could instantly become national heroes and heroines.

Gertrude Ederle, or Trudy as she was universally known both from affection as well as compact headlining, was one of these, and a shining example of the sudden magic that could envelop ordinary persons and overnight elevate them to fame and fortune.

One moment, as it were, she was an unknown, one of the faceless millions inhabiting our teeming cities, a young girl who enjoyed the exercise of swimming competitions and the companionship of her clubmates, and the next she was a world celebrity.

And had she but understood the nature of the excitement, love, and admiration she had touched off, had she been less modest, simple, and unambitious, she too might have become a millionairess, a Queen Midas, turning everything she fingered to gold.

As it was, the day after the news of her courageous triumph over self and one of the world's most treacherous bodies of water had been broadcast, merchants, promoters, manufacturers, and motion picture and theatrical producers were lined up in the offices of her "managers." They were trying to thrust large sums of money upon them for endorsements of articles, personal appearances, engagements, and services of every kind connected with the gilded name of Ederle, which could be expected to bring an equally gilded return from the almost hysterical Ederle-loving American public. The child had, so to speak, done nothing that was either useful, good, or serviceable to humanity, and yet as far as we of that era were concerned, she had done everything and we were prepared to drown her, who had survived the Channel, in a flood of dollar bills.

The fact that most of these offers were fended off with some arrogance by a group of "managers" that suddenly mushroomed around this celebrity, was part of a personal tragedy that dogged Gertrude Ederle, but did not alter the fact that here was an attempt for the first time in the memory of man to bestow riches upon a swimmer.

The art itself had barely become a sport. Up to that time, practically, swimming was something one did at the beach in the summer, or when one fell into the water or capsized when sailing, to keep from drowning. What, then, was there suddenly about this, and particularly women's swimming, which saw it in this decade elevated to the very pinnacle of publicity?

For the answer one looks again at our times.

Still heavy-handed, hypocritical, censorious prudes, we had but recently emerged from the age of the long-stockinged, full-skirted, bosom-swaddling bathing costume, the most ridiculous collection of woolen garments ever to conceal the female form divine. Men looked silly enough in their long drawers and half-sleeved, candy-striped, jersey tops, but it was the women dressed, apparently, more for going down into a mine than entering the sea, who really took the cake. One reason that swimming had failed to develop as a sport was simply that no one could move in the damn things. All they were good for was holding onto a rope and bobbing up and down in the Sea Bright, Sheepshead Bay, or Coney Island breakers. Any attempt at forward progress was soon brought to a halt by the drag of some twenty pounds of waterlogged clothing.

The revolutionary heroine who put an end to this nonsense and freed women from this form of bondage was an Australian girl by the name of Annette Kellerman, a polio victim who took up swimming at the turn of the century as therapy for her crippled legs. It was Miss Kellerman who claimed that no woman had the brute strength to swim the English Channel, for she had made several attempts to do so herself and once had gotten three-quarters across before being forced to give up.

But it was not for this that her name became world-famous, but the fact that she introduced the first one-piece bathing suit for women. A spectacular exhibition swimmer, she went into vaudeville and motion pictures clad, or rather unclad, in this daring garment and girls, forever thereafter freed from the drag of shoes, stockings, bloomers, blouse, and hat, bought themselves "Annette Kellermans" and began to swim.

When I was a boy Annette Kellerman was a household word and I remember her, smooth and glistening as a seal, performing in a tank on the stage of the old Colonial Theatre on Broadway and 62nd Street, a house devoted to high-class vaudeville. The s.r.o. sign was out at the theater, and the balcony spotlights were reflected from many a bald pate. The sellout attendance had come ostensibly to see her doing the crawl, the backstroke, the jackknife, and the swan dives, but nobody at the box office was being kidded. The original Annette Kellerman bathing suit was still a slightly bulky affair of jersey wool, even though skirtless and sleeveless. Nevertheless, it made the question of how ladies were put together no longer a matter of vague speculation.

The tight-fitting, black silk racing suit was only a few years away, and women's swimming and diving competitions became a major attraction. Newspaper publishers discovered that whereas reproductions of nightclub cuties in leotards or tights might bar them from the mails, due to the Nice-Nellies in the post office censorship in Washington, photographs of an octet of naiads, lined up at the end of the pool in their wet, clinging, one-piece garments were legit, even though far more revealing.

An appreciable part of the great Florida real estate boom was built upon photographs of girl swimmers used in advertising, and certainly no newspaper ever suffered a drop in circulation when it was able to publish this kind of cheesecake. Even as late as 1932 the publisher of the *News*, Captain Joseph M. Patterson, one of the canniest newspapermen ever to give the public what it wanted, commanded me to instigate and organize a great swimming meet to be held in the public parks, and which I staged first in Central Park and later at Jones Beach, filling our pages for days with girls, girls, girls. And what girls!

Back in 1917, a scattering of young secretaries and career women had formed an organization known as the Women's Swimming Association around a nucleus of a small pool on the

Lower East Side under the chaperonage of a remarkable woman, the late Charlotte Epstein, and coached by L. B. de Handley.

From this nucleus there exploded like fireworks the most astonishing and breathtaking collection of scintillating stars who were not only record-breaking championship swimmers and divers, but exquisitely lovely girls who became beauty queens and celebrities equal in fame almost to the reigning royalty of Hollywood. These included such unquestionable pippins as Aileen Riggin, Sybil Bauer, Martha Norelius, Helen Wainwright, Helen Meany, two sensational blondes named Georgia Coleman and Dorothy Poynton, Esther Williams, Josephine McKim and, of course, the one and only Eleanor Holm, the backstroke champion and one of the most beautiful nymphs ever seen in a bathing costume.

Gertrude Ederle, the daughter of the Amsterdam Avenue liverwurst purveyor, joined the Women's Swimming Association when she was thirteen and received all of her early teaching, coaching, and training there.

While Trudy was never a member of the W.S.A. beauty chorus, she was far from plain, and her somewhat Teutonic chubbiness, round, dimpled face, and fair-brown bobbed hair, were offset by agreeable features and an extraordinarily sweet expression.

She was of average height and not heavily muscled. Seeing her, you would have said there was just not enough girl there to pit against the thrust and slap of angry waves and relentless pressure of the winds prevailing across this tricky, punishing stretch of water. Perhaps her lack of beauty had something to do with her choice of ordeals. Certainly her decision to try to become the first woman to swim the English Channel was one of the most unselfish ones in the annals of sport. She wanted to accomplish this solely to bring a modicum of fame to the club she felt had done so much for her. She had not so much as the faintest foreshadowing of the celebrity it would make her personally, or the chance at fortune. And by that decision she touched off one of the supreme fairy tales of our times.

Trudy's specialty had always been long distance swimming; at the age of fourteen she had already made headlines by beating more than fifty opponents, including Britain's foremost girl swimmer, in a three-mile international race in New York Bay. A year or so later she swam from the Battery to Sandy Hook in record-breaking time. In 1925 the W.S.A. tapped its meager savings and Charlotte Epstein took Trudy Ederle abroad for her chance at the Channel.

No fanfare attended the attempt and even less its unhappy result. She failed. A turn in the tide accompanied by a sudden squall raised mountainous waves. Little more than half-conscious from nausea, waterlogged from the seas she had swallowed but still fighting, her limbs moving with indomitable automatism, she was pulled weeping and struggling from the Channel.

The naming of women as the weaker sex is a cliché which becomes even more frayed around the edges when such an example as that of Gertrude Ederle appears. In the failure this slight girl showed enough courage for a regiment, and displayed a fiber one never would have suspected in such a shy and otherwise ordinary person. Yet, as far as the American press and the rest of the world was concerned there was no story in defeat, and Miss Ederle was just another one of the many who had not swum the Channel.

There were two people, however, who were not convinced by this fiasco. One was Gertrude Ederle herself, and the other Captain Patterson of the *News*.

What brought these widely separated characters together was the fact that Channel swimming was an expensive business. There was transportation abroad and return, a long training period on the spot to become familiar with temperatures, eddies, rip tides, in short the nature of the enemy, the engaging of coaches and the hiring of accompanying craft. The resources of the Women's Swimming Association were insufficient to stand the cost of a second attempt. It was suggested to Captain Patterson that the *News* and the Chicago *Tribune* syndicate step in to back another try in exchange for the exclusive story should she succeed. With the prescience that made him the outstanding publisher he was, Captain Patterson agreed, gambling that if she made it, it would be the event of the year. But I doubt whether even he was aware of how big a story it would turn out to be.

A contract was prepared backing her with expenses, plus salary and a bonus. It called for a big decision on the part of an eighteen-year-old girl, for it meant giving up her amateur standing. Thereafter she would be a professional and denied all further amateur competition. It meant winner take all; loser forfeit everything. The iron determination and stubborn ambition concealed beneath that disarmingly gentle exterior left her no choice. She had challenged the Channel and she was unwaveringly resolved to defeat it. She signed.

We packed her off to Cap Gris Nez in France to train for her final effort. With her went her older sister, Margaret, herself a talented W.S.A. swimmer, Westbrook Pegler, then Chicago *Tribune* columinist and his wife, the late Julie Harpman, crack cityside reporter of the *News*. The coach who joined the party abroad was none other than that Thomas Burgess who, fifteen years before, had been the second to make the Channel crossing; his time, twenty-two hours and thirty-five minutes.

But in 1926 we were still innocents, not disillusioned. We had not yet had our noses rubbed into the fact that the dead of the 1914–18 war had indeed died in vain; that nothing whatsoever had been settled and that the democracies of the world were less safe than ever they had been before. To us virtue had scored a victory over evil in this war and we were established more firmly than ever in our belief in the favorite American fairy tale, the triumph of the artless good over the scheming iniquitous.

Such a story almost immediately began to build up at Cap Gris Nez, where the *News*-Chicago *Tribune*-Ederle party set up training quarters and Julie Harpman, covering, began to send home reports of cabals, disloyalties, and downright sabotage. We learned that our tender, guileless Trudy, the first All-American girl to arouse the nation to a frenzy of hysteria, had become enmeshed in a web of intrigue and hostility. In addition to having to contend with the furies of the Channel, it seemed there were those most necessary adjuncts of the bona fide *conte des fées*, ogres galore, and to the palpitating Americano, the best of all villains—furriners.

Neither the French nor the British wanted the girl to succeed in her attempt. As the *News* published Miss Harpman's stories with their unveiled hints of what was going on, the rest of the town and the country as well began to sit up and take notice, aware that being enacted daily before their eyes, as it were, and approaching its climax were all the elements of our most cherished type of dream. That climax failed no one.

The swim began the morning of August 6; the sea fairly calm, the forecast favorable. But weather prediction then was not what it is today. Evening and change of tide brought on a line squall, whipping the Channel into a hell of tide race and battering waves. With the chalk cliffs a few miles off Trudy would gain one yard and then lose two to the elements. Already the captain of the French escort tugboat had tried to break up the swim by bearing across her course until he was forcibly restrained by members of Trudy's party.

At twilight when she had been in the water for twelve hours, fighting fatigue, nausea, and all the devils of the deep against her, Thomas Burgess shouted from the tug that was lurching and wallowing in the heavy seas, "She must come out! But I will not take the responsibility of waiting for a sign from her indicating that she wishes to come out."

Whatever Burgess' motive might have been—perhaps sheer humanity rather than obstruction—it was the voice of authority and experience and once more the success of the adventure hung in the balance.

Someone leaned over the side and yelled into the teeth of the wind, "Trudy, you must come out!"

The girl raised her head out of the water and looked up from the deep trough of black waves, against which her legs were still threshing their six-beat trudgeon as regularly as the thumping of the engines from the accompanying vessel, and asked, "What for?"

With those two words, innocence and pluck triumphed. She battled onward. Two hours or so later Trudy walked out of the sea, up onto the sands of Dover to be met, I am afraid, if my memory is not tricking me, by a British immigration officer who solemnly kept her standing at the water's edge, demanding her passport, an idiocy which I note was repeated only this last summer in the case of another young girl swimmer who had just crossed for the exercise.

During her remarkable effort the story drove all other news off the front pages, and her feat was recorded in millions of words in thousands of columns of newspaper space. There had never been anything like it before.

In order to be the first to present the pictorial record of her accomplishment the *News*, as a picture paper, organized the swiftest and most expensive relay in the history of journalism up to that time. Sets of photographs were placed aboard four express liners departing from Southampton the same day. All of these were scheduled to arrive in New York simultaneously and practically at the same hour, which meant that our competition would have them as soon as we.

One of these ships, however, was a Canadian Pacific liner, an Empress steamer, whose destination was Montreal and thus, traveling the great circle route, reached the rim of the North American continent a day before the others. Employing two aircraft, one a sea and the other a land plane, a racing car with a famous driver, a railroad locomotive and an ambulance for the last leg, the photographs in waterproof wrapping were snatched from the ocean by the seaplane, where they were thrown overboard at the mouth of the St. Lawrence River, and then speeded on their relay through fog and dirty weather, to land in the *News* office twelve hours in advance of any others, a clean scoop. When we appeared on the street at eight o'clock that night with the picture of Gertrude Ederle greased, goggled, emerging from the sea near Dover, there was not another such picture in the whole of the United States. However, just as a wry epilogue to the journalism of those times, our competition, the rival *Mirror*, simply photographed our front and back pages and reproduced these in their next edition.

And thereafter all of America lay at her feet. The cornucopia of plenty, beyond the most fantastic dreams, awaited her, ready to be tipped and pour forth gold in an unending shower. She was at that moment the most famous girl in the world and promoters were queuing up, checkbook in hand.

To handle her affairs and sift these offers the family had engaged the services of a smooth and coony lawyer, the late Dudley Field Malone. But alas for Trudy, Mr. Malone was wise and smoothly practiced mainly in the matter of securing Paris divorces for American dollar princesses anxious to shed dull husbands. As an international lawyer this was his specialty; he was tops. But he was far from experienced in the handling of a new kind of celebrity, and particularly one of the caliber of Gertrude Ederle. So dazzled was he by the offers that came pouring in, that instead of confirming the best and bona fide ones accompanied by cash deposits immediately and thus assuring his client a lifetime competency, he held out for more. If so much was being offered while Trudy was still wiping the protective layer of grease from her body and shaking herself dry, how much more would one not be able to glean when she returned to the reception that was building up for her?

One can fault Mr. Malone for greed and inexperience, but it must be remembered that the greed was on behalf of his client. How was he to guess that the very sweetness, innocence, and guilelessness that characterized Gertrude Ederle was to prove his and her undoing and hand us our first jolt as to the inevitability of the happy ending?

For in spite of the furor that attended her achievement and the urging of our own reportorial staff that she return immediately to the United States, Trudy remained unconvinced either of her celebrity or the importance of cashing in at once. She was a stubborn girl, too, in her simplicity, and instead of catching the first packet Sandy Hook-bound, she went off to some little village in the Black Forest of Germany to pay a visit to *Grossmutterchen,* her dear old grandmother, whom she had never seen. There she spent some three idyllic and fatal weeks, during which time a second woman swam the English Channel.

Her name was Mrs. Mille Gade Corson, and she was the mother of two children, the first mother, then, to swim the Channel. In those days the word "mother" was still sacred in the U.S., still a tear-jerker *par excellence.* Only a scant ten years before, vaudevillians had been warbling a lyric that went something like: "M-o-t-h-e-r spells mother, the sweetest word in the world to me," leaving not a dry eye in the house.

It took Mother Corson an hour longer to negotiate the twenty-one miles between Gris Nez and the white cliffs of Dover, but it rubbed the edge off Trudy's feat and knocked the bottom out of her market. She was no longer the only woman to have swum the Channel and thereby a salable freak for public exhibition. One by one the would-be entrepreneurs, who had been sitting hat in hand in Mr. Malone's antechamber, slipped away. The gold and silver that would have made her comfortable and independent for the rest of her life, turned to ashes.

Her welcome, when she finally did return, was unstinted, for American hearts then were not fickle, nor were they commercially involved. Her journey through the canyons of downtown Broadway brought forth a most tremendous outpouring of love from the people of New York, and the thunder of her name as they cheered the girl with the exalted, tear-stained face, rolled and echoed from side to side of the tall buildings.

And here the fairy tale should have ended with, "And she grew rich, married a prince, and lived happily ever after." But that wasn't how it went.

Once, she had named as her heart's desire a red Buick Roadster. As a bonus for her courage, determination, and success, Captain Patterson bought her one and it was waiting at the Battery for her when she disembarked from the *Macom*. Her "managers," who were engaged in keeping everyone away from her, would not even allow it to be presented by us, and she only received it late that night before the delicatessen shop on upper Amsterdam Avenue. And in effect it was all she ever got for her pains, beyond some chickenfeed for one or two endorsements and personal appearances, much of which she used to reimburse the Women's Swimming Association for their original outlay on her behalf.

The cruel buffeting she had taken on the sides of her head during that grueling crawl permanently affected her hearing. Later, during an aquatic performance, she hurt her back and spent eight months in a plaster cast. A professional henceforth and forced to earn a living, she took a job as a swimming instructress to teach the young and quietly disappeared into the limbo of the forgotten—forgotten, that is, by all but her own friends.

She never complained about those who had mishandled and failed her. She remained wholly unspoiled by the great outpouring of adulation and publicity. She was never bitter, rude, or snobbish, nor wavered in that buoyancy and essential innocence which marked her character. The golden decade reached its end and America entered the crucible of change. Gertrude Ederle, for one, emerged from it a greater human being and one of the true Golden ones of the era.

Confessions of an Ex-Cheerleader

By Louise Bernikow

Louise Bernikow is a poet and journalist and editor of The World Split Open: Four Centuries of Women Poets in England and America. *In this 1973 selection, she looks back on her athletic career as a high school cheerleader in the fifties. Although rarely considered a sport, cheerleading requires physical exertion and athletic ability. Many cheerleading squads compete against one another annually in vigorous and complex routines. At the same time, cheerleading can also be viewed as preparation for stereotypical feminine roles that are supportive rather than independent. This realization has prompted some, like Bernikow, to recall their cheerleading days more critically than they experienced them.*

The trick is to be up in the air with a big Ipana smile on your face, touching the heels of your saddle shoes to the back of your head, bending your elbows as close as you can get them behind you. This makes your short red dress rise, revealing a quick glimpse of thigh and underpants. It also makes your 16-year-old tits, aided and abetted by stuffings of cotton or the professional padding of Maidenform, stick far out.

I am doing this of my own free will on a spring afternoon in Madison Square Garden. The year is 1957, half-way between my sixteenth and seventeenth birthdays. I have aimed at, plotted and waited for this moment. It is living up to my expectations. The Garden is crowded. This is the play-off game for the New York City championship: Forest Hills against Boys High.

The old Madison Square Garden smells like a locker room, which is what makes it such a triumph that I find myself the center of attention in it. I am a star at last on male turf. There are 10 of us at half-time in the middle of the wooden floor with all the lights out except for the spotlight shining on us. I turn my face upward into the smell of sweat, into the applause and whistles dropping like confetti from the tiers of spectator seats above me.

Tip of my head to Maidenform padding to saddle-shoed toes, dizzy with ecstasy, I go into the first cheer.

WE GOT THE T-E-A-M

I shake my shoulders and wiggle my ass.

IT'S ON THE B-E-A-M

I do some chorus-girl high-kicking, wiggle and shake a little faster, and smile my smile a little bigger.

COME ON, FOREST HILLS, SKIN 'EM ALIVE!

Up in the air, head back, back arched, trembling all over. I hit the ground squarely on my feet and run off to the sound of thunderous applause. The team emerges for the second half.

I am a cheerleader.

Forest Hills is defeated. I am sitting in the ladies' room, having changed the short red dress for a gray flannel skirt and button-down pinstripe shirt. The Garden is dark and silent. The cheerleaders are dark and silent, too. We are all quietly weeping. When we leave the ladies' room to meet the team in the corridor, each of us embraces each of them. I move from one boy to another, despondently hugging. No funeral has brought more grief.

On the way home, I see the *Daily News* centerfold photograph of the Forest Hills cheerleaders. We are lined up like chorus girls, grinning, shoulders back. I feel as though I am looking at faded glory. When I get home, the telephone is ringing. My mother answers and says it is for me. I can tell from her face that she does not recognize the voice, and she hovers near my shoulder, monitoring me.

"Hello?"

There is no sound on the other end, then there is heavy breathing, then faster huffing and puffing. I am terrified. I hang up.

"Who was that?"

"No one."

And not until 16 years later do I understand the connection: obscene phone calls are the other side of cheerleader glory.

Glory. I was hell-bent on glory when I started high school. On my awkward first day, I saw that cheerleaders were the queens of the school, and I determined to become one.

Forest Hills was a "rich" neighborhood, but not everyone at the high school was rich. I wasn't. In fact, I didn't live in Forest Hills at all, but in Kew Gardens Hills, on the other side of the tracks. I always felt like an outsider. When I became a cheerleader, every time I put on that red dress and went out there to jump and shout, every time I looked at the gold megaphone on my charm bracelet, and every time I walked through the corridors of the school knowing freshmen and sophomores were whispering and pointing with envy, I thought that I had managed, by hook and by crook, to wiggle my way into the ruling class.

Methodical, ruthless, ambitious, and manipulative, I studied the way "in" and discovered that, since cheerleaders chose their replacements, I had to learn how to charm women. Everything else in my life had depended on charming men and I, the original all-time Daddy's Little Girl, had that one down pat; but women?

Sororities were the key. Although they were officially outlawed, sororities ran things. The school cafeteria had special tables by custom for each sorority. As a sophomore, I would walk by those tables on my way to the nonspecial area where nobodies like me downed egg salad and Oreo cookies. I studied the sorority girls.

At night, I stood before the mirror "doing" my hair as I had seen it on the girls at those tables. I studied *Mademoiselle* and *Glamour*, full of girls who looked like cheerleaders, and there I discovered that fuzzy hair was my problem. Fuzzy Jewish hair. The girls in *Mademoiselle* had sleek blonde hair. Not me. The most popular cheerleaders at Forest Hills had sleek blonde hair. Not me.

I pin-curled as per instructions, every night, half going left and half going right. Still, in the morning, I combed it out to find kinks and fuzz. Somehow, in spite of it, I was "rushed" by sororities and, in blue serge Bermuda shorts and pink knee socks, was accepted.

I discovered how you charm women: you imitate them.

From Nora I picked up the names of painters and "acquired culture"; from Ellen I got my taste in plaid pleated skirts; from Arlene I saw how to bite my lower lip cutely. I was a sorority girl. I felt myself on shaky ground, always, but I hung in there, selling bananas on the streets of Manhattan as a "pledge," making the carfare back to Forest Hills where I joined my "sisters" who had dumped me off without a penny. We had an initiation ceremony; the fraternity boys came over afterward.

Two sorority sisters were cheerleaders. When "tryouts" time came, they taught the cheers to those of us who were going to try. We practiced all the time. I did cheers in my sleep and on the bus and in the shower. My family went nuts from the "Yea, Team" thundering from my bedroom.

"I wanna use the bathroom," my brother pounded at the door.

"Forest Hills—Forest Hills—THAT'S WHO!" I screamed from within, my teeth all freshly Ipana white.

If I made cheerleaders, my mother would stop clicking the hall light off and on when I came home from a date and "lingered" in the hall.

If I made cheerleaders, boys would arrive in rows and rows bearing tennis rackets, basketballs, baseball gloves, and fencing masks to lay in tribute at my feet.

If I made cheerleaders, Jimmy Dean and Marlon Brando would fall in love with me.

If I made cheerleaders, my hair would be straight.

Many tried; few were chosen. A jury of gym teachers and cheerleaders watched as we, with numbers on our backs, went through the cheers. I was Number Five. Something of the Miss America pageant in all this and something of the dance marathon. Girls were tapped on the shoulder and asked to leave the floor.

What were the criteria? I have gone over the old photographs in vain. They do not say. It was not "looks," for even by fifties standards, the cheerleaders were not the best-looking girls. My own photograph shows an ordinary middle-class Jewish girl. Her hair is short and flipped-up, with bangs. Her large nose has a bump on it. (I resisted the nose-job binge my friends went on. I have no idea where I got the courage.) She is wearing dark-red lipstick and her eyebrows are heavily lined. She looks older in the high school yearbook than she does now.

It wasn't looks that made a cheerleader, but "personality" or a certain kind of energy. Something called aggressiveness. Or bitchiness. Or pep.

Pep is what happened in American history before *vigah*, but it only applied to females. Pep was cheerfulness. It mysteriously resided in the Ipana smile. "Weird" or "eccentric" girls, moody girls or troublemaking girls did not have pep. We who had it became cheerleaders, committing ourselves to a season of steady pep, bouncy activity, and good clean dispositions.

I do.

We played some humid swimming meets in Far Rockaway and Flushing, tottering at the edge of the pool and getting our hair all fuzzy, but basketball was the main attraction. (There was no football. Rumor said a boy had once been killed on the field and the sport discontinued.) Cheerleaders as a group were married to the basketball team as a group. We played wife.

Our job was to support the team. We were the decorative touches in the gyms they played. We had some "prestige" in the city because the team was good that year. They had a little of our prestige rub off on them, too, for Forest Hills was known for the good-looking stuck-up bitches there. We learned to cater to the boys' moods, not to talk to Gary after he had a bad game (he would glower and shake us off), and yet to *be* there when he or Stanley or Steve came out of the locker room all showered and handsome. We were there for them always, peppy and smiling. Boys had acceptable temper tantrums on the court, but cheerleaders never did. We were expected to be consistently "happy," like the Rockettes at Radio City Music Hall.

We were the best athletic supporters that ever lived.

We paired off, cheerleader and basketball player, like a socialite wife and corporation executive, leading lady and leading man. My social life was defined by my "status." I only went out with jocks. "Who's *he?*" or "What a creep!" applied to boys who wore desert boots or girls who were "brains." We knew kids "like us" in other middle-class ghettos in the city, and we stayed away from the Greek and Italian kids in our school, from "rocks" like Howie and Dominic who played cards and drank and "laid girls," and from girls like Carole and Anita whom we called "hitter chicks" and who, we whispered, went all the way.

Cheerleaders had a reputation for chastity. No one ever said it, but we all understood it. On top of the general fifties hang-ups about sex, cheerleaders had a special role to play. Vestal virgins in the rites of puberty. Jewish madonnas.

Half the time, in real "civilian" life, I had to keep pulling those gray flannel skirts down, making sure "nothing showed," keeping my legs crossed. I would have been incarcerated on the spot by my mother if, one morning, I refused to layer the top of my body with a bra and all its padding followed by a slip followed by a blouse. Even if I were to evade Mother, my peers would have condemned me as a "slut" if I appeared less dressed.

The other half the time, as a cheerleader, I dropped a skimpy red costume over only bra and panties and got out there in the middle of a gym full of screaming spectators to wiggle my hips all over the place.

What does it do to the mind of a 16-year-old girl to be Marilyn Monroe one moment and Little Goody Two-Shoes the next? I don't know, but it sure wasn't sane.

For weeks before we went, the word was whispered from ear to ear among us: *Jamaica.*

Jamaica High School was the first "away" game we went to in my senior year. The word was full of terror. Jamaica had black kids. Forest Hills High School had been redistricted every year and there were *no* blacks in the school. Aside from the rocks and hitter chicks, nearly everyone was white, middle class, and Jewish. We held mirrors up to each other and told each other we were very heavenly and the whole world was like us, except we never really believed it. We called Manhattan "New York" or "The City." It was as far away and glamorous to us as it was to Clarence in Peoria or Pat in Kansas. Our mothers wouldn't let us go there.

I confess: when I left the Forest Hills ghetto for the first "away" game, I, Princess of the Pom-Poms, Our Lady of the Saddle Shoes, Culture Queen, carried with me, hidden in my purse, a menacing kitchen knife. For protection.

Every time I say "sure" when I mean "no," every time I smile brightly when I'm exploding with rage, every time I imagine my man's achievement is my own, I know the cheerleader never really died. I feel her shaking her ass inside me and I hear her breathless, girlish voice mutter "T-E-A-M, Yea, Team."

God knows, I tried hard to kill her. Forest Hills had a history of sending its red-skirted stars bouncing off for the big league at Cornell, and it looked for a few months just before I turned 17 as though I might follow their saddle-shoed footsteps, but something happened. I went to Barnard College instead.

Barnard was another kind of game, requiring a different kind of coin to play. No points there for having been a cheerleader. It was no longer a high-priced commodity, but now a social deficit. I, alert to the winds of change and being a good mimic, buried my cheerleader past. Fast.

"What did you do in high school?"

"I wrote poetry."

"I was in the theater."

"I listened to jazz."

And the cheerleader stayed buried until recently, when I had a series of strange revelations:

Beautiful, exotic Janet, painter-poet, was a cheerleader in Connecticut.

Acid-freak Nina, unwed hippie mother, was a cheerleader in Ohio.

Elegant Susan, theatrical and literary, was a cheerleader in Philadelphia.

Shaggy Bob, radical lawyer, was a basketball player at Midwood.

Junk dealer Joe was on the Bayside team.

I am not alone.

It *was* the only game in town for middle-class kids in the American fifties.

The world is full of us.

T-E-A-M.

Yea, Team!

THREE: The Structure of Women's Sports

Looking to the Future

WHAT IS THE FUTURE of women's sports? What should it be? All of the writers of the selections in this section favor equal opportunities for women in sports. But as Candace Lyle Hogan points out in her article on Title IX, equal opportunity can be interpreted in many ways. If we consider equal opportunity to

mean equal male and female athletic budgets, equal athletic scholarships, and equal pay for male and female coaches, it is clear that women are a long way from achieving equality in sports, although improvements are gradually being made. In her 1976 article, Hogan notes that, nationwide, women's sports budgets are only two percent of men's.

Even more complex is the issue of whether equality in sports means a completely sex-integrated sports system, including coeducational interscholastic teams; or whether it means two separate-but-equal sports systems. Most of the writers in this section favor the separate-but-equal approach for interscholastic and professional sports, although many advocate mixed

163

gym classes and mixed teams on the intramural level. Brenda
Feigen Fasteau argues that, although unappealing in theory,
separate-but-equal teams may, in practice, be the only fair
alternative. Fasteau and others note that creating integrated
teams might, in effect, exclude women even more thoroughly
from sports because, at present, the best male athletes perform
better in most sports than the best female athletes. In her
imaginative view of the year 2000, Lucinda Franks takes the
position that eventually sex-integrated teams will be successful: she suggests that training, not physiology, accounts for
most of the differences in men's and women's athletic performance.

Many of the selections in this section advise women, in
building their own sports system, to avoid duplicating the
male sports structure—or at least the excesses of its structure.
"Sports should [not] become for women what they have been
for many men: a display of aggression, a proof of toughness,
and a kind of primitive communication that replaces emotional intimacy," advises Brenda Feigen Fasteau. Sociologist
Harry Edwards writes, "The aim should be to set up a sport
system in which the emphasis is upon self-realization and the
value of participation." And Olympic discus thrower Olga
Connolly believes that women will help change the way
Americans look at sports: "It is women's task to educate the
spectators towards the appreciation of the esthetic qualities
along with the power display in sports. . . ."

Although criticism of the male sports system is deserved,
the complexities of creating a system based on more humane
values are sometimes overlooked. As some of the same people
who criticize the male system point out, sport does not exist
independent of the rest of the world. Sport both reflects the
dominant social values and helps to reinforce them, writes
Jack Scott. Similarly, Harry Edwards notes that important
American sports values—individual achievement, competitiveness, emphasis on winning—are also the dominant values
of the society at large.

It is precisely because sport is not an isolated arena, but an
integral—and influential—part of the society, that equal athletic opportunity for women is an important issue, not just for

athletes, but for all concerned with equality between the sexes. Harry Edwards notes that men's domination in sport "reinforces the attitude that national decision making is the sole province of *men*." Other writers, too, suggest that equality in sport may provide one of the bases for the development of full equality between men and women. In her piece on women's sports in China, Anne Gibbons remarks that, there, "women's carefully cultivated athleticism both reflects and reinforces their larger status in society."

At the same time, it is because of the central position of sport in society that achieving athletic equality is so difficult. By asking women not only to strive for equality, but to deny the values of the existing male sports system, an enormous burden is placed on them. Jack Scott suggests, more realistically, that women and men must both work to alter the sports system, without opposing it entirely. Scott's "radical ethic" embraces the value of competition and the quest for excellence. But it also says that "the means by which that excellence is achieved are as important as the excellence itself." To readers who may find his ideas rational and humane, but hardly radical, Scott remarks: "Anyone attempting to implement the radical ethic on a significant scale in the American athletic world today will quickly discover just how radical and revolutionary these ideas are."

Giving Women a Sporting Chance

By Brenda Feigen Fasteau

Brenda Feigen Fasteau, who shares a private law practice with her husband in New York City, has been active in the women's movement for several years. She has served as director of the American Civil Liberties Union Women's Rights Project and as vice-president of the National Organization for Women. Currently, she is on the advisory board of the National Women's Political Caucus and numerous other feminist organizations. In the following article, which appeared in Ms. *Magazine in 1973, Fasteau argues that schools should allocate separate-but-equal athletic resources for each sex in all interscholastic sports, and suggests how such a system might work.*

For the first few weeks of the season, two eight-year-old girls longingly watched the practice sessions of a Montgomery, Alabama, boys' football team. Finally, the coach broke down and let them play—but just for one season. I admire the stubbornness and audacity of these two little girls. I am also angry and sad that the same obstacles face them that faced me 20 years ago—when I was their age.

I wonder if they wish, as I once did, that they were boys. When you're that young, it's hard to see the value of being female because boys are permitted to do almost everything girls do, but not vice versa. It is especially hard when you love climbing trees and playing games, but are expected to play with dolls instead.

At about 13 years of age, it becomes even more painful, as boys, almost overnight, seem to grow stronger and bigger than girls. Although I was fairly good at sports and was on the girls' varsity field hockey, basketball, softball, and tennis teams, I was never as good as the best boys. It was small consolation that I was better at some sports—horseback riding and waterskiing. (Perhaps because these sports weren't as popular with boys.)

In athletics as we know them, the average man will probably beat the better-than-average woman. Scientists chalk it up to testosterone and the retention of nitrogen in men's muscles, which make them bigger and bulgier than women's. Even if this is true, the unhappy fact is that sports have been designed for men's rather than women's bodies—which means the emphasis is on strength. We have yet to see major promotion of sports utilizing women's unique flexibility (because of our less bulgy muscles) and better balance (as a result of our lower center of gravity). Gymnastics is the only widely practiced sport where women can outperform their male counterparts—especially on the balance beam.

I still haven't fully accepted what it means to be smaller and weaker than most men. From a practical point of view, it shouldn't matter; but it always has inhibited my activities in ways that make strength and sex matter a great deal. For example, in college I learned to play squash. When I got to law school, I discovered that women were banned from the university's squash courts. By disguising myself as a man, I managed to invade the courts with a classmate who is now my husband. We had fun, but I never beat him.

Still, as I remind myself, that may have been as much a matter of opportunity as biology: he's been able to play squash whenever he's wanted to and on courts where I wasn't allowed because of my sex.

Exclusion of women in sports is a concrete and difficult problem. But most young women never even reach the point of challenging their exclusion from their college's athletic facilities or varsity teams. By that time, they have been well conditioned to think of gym as a drag—often doing dancing and exercises, instead of playing football, soccer, basketball, and baseball. From early childhood on, girls are discouraged from taking pride in active and strenuous use of their bodies; boys, meanwhile, are encouraged to get "into condition," to enjoy their athletic ability.

Then there are the subtle discouragements: the unenlightened suspicion that a woman's interest in athletics violates the docile female stereotype and indicates lesbianism (remember the rumors about gym teachers?); the insinuation that if she shows too much interest in sports she may not be able to catch a man; and the general scoffing at women's athletic achievements. One Chicago high school teacher points to clear-cut evidence of sex discrimination in sports. "In the latest edition of the school paper, there were five articles on football and no mention at all of the girls' tennis team which had won its last three matches."

I don't mean to suggest that sports should become for women what they have been for many men: a display of aggression, a proof of toughness, and a kind of primitive communication that replaces emotional intimacy. Sweating, swearing, and grunting together as they play, men manage to create a fellowship which they find hard to sustain elsewhere. And sports provide men with yet another vehicle to test domination and preeminence. ("Let the best man win.")

Women, however, often do communicate with each other in noncompetitive, nonathletic situations; they are generally better able to express emotion, and seem to care less about beating each other into submission. Our self-images (unless we are professional athletes) aren't much affected by winning a tennis match. While this may reveal something positive, it also unfortunately indicates that women are conditioned not to take themselves seriously in sports.

Of course, the majority of men do not take the sportswoman seriously, either. I notice that whenever I'm interested in playing tennis with a male partner, no matter how well matched we might be, he invariably prefers to play against another man no better than I. Partly, this reflects his fear of losing to a mere woman. But, in a deeper sense, playing with another man seems to reinforce his own competitive sense of masculinity. If he beats another man, he's somehow more of a man himself. If he beats me, it's irrelevant, predictable. Losing is a blow to his ego whether it's to me or a man, but it's a diversion to play with me; the real contest is man-to-man combat.

However, there are encouraging signs that participation in sports is becoming important to women of all ages. Women are beginning to demand their rights as athletes. In New Jersey, for instance, the State Division on Civil Rights found probable cause in a case brought by a local National Organization for Women chapter because girls were barred from the all-boy Little League team. Most often, sex discrimination charges are filed when girls want to engage in a particular sport which a school offers only to boys. Lawsuits or the threat of legal action have led many schools to accept girls on boys' teams, especially in noncontact sports.

One of the highest courts to rule on the issue of integrating high school teams on the basis of sex is the U.S. Court of Appeals for the Sixth Circuit. In the case of Morris v. Michigan High School Athletic Association last January, that court affirmed a lower court order that girls may not be prevented from participating fully in interscholastic noncontact athletics.

As a result of the desire of Cynthia Morris and Emily Barrett to participate in interscholastic tennis matches, many high school girls have benefited. In addition, after this complaint was filed, the Michigan legislature enacted a law guaranteeing that all female pupils be permitted to participate in noncontact interscholastic athletic activities and to compete for a position on the boys' team even if a girls' team exists.

New York and New Mexico now also have new regulations which call for the integration of the sexes in all noncontact sports wherever there is a high school team for boys but not for girls. And lawyers of the American Civil Liberties Union have caused at least five other states—Connecticut, New Jersey, Indiana, Minnesota, and Nebraska—to integrate noncontact sports in their high schools. As a result of litigation, female track stars in Connecticut and Minnesota have made their way onto the men's teams. A young Minnesota woman is now on the boys' skiing team of her high school; another has joined the boys' tennis team of hers.

The Indiana Supreme Court, responding favorably to a class action by a female high school student wishing to play on the boys' golf team, held that the Indiana High School Athletic Association rule against "mixed" participation in noncontact sports was a denial of equal protection under the 14th Amendment to the United States Constitution. (Any institution receiving federal or state money may be in violation of the equal protection clause of the 14th Amendment if it discriminates against women students and coaches in athletic programs; sex discrimination in schools which receive federal funds also violates the Education Amendments of 1972 which recently became federal law.)

In New Jersey a high school sophomore successfully challenged a rule of the state Interscholastic Athletic Association that prohibited high school women from competing on varsity tennis teams. A pilot program has begun in New Jersey to allow girls to compete with boys for positions on varsity teams and to encourage schools to upgrade physical education programs for girls. Specifically, the ruling makes clear that outstanding female athletes receive opportunities for training and competition at their ability levels. Lawsuits have also been won in Louisiana and Oklahoma.

In many of these cases there are no girls' teams, so it's easy to decide that interested girls must be allowed to play with the boys. It is more difficult to resolve the question where a girls' team and a boys' team exist for the same sport. If the highly talented girl athlete is encouraged to join the boys' team at the high school level, why not at the college level? Or in the Olympics and other amateur athletic competition? And if at the Olympics, why not in professional sports?

Unfortunately, no American woman would have made the Olympics if the team had been integrated and if the same criteria for selection were applied to both sexes. The very best men—the ones who enter the Olympic tryouts—are still better than the very best women. And certainly at the professional level, women in direct competition with top men would be in trouble in almost every sport. It is debatable whether Billie Jean King, the Number One woman tennis player in the world, would even make the top 10 if male and female professional tennis players competed against each other.

At the professional level, the point is occasionally made that because women aren't as good as men, the purse in women's tournaments is legitimately smaller. This argument overlooks the fact that women pros, such as Ms. King in tennis, draw crowds just as large if not larger than the men they can't beat and that such women regularly capture the headlines in sports columns.

In any high school or college, integrating teams on an "ability only" basis could result in a new form of exclusion for women players. It would effectively eliminate all opportunities for them to play in organized coached competition.

Obviously, therefore, school athletic training programs have to be developed to balance the scales, and equal financial attention must be paid to both sexes. To begin with the human resource, coaches of women's teams must be paid as much as coaches of men's teams. A woman high school basketball coach recently produced figures showing an allocation by the Syracuse Board of Education of $98,000 for male coaches and $200 for female coaches. Discrepancies between women's and men's salaries may violate not only the 14th Amendment to the Constitution but virtually every piece of legislation in the area of sex discrimination in employment and education.

Scholarships, too, must be equalized. The first and, it seems, the only university to establish an athletic scholarship for women is the University of Chicago.

As for the students themselves, Minnesota and Utah lawsuits are asking that equal resources—money and personnel—be devoted to physical education for girls and boys. From the first grade through college, girls and boys should have gym classes together with equal access to athletic facilities and instruction. Students, regardless of sex, should be encouraged to perform to the best of their individual ability.

Until puberty, there are insufficient height or strength differences between girls and boys to justify predominantly female or male sports below the junior high school level. Girls and boys from an early age should be taught judo or other skills which convey a sense of their own individual strength and agility. If at some point girls and boys prefer different sports, they can individually separate themselves according to these preferences.

Until there is a relaxation of the external cultural pressure for males to prove their masculinity, boys may well choose sports like football, wrestling, and boxing. In any case, a girl wanting to play football should be permitted to try out for the boys' team if an entire girls' team cannot be formed. Girls with the skills to make the boys' team should have the opportunity to play. I am now arguing in court for the right of a woman student at City College in New York to participate in a men's basketball course because there is none offered for women.

That only noncontact sports are considered suitable for sex-integration is nonsensical. As one proponent for the integration of contact sports puts it: "If we are worried about girls' breasts and internal organs, then give them chest and belly protectors. We haven't spared our male football players any expense in that department. We can't declare that because we think many or even most girls cannot or will not play in certain sports that *none* may therefore be allowed to." To match this myth about women's participation in contact sports, there is also a long-standing controversy over the definition of "contact sports." (Baseball and basketball are considered contact sports.)

Because girls have not enjoyed the same physical and psychological opportunities as boys to develop athletically, I believe that resources must be made available for at least two interscholastic teams per sport: one for girls and one for boys. While sex-segregated teams may sound like the long-discredited separate-but-equal doctrine, it is through a process of careful elimination that this policy emerges as the most viable. The four other alternatives listed below are simply *not* equitable:

1. A system involving ability-determined first- and second-string teams will undoubtedly result in two mostly male teams and no greatly increased participation for females.

2. A first-string team that is sex-integrated to absorb top talent of both sexes plus a second-string all-girl team would increase girls' participation but it runs afoul of boys' rights by excluding them from the second team.

3. If the first-string team is based solely on ability and the second-string team members are evenly divided, boys and girls, the system ends up favoring boys again by assuring them representation on what amounts to one and one-half out of two teams.

4. The quota solution requiring half boys and half girls presents both practical and psychological problems: intrateam ostracizing of the girls who dilute the overall performance, and interteam exploitation of the "weaker" sex members of the opposing team.

So we're left with the separate-but-equal solution. While it may penalize the outstanding female athlete who must play on girls' teams regardless of whether she qualifies for the boys' team, it has the singular advantage of giving boys and girls an equal opportunity to compete interscholastically. This is, in my view, an adequate response to the argument that in sports, as in other areas, women should be compensated for past discriminations. The contention that women should be allowed to try out for men's teams, even if there are comparable women's teams, is potentially unfair to the men who can't make the men's teams but might make the women's teams. Even more importantly, it cheats the women's team which would lose its best athletes to the male squads, thus setting women's sports back even farther.

Where girls' sports are taken seriously at the high school and college level, the results are striking. Throughout Iowa, for instance, girls' basketball draws the bigger crowds. The coaching is excellent, and the facilities and equipment are first-rate. Because women's basketball is a matter of state pride, high school and college women in Iowa eagerly try out without feeling the traditional stigma and scorn so frequently associated with women's sports.

Marcia Federbush of Michigan suggests an Olympic-style system to solve the inevitable imbalances of participation, resource allocation and spectator interest: the girls' varsity and the boys' varsity would *together* constitute the school's varsity team. On the same day or evening both teams would play their counterparts from another school (alternating the game order since the second game is inevitably the star attraction). At the end of the two games the point scores would be totaled. If the boys' basketball squad won 75–70 and the girls' basketball team lost with a score of 60–80, the final school score would amount to a 15-point loss.

The girls' and boys' teams would travel together and use the same facilities. They would enjoy equally skilled (and equally paid) coaching staffs, equal budgets, game schedules, uniforms, equipment, combined publicity attention, and a shared spotlight.

Clearly, when interdependence leads to team success, the primary advantage would be the shared commitment in *two* strong separate-but-equal teams.

Shedding Light on Title IX

By Candace Lyle Hogan

Candace Lyle Hogan writes a nationally syndicated biweekly sports column and a weekly column for Soccer USA. *As an associate editor of* womenSports *Magazine from 1974 to 1978, she regularly reviewed the progress of Title IX. In this 1976 article, she explains the legislation's origins, limitations, and possibilities.*

Woody Hayes narrowed his eyes at the squad he had assembled on the 50 yard line. For the first time in his career the coach wasn't sure if good blocking could save the day for the Ohio State football team. With that female jock bill a scourge on the land, no honest, red-blooded American citizen was safe on his own football field. Why any minute now a lassie from the distaff side could sashay up demanding to throw a tackle or two. Thus Woody's pep talk, or last hurrah, as it were, to his football team:

"This could be the 'Big Game' to end all big games, you big lugs. Losing could mean flying second class, less free tickets to scalp, I mean it's all laid on the line, men. This time losing will really be like death. What I'm telling you is that this could mean settling for a cheaper cut of beef or (shudder) . . . chicken on the training table!"

With that, two linebackers fainted dead away. Drawing their wallets, several alumni rushed over trying to revive them. In the distance could be heard the thundering approach of the angels of vengeance. It was the women of Ohio State.

"Oh, why couldn't it just be George Plimpton?" Woody whimpered. "This might do more damage to the Saturday afternoon college football ratings than cartoons."

The women, wearing tattered shorts and knee pads yellowed with age, were led by their new athletic director Phyllis Bailey. She halted them for a huddle before charging out onto the field.

"Now ladies, like I've always told you, 'she also serves who only stands and waits,' and those who abide tacky equipment and hand-me-down uniforms get points in that great scorebook in the sky. But all that's changed now. See this document tacked to my pinney? This is Title IX, the stone tablet of women's sports. This means the world is ours. We can get whatever the men have (she leafs through it) as long as, according to Paragraph 86.41, Subpart C, we can prove interest and need. That's why I've called you together today. We're going to prove we're 'interested' and 'needy' by smearing those over-sized budget-eaters all over the football field. First string ready? Tighten your flanks and go for it!"

The outcome of that grueling gridders' gouging was never reported in the <u>Columbus Dispatch</u>—just a photo ran the next day. It pictured the entire Ohio State football squad limping back to the locker room, each player half-barefoot. You see, the women had wrenched the left shoe from some, the right shoe from others. They had taken the "opportunity" to be "equal" because, after all, the spirit of Title IX says "fair share."

Title IX. Title IX of the education amendments of 1972 is official . . . it's on the books . . . it's the law of the land. The long-awaited final regulation implementing it was signed by the President on July 21, 1975. It is illegal for schools to discriminate against people on the basis of sex. Title IX puts the force of law behind the fact that women are entitled to a fair and equitable share of whatever opportunity a federally-assisted educational institution offers. That means no sex discrimination in admissions, scholarships, employment, rules and regulations, physical education . . .

And yes, that means athletics too.

But no, Title IX doesn't say Uncle Sam has to *give* your share to you. It says, in short, it's yours *if you can get it.* Equal opportunity—not necessarily equal funding—is yours, if you can convince school administrators that you need it.

Ay, there's the rub. Although some of us might like to see legions of women (as whimsically described above) making up for lost time, and although some men (notably those who run the NCAA) envision such a mob invading their turf, it's just not working that way.

Confusion. But which way is it working? As Cal Papatsos, Associate Professor of Queens College, in New York, puts it: "The tragedy is that when Title IX initially came out in 1972, it set high expectations because HEW promised all things to all people. Since the final regulations came into effect, I've been up and down the eastern seaboard and the only action I can see is people trying to figure out what it is. I see most people in a holding pattern."

The confusion was apparent even before the bill was signed. The Congressional debate on the issue produced such an outpouring of response that the bill was doomed to ambiguity.

Although it prohibits sex discrimination across the board, it was Title IX's athletic clause that aroused the intense controversy, which lingers in confusion. The "guidelines" were three years in the making, a span that promoted a storm of debate over the dollar as well as educational value of intercollegiate athletics. There was an unprecedented whirlwind, 10,000 public comments, over the draft regulations, and there were several unsuccessful legislative attempts to alter the law by exempting revenue-producing sports.

According to Margaret Dunkle, associate director of the Project on Status and Education of Women of the Association of American Colleges: "As the battle lines were drawn, it became clear that Title IX was stimulating new and unique coalitions. The various sides on the issues could not be identified by labels, party, geographical, liberal/conservative, or even sex."

But on one point there is no disagreement. Title IX, all buffed out in its final form, thrilled no one. Women's sports advocates, expecting equal funding, got diluted, undefined "equal opportunity." NCAA honchos, after spending more than $200,000 lobbying to avoid sharing a dime with women, went home to the unnerving prospect of revamping bloated football budgets.

What Title IX Is Not. Everyone was expecting fixed guidelines to untangle the chaos wrought by 50 years of discrimination. Those expecting a stone tablet got vague outlines instead. The breath of the bill, however, was etched in stone: "Be it resolved that no person in the United States shall, on the basis of sex, be excluded from participation in, be denied the benefits of, or be subjected to discrimination under any education program, or activity receiving Federal financial assistance."

That means 16,000 public school systems and nearly 2,700 post-secondary institutions have lots of changing to do. HEW is in a state of change too and may be bowing out of its role as the enforcer of Title IX and other civil rights laws. Weinberger said, "The most effective enforcement of all is a public which supports the law." Since elementary schools have until July, 1976, and secondary and post-secondary schools until July,

1978, to comply with Title IX, federal litigation will not be an immediate way to force schools into compliance.

There may be teeth in the law yet. A letter from HEW's Office of Civil Rights last September emphasized that the three year adjustment period is not a grace period. HEW expects schools to have taken firm steps toward compliance in the first year. Responding to this, the board of regents at the University of Maryland ruled that the university must comply with Title IX within the first year. The board directed the head of men's athletics to submit monthly reports specifying what actions he was taking.

In other action, a group spearheaded by WEAL (Women's Equity Action League) is already suing HEW and the labor department for failure to enforce anti-sex-discrimination laws for schools. It is expected that the WEAL suit will prod HEW grudgingly into enforcement.

Support for women in sports was increasing even before the law was written. As long as women wrangle with their schools for a piece of the pie, opportunities for women should continue to increase.

Title IX may be as meaningful in what it is not, as in what it is. It does not prohibit anything except sex discrimination. Title IX allows a school to sponsor separate teams for men and women in contact sports, but it does not forbid coed teams in contact sports—unless, by making a program coed, a school is limiting a woman's opportunity to compete on that team. It says that a school may not need to provide equal funding, but it does not forbid equal funding.

Flexibility. The vague law almost encourages schools to experiment. From school to school you may see differing patterns of development, which is legal under Title IX as long as a school is actively evoking student interest and responding to student needs in a non-discriminatory manner. You might see a school's number one female tennis player leaving her teammates to fill a number-three spot on the boys' tennis team. It is not likely, but you might see a boys' football squad trimmed so that the school can afford to field a boys' volleyball team. (After all, it can be argued that some boys as well as most girls have had their opportunities previously limited when so-called minor sports have been squeezed out by football and basketball.) You might see a girl playing on the boys' football team in a school that has no girls' team. You might even see Darrell Royal's gridders flying second class once in a while, so the women's gymnastics team can practice on balance beams that don't wobble.

Whatever you see will probably have the inconsistency that occurs when people clinging to tradition try to adjust to change. School sports are in a state of transition. Since Title IX is more a blueprint for the future than a manual for the present, many school programs are developing on a trial and error basis.

Nationwide, women's sports budgets only equal two per cent of the men's budgets. Walter Byers, executive director of the NCAA, has been quoted as saying, "Two per cent is enough." Those who are able to influence budgetary decisions will determine whether Title IX's leeways turn into loopholes. It may well be that people with more concern for the big business of athletics and less regard for equal rights will determine Title IX's effects.

Margot Polivy, legal counsel for AIAW (Association for Intercollegiate Athletics for Women) and considered to be the nation's foremost authority on Title IX, says it's up to people on the local level to monitor Title IX's effects. "It's a game that everybody has to play. All the foot soldiers have got to be generals on their own campuses," she says.

What It Is. When it was originally proposed, Title IX required that all physical education classes be co-educational. The final stipulation modifies that requirement by allowing separate instruction for boys and girls in contact sports and in sex education classes. The law explicitly permits grouping of students by ability, and it allows separate toilet, locker room, and shower facilities, as long as the facilities are comparable.

Title IX requires that schools provide equal opportunity for both sexes to participate in its interscholastic, intercollegiate, club, or intramural athletic programs. Although "equal opportunity" is not defined, HEW will determine if it exists by considering whether the selection of sports and levels of competition "effectively accommodate the interests and abilities" of both males and females. HEW will also consider such factors as equipment, travel, coaching, medical services, training, housing and dining facilities, and publicity.

Schools may field separate teams in contact sports, and where competitive skill is the basis for selecting team members. If a school operates a team that excludes one sex, it must allow members of that sex to try out for the team, unless it's a contact sport. Title IX does not, however, rule out the possibility of women trying out for a contact sport team. In fact, last fall the Supreme Court in the state of Washington ruled that a high school girl be allowed to play on the boys' football team.

A school does not have to spend equally for both sexes, but it must provide funds necessary for equal opportunity. If there is sufficient "interest" a school *must* provide funds.

In its clarification letter HEW stated that by July 21, 1976, each school is required to perform self-evaluation of its athletic program including: 1.) comparison of Title IX requirements to current practices, 2.) determining interest and abilities of both sexes by seeking information from all segments of the community, and 3.) developing a plan and publicizing it.

Title IX still applies to programs which are funded by sources other than the federal government like booster clubs and gate receipts. Schools which are not complying with Title IX risk losing their federal funding.

What's Happening. Title IX is a catalyst forcing schools into intense review, discussion, self-examination and re-evaluation. It is important to remember that with or without Title IX many schools have already increased opportunities for women in sports, and are on the road toward what Blaufarb calls "eventual equality." Speaking for the National Association of Physical Educators, she says, "Title IX puts the force of law behind what we've approved of for years. Most elementary school sports are coed now and have been for years. The majority of high schools in the nation have run two programs, one for boys, one for girls.

"Over the past six years most high schools have started to

offer coed physical education classes. Women are divided about the value of coed activity in respect to athletics. There is no reason the so-called lifetime sports, such as swimming, tennis, golf, handball, racquetball, shouldn't be coed. But contact sports and sports which involve regional and state-wide competition will probably remain single-sex and separate."

Most physical education professionals believe that to maintain the educational emphasis of sports, schools must eventually provide three types of programs: coed classes (intramurals included), men's interscholastic teams and women's interscholastic teams—separate league competition for each.

Schools which see Title IX mainly as an economic threat are acting impulsively and, according to Papatsos, negatively. "Some schools are mandating coed in everything. They are trying to eliminate the girls' program by making both into one athletic program. That's a distortion of Title IX."

Elinor Nickerson, women's Athletic Director at San Ramon High School in Northern California wants her program in the East Bay Athletic League (EBAL) to continue. In a position paper she wrote, "It is not the intent of Title IX to pre-empt, harm or destroy existing programs. To change the character of a sport or a thriving program by making it coed constitutes pre-emption."

She turns down the boys who want to try out for the girls' volleyball team by explaining, "It's a different game and it wouldn't be fair for you to compete with the girls. In boys' volleyball the net stands eight feet high, while the girls' net is 7⅓ feet. Now what you've got is a handle to use on the men's department to try and get your own volleyball team."

Nickerson recognizes that some coed competition may be an expedient way to provide girls with athletic opportunity. For example, if there are not enough skilled girls the school cannot field a girls' tennis team. Title IX says that a sufficiently skilled girl may compete on the boys' team, but that does not preclude the school's obligation to provide a girls' team when sufficient interest warrants it.

At San Ramon, the top girls' tennis player left her team to join the boys' team as the number-three player. "As far as the kids are concerned," says Nickerson, "the boys' league is the real league. She has the glamour position on the boys' team and it's not her fault that she gets prestige by being regarded as a sex kitten. But it means that the girls on the other schools' teams in the league don't have the opportunity of competing with our top girl tennis player."

The stage is being set for a workable solution. The all male board of governors of the EBAL asked Nickerson to be the first woman athletic director to attend its meetings. The California Interscholastic Federation (CIF), which governs most of the state's high school league competition, ruled that any school wishing to join CIF must affiliate both its boys and girls athletic programs. "Now high school athletic directors are begging for women coaches to start attending their meetings," says Nickerson.

Women athletic directors have been hired at UCLA, University of Kansas, Kansas State University, University of Colorado, University of Missouri, Northwestern University, University of Texas, to name a few. But even at UCLA, which Weinberger called a "model program," the women's athletic director is not assured of controlling her own programs. In many schools, the men's athletic director is ultimately in charge of both programs. He acts as liaison with administrators, and it's up to the women's director to work well with him.

Go For It (or What You Can Do). A women's coach raised the penetrating question: "Say I do find policies in my school that do not conform to Title IX. What could I do to change that? I could jump up and down, scream and holler, but I don't know what else I could do."

Many woman teachers and coaches have been effective in improving the lot of women athletes already . . . Joan Joyce, for example. When Joyce began to coach volleyball at Mattatuck Community College in Connecticut, she discovered that the women could only practice in the gym twice a week, usually during the worst evening hours. "So I went over and sat down with the guys on the men's team, smoked a couple of cigarettes, and we got to know each other. From then on I'd go every afternoon and have the gym all to myself for the women's team.

"That's how it can work. I didn't come into the men's athletic director and crash his program. If you start off by bucking them, you're in trouble."

Another successful coach said, "You can be more effective if you promote good will. Listen to their expertise and offer yours. Don't ask for more money, equipment and playing schedules than your athletes are ready for. Tell the men 'we couldn't do it without you'."

If you have to do it without them, you can. One woman who is working to develop her interscholastic program suggests, "If you need to, you can go over the principal's head, directly to the superintendent of schools. But garner your forces first, through booster clubs, parents, media, students. . . .

"We attend booster meetings each month. If we don't show up, they figure the girls don't need any money. If you can get the boosters behind you, they're the ones who are not at all cowed by the board of education. They're loud and they're vocal, and they love it, particularly the ones who have a daughter on a team. The boosters can help you prepare fliers, surveys and questionnaires to send to the parents.

"Just by communicating, good will is growing. The men's and women's teams sometimes practice and raise funds together. The girls sell programs at football games, but at the same time, I hear girls telling their boyfriends they can't go out on a date because they have to go to basketball practice. So now some of the guys are going to watch the girls practice. They're forming a rooting section."

A Radical Ethic for Sports

By Jack Scott

Jack Scott, author of The Athletic Revolution *(1970), former athletic director at Oberlin College, and director of the Institute for the Study of Sport and Society, is widely known for his radical critique of American athletics. In this selection, he argues that competitive achievement and*

humane cooperation do not have to be mutually exclusive
values in sport. Excerpted from a speech before the
American Association of Health, Physical Education and
Recreation, this article appeared in a 1972 Intellectual
Digest.

The dominant American sport ethic is best captured in Vince
Lombardi's famous remark that "winning isn't everything,
it's the only thing." If this ethic ruled only the relatively small
realm of professional athletics, it might be of no serious
concern. But as we all know, the Lombardis, the Tom Landrys,
the Darrell Royals are the high priests of American athletics.
The Lombardian ethic is the rule of the day from the professional ranks down to the colleges, high schools and junior high
schools. Even rather conservative athletic figures, such as Fran
Tarkenton and Harry "the Hat" Walker, have begun to speak
out in alarm about the influence of the Lombardian ethic on
Little League and Pop Warner sports.

It must be admitted, however, that the Lombardian ethic
has guided those who live by it to some of the highest levels
of athletic excellence known to man. This ethic is oriented
toward the product, to be sure, but the product it turns out is
an excellent one. In any sport that Americans have taken
seriously, we have invariably developed some of the finest
teams as well as individual athletes seen anywhere in the
world. Though we sometimes get carried away with our own
chauvinism, as when we declare the Super Bowl a world
championship, our myriad accomplishments in the international athletic arena, including the Olympic Games, speak for
themselves. . . .

In American sport, the opponent is the enemy—an obstacle
in the way of victory. During an interview that I did with
George Sauer, he commented that this aspect of football was
one of the primary reasons he chose to leave the game despite
his tremendous love for it. "We shouldn't be out there trying
to destroy each other," Sauer said, "but some people try to
make the game that way. They have the idea that in order to
be really aggressive and attain the height of football excellence,
you almost have to despise your opponent or even hate him.

I think when you get around to teaching ideas of hatred just to win a ball game, then you're really alienating people from each other and from themselves and are making them strive for false values."

The antithesis of the Lombardian ethos is the counter-culture ethic. A saying that was around a long time before the birth of the counter culture sums up this ethic: "It's not whether you win or lose, but how you play the game that counts." The counter-culture ethic looks at the product orientation of the Lombardian ethic and demands that we focus on the process instead. We should enjoy sport for sport's sake, not for any extrinsic reward it might bring. Not too surprisingly, some counter-culture proponents have even suggested that we abolish scoring. A counter-culture runner wants to be concerned with how his run felt, not with how fast he covered the distance.

The counter culture has looked at the extreme competitiveness of the Lombardian ethic and has quite correctly been upset with its many abuses. Many counter-culture proponents have suggested we replace competition and aggression with gentleness and cooperation.

According to them, the rigid authoritarian structure of the Lombardian ethic stifles self-expression and spontaneity, so this structure must be eliminated in order to allow these qualities to emerge. Likewise, teamwork under the Lombardian ethic often develops at the expense of individuality, so the counter culture usually prefers individual to team sports.

The Lombardian ethic views sport as a masculinity rite from which women are excluded. (Lombardi often motivated his players by indicating none too subtly that to lose a game was to lose one's manhood. One of his greatest players, Willie Davis, after a Green Bay Super Bowl victory, commented, "We went out and won the game and preserved our manhood.") Upset by this supermasculine approach, the counter culture advocates coeducational activities. Frisbee, where there is no violent body contact, is seen as a replacement for football.

In *Athletics in Education* (1936), Jesse Williams and William Hughes addressed themselves to the counter-culture advocates of the day: "Some parlor athletes and some splendid though misguided sportsmen talk about sport for sport's sake and condemn winning. They neither understand nor contribute to the problem. Sport for the sake of sport might be the worst dilettantism possible. As a slogan expressing abhorrence of corrupt practices, it is admirable; as argument that victory should not be striven for, it is mere nonsense."

I could not possibly agree more with Williams and Hughes. To tell a competitive athlete, man or woman, who is training three and four hours a day, day-in-day-out, year after year, to not be concerned with victory is liberal snobbery; or at best it is the remark of someone who simply does not understand the agonistic struggle that is an integral part of the competitive sport experience. It is just as wrong to say winning isn't anything as it is to say winning is the only thing.

Like all other institutional activities, sport reflects and in turn helps to reinforce dominant social values. If the dominant values of a society are alienating and destructive, then any major institutional activity in that society will reflect these values regardless of how pure and intrinsically valuable that activity may be. Not understanding this relationship, the counter culture looked at the institutional manifestation of sport in American society, saw its dehumanizing nature, and concluded that something was wrong with sport itself. The mistake was to not distinguish between the essence of sport and its institutional manifestation. The counter culture has performed an invaluable service by highlighting the abuses of the American system, but it has been rejected by the overwhelming majority of American people because it does not offer a sound, rational, humane and viable alternative. The radical ethic of sport is a synthesis of these two positions, and it does offer such an alternative.

The radical ethic says there is nothing fundamentally wrong with the essence of competitive sport. It says that the agonistic struggle in sport of team with team, individual with individual, individual with him/herself or individual with nature is a healthy, valuable human activity. It does not view sport as either solely competitive or solely cooperative. As many fine physical educators have tried to point out, there is a vital interplay between competition and cooperation in healthy sport activity. Competitive sport is in trouble when this balance is tipped toward competition, as it is today, or toward cooperation, as the counter culture would prefer.

Rather than replace the Lombardian emphasis on the product with the counter culture's emphasis on the process, the radical ethic wants to view the human experience in a whole, non-fragmented manner. The radical ethic has no quarrel with the Lombardian quest for excellence. It only says that the means by which that excellence is achieved are as important as the excellence itself. A "winning-is-the-only-thing" philosophy could easily be translated into "the end justifies the means." The radical ethic does not support authoritarian coaching techniques or the plying of athletes with amphetamines in the quest for victory—practices that are common today.

There is nothing wrong or dehumanizing about a person taking pride in accomplishment, whether it be in athletics or in any other human endeavor. But his/her quest for excellence should not be accomplished at the expense of him/herself or others. The radical ethic has a deep underlying faith in human beings. When a humanistic process—a process that will allow and encourage individuals to develop their full potential— replaces the present dehumanizing system, the sport experience will be even richer than it is under the Lombardian ethic.

The radical ethic views the athlete as an artist who is struggling to express him/herself, but like the followers of the Lombardian ethic, radical proponents understand the need for dedication and hard work. No matter how aesthetic a setting may be, a counter-culture long-distance runner will not have a peak experience during a run if his/her physiological conditioning is such that he/she has cramps after the first mile. You have to put in a lot of hard work before you reach a level of fitness that enables you to enjoy the process.

The radical ethic sees nothing wrong with team spirit as long as it stems from a genuine development of community rather than from authoritarian intimidation. Sharing and co-operating with others in a healthy team setting makes one more human rather than less. Under the radical ethic, team spirit would flow from a genuine concern for one's teammates rather than from a superficial and imposed conformity.

But perhaps the most fundamental aspect of the radical ethic is how the competitor sees his/her opponent. The opponent is not simply an obstacle in the way of victory or an instrument to be used for one's own glory. In a very real sense, the opponent is a brother or sister who is presenting you with a challenge. You cannot experience the agonistic struggle of sport without him/her. The champion radical athlete will share his/her knowledge and skill with lesser athletes in the hope that they will rise to his/her level. His/her pride in victory comes when he/she struggles courageously in the face of a real challenge.

The radical ethic assumes women should have equal access to the competitive sport experience. Allowing women to compete against men, however, does not provide women with equal opportunity. As Simone de Beauvoir points out in *The Second Sex*, the difference between the female and the male athlete is similar to the difference between the heavyweight and lightweight boxer. The athletic experience is no less rich for the lightweight even though the heavyweight could of course beat him. Consequently, the radical ethic says that women who want competitive sport experience should be provided with the economic and institutional support that men receive.

Rather than denigrate the many accomplishments of those who have been guided by the Lombardian ethic or the counter-culture ethic, the radical ethic attempts to build a system based on the achievements of these two systems while avoiding their abuses and excesses. The radical ethic is indebted to men like Knute Rockne and Vince Lombardi, though it does not see them as the apotheosis of the sportsman. It has a commitment to excellence along with a desire to achieve that excellence by a process that would humanize rather than dehumanize.

These ideas may not appear radical or revolutionary. However, anyone attempting to implement the radical ethic on a significant scale in the American athletic world today will quickly discover just how radical and revolutionary these ideas are. That a rational, humane ethic must be classified as radical or revolutionary should tell us something about the nature of contemporary American society.

Desegregating Sexist Sport

By Harry Edwards

*Harry Edwards, professor of sociology at the University of
California at Berkeley, is the author of* The Revolt of the
Black Athlete *(1969) and* Sociology of Sport *(1973). In 1968,
he organized the black protest at the Olympics in Mexico
City. In this selection, he urges that women not merely
duplicate or integrate the American sports system, but make
it more humane and democratic. Originally presented
at the University of Wisconsin Forum on Sport and Society,
this article appeared in a 1972* Intellectual Digest.

The contention here is that the conditions of American sport
constitute a fundamental obstacle to the achievement of
women's equality in American society. No matter how vocif-
erous women become in their quest for human rights, until
they have succeeded in overthrowing male domination of sport,
they might as well be running on a treadmill.

As religion in America has become more secular, sport,
perhaps the basic institution allowing for communal reaffir-
mation of secular values, has become more sacred. Sport
manifests every characteristic of a formal, thriving religious
movement. It has its gods (superstar athletes), its saints (those
high-status sports figures who have passed to the great beyond—
Lombardi, Rockne, Gipp, Thorpe), its scribes (the hundreds of
sports reporters and sportscasters whose object is to dissemi-
nate the "word" of sports deeds and glories), its houses of
worship (the Astrodome and other facilities that rival anything
ever constructed to house traditional worship services). And
sport has one other feature that traditional religion has long
since lost in American society—massive throngs of highly
vocal, maniacal "true believers" in the creeds and values
relating to sport and its contribution to the maintenance of
the "American way of life."

Thousands of hours are spent each year by the citizens of
this country viewing sport. And who are some of the most

dedicated fans? One need only explore the alumni rosters of our major sports institutions to understand that businessmen—those individuals whose decisions influence the dispersion of opportunities for achievement—dominate and control most of our collegiate athletics. Senators, congressmen and the President of the United States—the self-designated "Number One" fan in the country—identify so thoroughly with sport that the lexicon and imagery of athletics have crept into their political phraseology (the Nixon "game plans" for Vietnam, the economy, the 1972 presidential elections).

Women live in another world. If the American female is fortunate, she may achieve the status of "superintake valve" epitomized by Hollywood sex symbols and the winners of countless "meat parades" from the "Miss Broken Jaw County Fair" beauty pageant to the "Miss America" and "Miss Universe" contests. The beauty contest, once only peripheral to chauvinistic male exploitation of women, has become the most substantial avenue by which a woman may achieve self-actualization within the context of established sex-role definition. A negligible number of women achieve status via this route. For the others, the empty drudgery and boredom of performing trivial household duties and participating in suburban "morgue sessions" cast in the guise of card parties and social gatherings stretch out like a vast wasteland.

When we consider the factors influencing the emerging condition of women combined with an understanding of the functions of sport in American society, the role of sport as a prime perpetuator of female subjugation becomes clear.

In any society, sport as a social institution disseminates, reaffirms and reinforces the secular values regulating human interaction. All other functions are secondary and stem from this—particularly spectator entertainment. Ultimately it is the commonality of values governing behavior in both sport and the power centers of American life that creates the predominantly male enthusiasm for and identification with athletics. Foreigners and often women have a difficult time appreciating the mania exhibited by American men over, say, football.

In America, sport values stress individual achievement, competitiveness, a manifestly Protestant-ethic brand of discipline and an exaggerated emphasis upon winning. It is not coincidental that these values reflect precisely those regulating interaction in the larger society.

As early as the 1950s, General Douglas MacArthur stated that sport is "a vital character builder . . . that molds the youth of our country for their roles as custodians of the Republic. Fathers and mothers who would have their sons be men should have them participate in sports."

General MacArthur clearly did not have women in mind when he made this statement. Few of the expressions depicting a cause-effect nexus between the benefits of sport and the maintenance of America's integrity as a nation refer to women at all. Females are not only cut out of most sport involvement—varsity-level collegiate athletics, coaching, officiating—but even in those sports in which they are encouraged to participate, they conform to the behavior considered appropriate for women. A review of the work of Eleanor Metheny and Marie Hart, among other scholars, reveals the degree to which this occurs and indicates that in America it is deemed inappropriate for women to engage in sports requiring bodily contact, aggressive action against an opponent, lifting or throwing of even moderately heavy objects or assuming awkward or "unbecoming" positions. It is quite appropriate, however, for women to engage in sports where a physical barrier separates opponents, where gracefully choreographed and aesthetically pleasing movement is demanded. Thus, while males are participating in football, basketball, baseball, boxing, wrestling and preparing themselves for their roles as "custodians of the Republic," women are propelling themselves gracefully and athletically over the ice or through the water or they are slapping a ball over a tennis net.

In America a female's athletic competence is seen to detract from her womanliness ("she can throw a ball, bat and run like a boy"). For this reason, many females never become involved in the most popular sports. Those who do participate even in those sports open to women (track, swimming, ice skating, tennis) often retire before their prime. Most women are forced by cultural definitions to choose between being an athlete (thereby facing the barely hidden suspicions as to their heterosexuality) and being a woman. What do the people responsible for legislating, enforcing and implementing laws to erase female oppression see when they view sport? They see *men* exercising leadership, *men* manifesting the complex of values (character and coolness in a situation of aggressive attack, discipline, mental acuity) that supposedly made this country great and will insure its greatness in the future. All this reinforces the attitude that national decision making is the sole province of *men*. Little wonder that much of the legislation aimed at ending sexual discrimination is inevitably more cosmetic than meaningful.

I am not advocating that women demand an equal opportunity with Bob Brown to knock heads with Dick Butkus in professional football. I am six feet, eight inches tall and weigh 265 pounds, and I would not relish the idea of a physical confrontation with Dick Butkus, Bob Brown, Muhammed Ali or any other person professionally trained to crush skulls. What I am stating is that there is no rational reason why a woman should not be encouraged and allowed to become a jockey, a coach, an umpire, or a sportscaster or reporter. There is no rational reason why female students should continue to pay the same tuition as male students yet be denied access to varsity sports programs except in the role of pom-pom girl or cheerleader or some other position that is primarily part of a flesh exhibition on the sidelines, peripheral to the center of action. Sexually, the most segregated department on any major college campus is the athletics department. It takes only a glance at its budget and the degree of public and administrative concern over its functioning to understand that it is also the most important.

I am proposing that along with their efforts toward greater opportunities in education and work, women should organize an intensified campaign demanding opportunity for leadership and control positions in sport across the board and participation as athletes *with men* in all sports where the structure and physical requirements of the activity allow. The short-run advantage to be gained is a diminution of the male-dominated image of major sports—especially if female involvement is

(text continued on page 196)

Sports for Everyone

The images on these four pages suggest a future where girls and women can participate fully in sports. Some of the photographs also hint at the desirability of creating a more humane sports system that can serve large numbers of people— young and old, male and female. **1:** Runner in the 6-mile Mini Marathon, New York, 1976. **2:** Delta State vs. Queens College, 1976. **3:** Training for the Olympics, 1977. **4:** Child learning gymnastics. **5:** Mass calisthenics during a factory break in China. **6:** Cindy Meserve, first woman on a men's NCAA basketball team. **7:** Fencers, Brooklyn College. **8:** Gymnastics class. **9:** Hoboken Little League. **10:** Mini Marathon, 1976. **11:** Karate Exhibit, 1973.

5

explicitly linked to the increasingly prevalent denunciation of beauty contests and a refusal to become engaged in sport as half-clad pom-pom girls and cheerleaders and baton twirlers.

By settling for involvement in male-dominated sports as now structured, women run the risk of making the same mistake made by blacks in their liberation struggle. Upon close examination, the "change" demanded by black liberation groups from the most militant to the most condescending is only superficial. The black liberation struggle has emerged not as a struggle for *change* but as a battle over the *terms of exchange* between black men and white men; the struggle is essentially over how much social and moral tranquillity black men will allow white men in *exchange* for how much power. Thus, if interracial tranquillity and harmony were established tomorrow in the United States of America, this nation would still have to face the fact that more than 51 percent of its population would still be subjected to the frustration and degradation of abject sexist oppression.

Women should not only demand access to the sport structure as now established, but they should also campaign to gain their just proportions of public funds and institutional budgets as well as access to publicly owned and institutionally controlled athletic facilities. The aim here should not be to organize a sport structure that mirrors or mimics the present afflictions of male-dominated sports in America (vulturistic recruiting, economic overextension, drug abuse, heavy emphasis upon winning, etc.). Rather, the aim should be to set up a sport system in which the emphasis is upon self-realization and the value of participation; where anyone, male or female, has the opportunity to engage in sports that do *not* demand that a participant pound his opponent into submission or force him into abject defeat and humiliation in order to achieve the singular goal of American sport—winning. Some sports such as football and boxing would be excluded from such an athletic program completely. But hopefully, America would gain far more than she would lose through initiation of such an alternative sport structure. For women could very well succeed where the black civil rights movement has failed—and that is in developing an alternative social model in which the younger generation can be socialized with values stressing cooperation rather than antagonism, participation and self-actualization rather than confrontation and domination. In doing so women may succeed in injecting the seeds of humanity, justice and equality not only into the moral and ethical "no woman's land" of American sport but into American society.

Women's Sports in China

By Anne Gibbons

*Anne Gibbons is a feminist physical educator who
teaches at the Bank Street School of Education in New York
City. She has long practiced sports, but was inspired
to learn basketball as a result of her experiences in China.
This article, based on her 1976 trip to the People's Republic
of China, describes some particularly striking aspects
of Chinese women's—and men's—athletic participation.*

Physical educator Marie Hart has noted that women in other areas of the world engage in sports with less stigma and greater acceptance than do American women. This applies to many Eastern and Western European countries and is true of the People's Republic of China. The results of national athletic programs in which the sexes are trained nearly identically have been astounding, as viewers of the past decade's Olympics know. On a tour of the People's Republic of China in 1976, as part of a sports delegation, I was able to gain some insight into the athletic experiences of women there.

A visit to a spare-time sports school in the city of Hangchow was particularly illuminating. As we entered the gymnasium, a women's basketball team was practicing on one end of the court. Some of the men in our group began to shoot baskets at the other end. However, most of the American women didn't know how to play. Even those of us who did had never competed, so we felt awkward trying to shoot baskets with men who were far more skillful. Oblivious to our discomfort, the men caught most of the rebounds and dribbled freely around us. When the Chinese women invited our whole group to join them in a game, all but two of the American women sat down. Even they dropped out before long, to watch from the sidelines, frustrated at their inability to participate.

There were visible differences in style between the Chinese women and the American men on each team. The women used a great deal of teamwork, constantly passing to other players and including everyone in the game. The men preferred dramatic individual shots at the basket and played their roughest, with little concern for the possibility of injuries. The Chinese stopped immediately to help fallen players, even at the price of a basket, while the Americans played on without noticing. Aggressive and cooperative at the same time, the Chinese women were excellent players.

This difference in style holds true for Chinese men as well as women, as thousands of Americans saw firsthand in 1975. Chinese men's and women's teams toured the United States, startling spectators by helping fallen players as a matter of course. Unlike the American image of the male sports hero as super-masculine and rigidly competitive, the Chinese male athletes combined superior playing with human feelings of concern and support. They were no more "unmasculine" than were the female players "unfeminine."

One need not possess superior ability to be physically active in China. Athletics permeate daily life, and nearly every Chinese citizen participates in sports. At 6:00 A.M. we arrived at a park filled with hundreds of people starting their day with physical activity. This happens each morning in China: men and women seventy to eighty years old do tai-chi-chuan (shadow boxing); groups of young boys and girls practice wu shu (a martial art); volleyball and basketball games are played; people run together and do calisthenics.

This is just the beginning of a typical physically active day. Rush-hour traffic consists mainly of bicycles, even in large cities such as Peking and Shanghai. Although public transportation is inexpensive and accessible, many people prefer riding their bicycles to work. Twice during the day, workers in all government offices, industries, and commercial enterprises take a break to do exercises to music broadcast nationally over the radio.

In China, a person's workplace might well be the focus of his/her athletic involvement. Workshops within plants play one another, and factories compete with each other at the city, provincial, and national levels. Costs are covered by trade union and government funds. At the Kwangchow Table Tennis Ball Factory, for example, a member of the Revolutionary Committee, the factory's administrative body, organizes ping-pong, basketball, and badminton teams. Men and women alike use the recreation room, basketball court, and outdoor exercise area. Large factories employ full-time sports instructors. On days off, many workplaces sponsor trips to the countryside for swimming, hiking, and mountain climbing, at no expense to the worker.

Physical training is considered an integral part of the cur-riculum in kindergarten, primary, and middle schools. In addition to at least two weekly gym classes and daily exercise periods, all schools provide extensive after-school sports pro-grams widely attended by girls as well as boys. The same is true of spare-time sports schools, where exceptional athletes of both sexes are trained. Women basketball players we met at one such school told us that they were coached the same as men, had similar training routines, equal access to facilities, and equal funding.

Athletics are strongly encouraged and widespread in China mainly to keep people healthy. Before the founding of the People's Republic in 1949, poverty, disease, and the constant threat of starvation were a way of life for most Chinese people. The YMCA organized sports for foreigners; the referees couldn't even speak Chinese. A park that is widely used today once posted signs which read, "No Chinese and Dogs Allowed." The development of sports since the establishment of a socialist government reflects dramatic improvements in living condi-tions, tremendous economic growth, and, most importantly, China's concern for the health and emotional well-being of its people. In order to industrialize as well as to increase production in an economy that is still 80 percent agricultural, both men and women have to work hard and be in good physical condition to do so. Sports physically strengthen the population and serve as a means of preventive health care.

This is particularly significant for women, who have made enormous strides over the last thirty years. Before 1949, Chinese women were totally dependent on their fathers and husbands for survival. In *China Shakes the World*, Jack Belden described the marriage of Goldflower, a poor peasant girl, as typical:

She had to wait on him day and night. When he went to sleep she had to take off his shoes and clothing; in the morning, she had to put them on again. She had to light his cigarettes, pour his water, hand him the cup with both hands and a subservient smile on her face. He struck her daily as a matter of course and beat her unmercifully if she did not obey his commands on the instant.

For many women, beauty and desirability were measured by the size of their bound feet. The physical restrictions imposed on them were thus extreme. Ning T'ai-t'ai related her experience in Ida Pruitt's *A Daughter of Han:*

They did not begin to bind my feet until I was seven because I loved so much to run and play. . . . When I was nine they started to bind my feet again and they had to draw the bindings tighter than usual. . . . My feet hurt so much that for two years I had to crawl on my hands and knees. Sometimes at night they hurt so much I could not sleep. I stuck my feet under my mother and she lay on them so they hurt less and I could sleep. But by the time I was eleven my feet did not hurt and by the time I was thirteen they were finished.

Although Chinese women have not achieved total equality with men, they are no longer weak or subservient. Almost all females work for pay outside the home. While the heaviest manual labor is still done mainly by men, and housework and teaching young children are female jobs, women perform many functions traditionally considered male. They are welders, crane operators, printers, pilots, bus drivers, and agricultural workers. Women have complete legal equality.

Sports have played an important role in strengthening Chinese women both physically and psychologically. Women's carefully cultivated athleticism both reflects and reinforces their larger status in society. A martial arts demonstration we watched at a spare-time sports school in Peking shows how the Chinese encourage women to be strong and forceful. A small girl holding only a dagger tries to defend herself against three boys armed with spears. Through a sequence of various skillful maneuvers, she manages to defend herself against her attackers and emerges victorious.

Chinese women are fortunate to experience the physical and emotional rewards inherent in athletic competition. Given their history, it is remarkable and perplexing that they have already surpassed American women in sports. Their athletic progress has resulted from larger political change. At a spare-time sports school in Shanghai, we asked a female coach how American women might improve their situation in sports. She replied, "Oh, you have to change the political system for women to be equal to men." Is this true? Or can American women, in the absence of overall political change, win athletic equality and opportunities for masses of people to participate in sports?

Women in Motion

By Lucinda Franks

See page 94 for biographical information on Lucinda Franks. In this article, from an anthology entitled Woman in the Year 2000, *edited by Maggie Tripp, Franks imagines what sports might be like in an egalitarian America of the future.*

Turn your thoughts back about twenty-five years. When the Total Human had not yet been born and the average body was just a neglected dormitory for the mind. Try to remember those sedentary days when the finely-tuned work of art called the human anatomy was pounding and screaming to get out from under dimpled scallopped layers of fat, sagging muscles, and aching bones entering the final and fatal stages of benign neglect. Who would have thought then that society would rediscover a secret as old as civilization, a secret that would intensify a human's joy in life, that would cleanse the brain, and turn agitation and unrest into peace of mind.

There is a quaint and amusing quality to our memories of the late Sixties and Seventies. The picture of the Halls of Academia, encrusted with myths, where the professor sniffed at the thought of wasting precious brain cells in the pursuit of brawn; the housewife driving the car a mere half-mile for cigarettes; the middle-aged man huffing and puffing to chase the dog; the teenage girl "getting out of gym" by pleading it was that-time-of-month; the low esteem with which any form of physical exertion, save sex, was regarded; the inability of the general populus to extract pleasure from participating in sports.

Now that we are in the Year of Our Lord 2000, with modern technology and a rebirth of the age of reason having joined forces to put a world hurtling toward catastrophe back on course, it is hard to move back in time—to recall a period when there were no integrated golf and baseball teams, when women athletes were not vying for football scholarships, when indeed it was not known that women are capable of being as strong pound-for-pound as men and, with equally strenuous training, can match or surpass them in many sports.

Lest we forget, however, there *was* a time when Little League and high-school ball teams were all-male, with coaches swearing they'd dynamite the field before letting girls in, and actively defying court orders for integration. There *was* a time when women were regarded, in the words of one sports philosopher of the Seventies, as "truncated males, which should be permitted to engage in such sports as men do—but in foreshortened versions." There even was a time when acrobatics, diving and equestrian sports, where women had proven themselves uniquely superior, were not popular spectator events in this country; the same people who now thrill at watching fine performances of balance, quickness of manipulation and rapid reflexes in these events were the ones back in the Seventies saying that those singularly female skills would never draw sports crowds, which counted on sheer male rough-and-tumble, blood-and-guts spectacles for their enjoyment.

It was somewhere around the mid-Eighties when sports finally became an "in" thing. It took years and years to arrive, having begun in the early Sixties with President John F. Kennedy's physical fitness campaign. Yet it was almost as if the door opened overnight. Suddenly the concept of sports had changed, and the very word shifted in its connotations. Just as in the Seventies, good nutrition suddenly became faddish with "natural and health foods," so did exercise and games skyrocket in status. They no longer evoke images of smelly locker rooms, tile floors, exhaustion and former ninety-nine-pound weaklings with muscles the size of watermelons. And female athletes all at once were transformed from "Amazon Lesbos" to "goddesses," thanks to the appearance of Billie Jean King and other coolly feminine tennis pros, who started Americans down the road to female sports-star worship. The emergence of these female superstars signaled an era of enlightened spectatorship. They liberated the world of sports by shifting the emphasis from the love of size and brute power to a broader appreciation of beauty, virtuosity and intricate skill. Sports began to be a multifarious experience for both spectators and participants—a physical and spiritual reaching out, transporting the individual to realms undreamed of by the "acid-eaters," of past decades; or simply a rediscovery of the historic and delightful activity in which our primal ancestor indulged: playing with his fellow.

At the heart of this change was a realization of what coordinated bodily movements, as expressed in a sport, could do for a sense of well-being. The idea was as old as man. The Greeks had known that a sound mind is inside a sound body. Kierkegaard had used the word kinesis—Greek for "motion"—to signify a deep existential change in the mode of being. It was a truth well-known, but somehow buried beneath the surface of man's consciousness—like the cat that looks all around the room for the bell that is tied around its neck.

People began to examine the generally well-balanced state of mind that many athletes seem to have. Statistics were taken, polls and studies were made, and the reasons were sought.

Athletes came forth with personal descriptions of the almost religious feeling that came upon them after they had stretched their bodies to the limit; runners spoke of the trees merging with the ground as they raced, swimmers told of the moment when the water seemed to propel them forward, persons who exercised regularly professed to be in harmony with nature and themselves—a quality they feared would disappear if they stopped their regimen.

Remember the famous experiments at Pennsylvania State's Health, Physical Education and Recreation College, when finally someone decided to put the old maxim "a sound mind in a sound body" to the test of science? Two groups of high-school seniors were chosen and given Scholastic Aptitude Tests. One group then went through a six-month program in which members trained two hours a day doing a variety of physical exercises; the second group, the control group, simply continued its normal study and play schedule. At the end of the experiment, the two groups again took the SATs, and, while the control group's results remained generally the same, the exercise group members' scores rose dramatically. Some youngsters who had not previously qualified for college—save an occasional "finishing school"—now achieved scores which met the admission standards for some of the toughest Ivy League universities. The experiment made headlines everywhere.

It was that experiment—there had been similar less dramatic tests of the relationship between exercise and mental functioning which had been largely ignored by the public—that put exercise on the top priority list for Americans. Pop phrases and catchwords were coined: "Body in motion," "Let's play" and "Jog awhile." It could not be denied that exercise improved clarity of thinking, alertness, ability to absorb complex ideas; it increased blood flow to the brain, strengthened the cells, and without a doubt acted on the regions of the brain to decrease anxiety and induce confidence and inner harmony.

And then "gamesmanship" was redefined. One must remember that in the Seventies, the need to win, and the need to have one's favorite team win, was crucial—so crucial, in fact, that the means used, the art of the game itself, was secondary. It's hard to imagine when winning was so important that it could make or break a man's self-esteem. Now, the conquering of one's opponent is not the prime mover in games; it is conquering *one's self*. Dr. Seymour Kleinman of Ohio State University, one of the first to stress this new dimension to sports, this inner contest with the self, used to cite the words of Michael Marine, who wrote about boating in an American Youth Hostel newsletter:

When I first started boating, I thought my satisfaction and elation came from competing with the river and winning. I would attack it again and again, trying ever-more difficult maneuvers . . . occasionally, I would even have delusions of winning the war over this inanimate river. Finally, however, I came to the realization that it is not a struggle between me and the river. The river, with all its dynamic action, is only a catalyst. Boating is a means of self-expression and my competition with the river is me overcoming myself, affirming myself, and realizing myself in my struggle toward victory, toward the absolute, toward self-control.

Both spectators and participants have now come to place less emphasis on winning or losing than on the way the game is played. In elementary schools, young children now devote half the school day to playing outdoors. Although supplied with balls, nets and other equipment, they are left to make up their own games with their own rules. Older children's games are structured in a way that lets everybody win. The Harris Games, named after Dr. Dorothy V. Harris of Penn State, are designed to reverse two traditional but still disquieting facts about sports: there are many more losers than winners, and the ones who need to win most generally lose. The Harris Games are intricately structured so they do not discriminate against the weak, the fat, the clumsy or the slow. Instead, the complicated series of games favors each player and brings out the one particular thing each can do better than anyone else: the fat child wins the game where weight is important; the small boy, where smallness is crucial. This early conditioning has been proven to have dramatic effects on ego and body image, teaching young people to feel comfortable with their bodies, to be proud of themselves and to move with greater ease.

It is well-known that more high-school students than ever

are qualifying for athletic teams, that more are passing physical fitness exams with high scores. Psychologists say this is not only because of the intense national popularity of sports, but also because children who used to shy away from physical output—because it was a source of pain and humiliation—are now allowed to enjoy it without the threat of being harshly judged.

The People's Republic of China was decades ahead of us in learning about the mysteries and gifts of the body in motion. Peking and Shanghai thirty years ago looked like our big cities look today—free of polluting cars, full of bicycles and joggers. In the old days, people used to pass the time having parties, drinking liquor and watching television. If they did venture outdoors, it was to rest on park benches and on beaches. Only the kids, sometimes with their father, played games. Now, of course, people celebrate their bodies. Schools, gymnasiums, neighborhood baseball diamonds and playing fields have replaced the corner cafés and "singles bars" as adult hang-outs. And just as years ago, the Chinese started the practice of rigorous exercise each morning, so now has a dawn jog for every family member—from toddler to grandmother—become as essential as brushing the teeth.

Much of the credit for all these changes belongs to women. Their full and equal entry into the sports arena, after years of chipping away at this narrow and selective male-dominated field, expanded it into a healthful and consciousness-raising pastime for everyone. It is ironic that women should be at the forefront of the "Body Movement," having launched their modern liberation campaign in the Sixties and Seventies with a demand for men to stop ogling the female body and start paying attention to the female mind. Once it was generally accepted that the female mind was as sound as the male mind, the battle turned back to the body—to prove that it was more than just a pleasure trove for man.

The array of myths about women and sports fell like dominos. It was proven that, up until menopause, a woman's bones, though smaller, were no more fragile than a man's, that a woman was *not* more likely to be injured while playing than a man, and that in fact the injury rate per participant was generally lower for girls than boys—in both contact and non-contact sports—because of the girls' extra padding of fat. Breast pads were soon devised for women athletes, similar to men's jock straps. Coaches were convinced by medical testimony that the well-guarded uterus was one of the most shock-resistant internal organs in the body and that strenuous activity actually increased muscular support around the pelvis. Similarly, it was accepted that vigorous exercise helped both menstruation and pregnancy (the U.S. Olympic Committee stopped advising its swimmers and other athletes to use the pill to prevent menstruation from coming during their contests). The scientific discovery that men also enjoy monthly cycles, with attending emotional highs and lows, also helped to dash the legend of the "female curse." The widely-held belief that women athletes developed bulging muscles turned out to be scientifically unprovable—a woman's physique is genetically determined at birth, and no amount of exercise and training can radically change it. When women began to train strenuously for serious athletics in the Eighties, it turned out that with the same amount of training they developed less musculature than men, and instead used a higher percentage of already-existing fiber. Those shotputters with bowling-ball shoulders turned out to have had the basic bulges in the first place.

Centuries of ignorance about and lack of research on the female physiology were overcome. Women, exhilarated with this new sense of physical power, began the slow process through the Seventies and Eighties of throwing over the "femininity game"—luring, baiting and netting a husband—for the far simpler and honest games that men had enjoyed for years.

After long research into the female physiology, there now appear to be only a few sex-linked differences between the male and female performance in the sports arena. The average female is still born smaller than the average male, and thus is at a disadvantage when at a random sample women are pitted against a random sample of men. Moreover, she is at a disadvantage when performing in a climate where heat and humidity are high, since the body temperature of a woman must rise two to three degrees higher than that of a man before she begins to perspire and cool off. It was this discovery that led to the successful movement to have lacrosse and field hockey meets postponed from the traditional spring and summer season to late fall and winter.

Women athletes who have undergone steady and rigorous training also have overcome the historic heat dissipation handicap of the average female—that is, that the female has fewer functional sweat glands than the male. It was definitively established that women in fact had, in earlier times, not exercised as much as men had, and had thus lost the use of a high percentage of their sweat glands; these needed to be reactivated, and were, by rigorous exercise. The change in conditioning has not altered a basic difference in the female frame, however, and her wider hips and lower center of gravity still place her at a disadvantage in some sports.

Nevertheless, women keep closing the gap between men's and women's world records, and it now appears as if a woman may well become the fastest long-distance runner in the world. Blossom Larrieu broke a new world record for the mile run for women last month—2.45.1 minutes, just 20 seconds behind the men's record; women, who were more than fifteen percent slower than men when women's participation in this event began back in the Sixties have enjoyed a much greater improvement level than men. The records for the one-hundred-meter dash have also come closer together (9.9 seconds for women against 9.6 for men) with women catapulting ahead while men have shaved much less off their time of twenty-five years ago.

Women have long equalled—although not beaten—men in swimming events (the record for the men's and women's four-hundred-meter freestyle is the same), with the sexes running neck-in-neck in improvement levels over the past ten years. The reason for this, of course, is that, although women over the years have reduced body-fat deposits to perform better, they have also proportionately lost the original advantage of buoyancy in the water that the extra fat provided them.

For years, women have been surpassing men in equestrian sports where their sensitivity in handling the reins gives them a distinct advantage. They have also excelled at diving, gymnastics, and acrobatics, recognizing and exploiting the special

feminine qualities of grace, elasticity, and rapid motor adjust-
ments which these sports demand. Of course, women have
long shown themselves men's equals in riflery and archery
and, more lately, in golf. For many years, the record for
swimming the English Channel has been held by women,
because of the insulation against cold that their extra fat
(always slightly more than men's even after heavy life-long
exercise) supplies.

What are the reasons for women's fast-approaching equality
with men in many sports? To understand them, we must
return to the misconceptions of the Seventies and trace the
process of enlightenment. Back in 1974, when the bulk of
research on the female physiology could barely have filled one
small library shelf, it was recognized that the trained woman
athlete could always beat the untrained man. But given a man
and a woman of the exact same build and training, it was
believed that the man would always win because of his greater
muscle mass, larger maximal oxygen uptake—or aerobic
power—and proportionately bigger heart and lungs. Women
were believed to have less stamina and less potential for
reaching the heights of male athletes. It took a long time but
eventually it was recognized and accepted by coaches—who
had long been as moveable as the Pyramids on the issue—that
women's physical inferiority was the result less of physiology
than of a lifetime of deprivation. It had been so socially
unacceptable for a woman to engage in strenuous activities,
and she had been encouraged so often to depend on others to
defend her—to act as her arms and legs—that she did not know
she was capable, for instance, of even lifting a television set.
Careful conditioning from a very early age taught her to use
only a fraction of her strength, to draw back her hands at the
last second when hitting out or throwing, to equate muscle
power with scorn and rejection. This conditioning was intensified from the time of menstruation and was discovered to be
the main reason why she sharply declined in performance
ability after puberty, in comparison with her brother's contin-
uing improvement.

At first it was thought that even if this conditioning were
removed and woman given opportunities to develop in the
same way as man, her innate biological inferiority would

prevent her from ever being able to compete with the male athlete. It took research by physical education scientists at Penn State, the University of California and others to finally break the last ball and chain of opinion that was holding sportswomen down.

Until the late Seventies, an athlete's maximum aerobic power (the capacity to extract oxygen from the air and deliver it to the working muscles) had been measured relative to his total body weight and was considered the best indication of his endurance capabilities. According to tests, the aerobic power of the female was only seventy to seventy-five percent of that of the male.

A number of scientists decided that it would be fairer to measure aerobic power in relation to fat-free body weight—in other words, the working muscle. It was found that square-inch for square-inch of muscle, women are as efficient as men in the use of oxygen. The discovery that at least in the laboratory women had as great an aerobic work capacity as men led to other tests to see if women's muscle power pound-for-pound was also as great. Not only were women found to be as strong as men in relation to lean body weight (total weight minus the weight of fat), in many tests their muscles proved to be stronger.

The problem, of course, was how to reproduce these laboratory results in real life. The solution was to get rid of the fat deposits, the padding, the dead weight that slows up women's performance, and to utilize more of the already existing muscle fibre. That is exactly what women did. They trained as hard and as long as men—after years of being restricted to moderate practice, which insured they would be only half as good as men. The long-distance runners were the first to lose the extra body fat because of the miles and miles they ran in training and the resulting caloric expenditures.

The fact that men have about twice the muscle mass of women was finally discovered to be meaningless. Just as men and women utilize only a small percentage of brain cells, so they use only about a quarter of their muscle fibre. This discovery put an end to the practice in the Sixties and Seventies of feeding female athletes, especially in the Eastern European countries, steroids. Women athletes who trained as strenuously as men were found to slowly increase use of muscle fibre, and reduce fat. Today, there is virtually no difference in strength between the average-trained male athlete and the average-trained female of the same body weight; the relative values for fat and lean weight are similar for both of them and although the woman generally retains slightly more fat padding than the man, she makes up for it by a greater use of her muscle fibre. It appears that the sedentary lifestyle of women has been largely responsible for the longstanding belief that nature meant her to be weaker.

Because men and women no longer have different training programs, U.S. women no longer are at a disadvantage in international meets—as were the U.S. Olympic team women back in the Seventies. Coaches found long ago that women could endure, and in fact needed, the kind of tough practice that men underwent. They have proved themselves able to do three hundred sit-ups; to run one hour straight; to lift seventy-five-pound weights. Such training has helped them develop endurance—a quality in which men always had the edge, until now.

An integral part of training for women had, since the mid-Eighties, been a reeducation course aimed at erasing societal conditioning and bringing out the natural competitive instinct and achievement motivation in them. Utilizing psychotherapy, psychodrama and hypnosis, the courses were mandatory for members of the Amateur Athletic Union and the Association for Intercollegiate Athletics and were used in physical education courses in most high schools and universities. They were aimed at wiping out the traditional female need to fail when competing with a man, as well as severing the link between success motivation and the voracious feminine need for praise and approval. Results were so good, with women shedding their fears and feelings of inadequacy and finally throwing themselves into the game for its own sake, that most courses have now been discontinued.

Little League teams now generally have a preponderance of girls, which is ironic considering it has been only twenty-six

years since the Little League Baseball Organization was forced
by court orders to allow girls on its teams. Medically, however,
it was inevitable. It has long been known that girls aged nine
to twelve are larger and stronger than boys, because they
mature earlier.

At the high-school level, all sports are integrated and there
are no longer "boys" and "girls" squads; such teams as golf,
tennis and swimming generally consist of equal numbers of
each sex. Because of the larger size of the average male, and
thus the greater strength, only a few of the best women athletes
make the football and wrestling teams, however. At first,
desegregation had to be won through separate suits by individual athletes and in a few cases by an agency of a state like
Pennsylvania, which challenged the school systems' right to
sex-segregated sports. Finally, the passage of the Equal Rights
Amendment forced every high-school physical education department in the nation to integrate teams and provide equal
facilities and equipment to young women and young men.

On the college and university scene, the passage of the
Education Amendments of 1972 forced educational institutions
receiving Federal assistance—virtually every college in the
nation—to give early equal treatment to men and women.
Title IX of the Act prohibited colleges to exclude anyone on
the basis of sex from participation in, or benefit from, any of
its educational programs or activities, including sports. Although the regulations governing Title IX were slow in being
issued and even then vague and open to many tests and
challenges, they finally forced colleges to slice up athletic
budgets evenly between men and women. Before that, most
universities were allocating only a fraction of their budgets to
women's sports, even though half their student bodies were
female. The universities, after much rancor and protest, were
forced to cut back their men's athletic budgets and skimp on
the revenue-producing sports such as football and basketball
to give the women a greater share. Women, freed from having
to throw bake sales to raise funds for their travel, spent more
time in rigorous training and eventually reached levels in
which they could compete with men. Now, of course, since
most sports have become integrated, the men have their money

back. The Association for Intercollegiate Athletics for Women, which had traditionally forbade its member colleges to give athletic scholarships to women, changed its policy to fit the times, and now women are receiving scholarships for everything from lacrosse to football.

Title IX, as well as the ERA, totally reversed the college sports scene. No longer were women prevented from taking courses in wrestling or men from volleyball. No longer were squash or handball courts closed to women, and no longer were tables of "high protein food" open only to male athletes. Sportswomen were allowed equal access to swimming pools and other training grounds, given equally good equipment (goodbye to the cast-off mitts, "old gyms" and torn uniforms), and eventually given an equal number of athletic scholarships. After a number of experiments with integration and semi-integration of teams—rich colleges tried three teams for each sport; one female, one male, and one mixed, while others tried two "separate but equal" teams—women have finally gotten good enough to make mixed teams a reality. The most successful mixed teams are in swimming and track where relays can be played, but baseball, basketball, lacrosse, field hockey, soccer and some individual track events have also been successful, with the average woman not being far enough behind her male counterpart to be considered a liability. Although a very few women have "competed up" to join the male-dominated college football teams, most are satisfied to play on the women's teams. Football, as well as rugby, ice hockey and wrestling still have one team for each sex.

On the professional circuit, there used to be a vicious circle in the Seventies whereby tournaments of women's golf, tennis and bowling would not get television coverage unless there was a big purse offered, but sponsors wouldn't provide the big purse unless the tournament was televised. That Catch 22 of women's sports was soon ended, and by the Eighties men and women were earning equal prize money.

Women have come a long way in twenty-five years. Perhaps that is why all this uproar is happening now. Men are frightened by the sight of all these lean compact women—most young girls today do look like they stepped out of an Egyptian fresco.

It is not that women no longer look like women—their muscles, though more outlined, are no bigger, and the sloping feminine lines are still there. It is the uniform absence of a traditional *thickness* in the female form that seems to be disquieting to the people making the most noise. "You can't pinch women any more, you can't even get hold of them," grumbled one of the leaders of the New Male Chauvinism Movement recently. And it is true that flesh seems to be the sole province of the over-forty these days. The NMC complains that women have usurped every last asset unique to males: "First, women have a stronger constitution and a longer life—their survivability is superior to ours. Then they equal us mentally, and moreover claim they have the secret of the universe stashed somewhere in their consciousness. They give birth to life, and now they're just as strong, if not stronger, than we are." One of the more legitimate concerns of the NMC Movement is the fear that with the decreasing fatty tissue in active, exercising young women today, a danger is being posed to the species. If the female fat layer is not there to protect sex tissue and the stomach during pregnancy they ask, are we not raising a generation of female bodies that will be unable to protect their unborn babies? Are we gradually making female fat obsolete, and will the reproductive organs be the next to go? NMC sportswriters are calling sportswomen puppets, charging that they are mimicking males instead of being what they are best at. They are demanding that women quit competing with men. The hue and cry is great. You would sometimes think we were back in the Seventies.

Last Word

By Olga Connolly

Olga Connolly, a five-time Olympic competitor, won a gold medal in the 1956 women's discus throw. A Czechoslovakian expatriate, she was selected to carry the United States flag in the opening ceremonies of the 1972

*Olympics, an honor traditionally reserved for a man. At the
1972 Olympics, she mobilized athletes to send antiwar
telegrams to President Nixon. She is now director of
recreation at Loyola-Marymount University in Los Angeles.
In this 1974* womenSports *article, Connolly argues that
male-female athletic comparisons obscure the real purpose
of sports competition.*

I have long believed that physical fitness is the key to
woman's emancipation. After all, the ability to stand firmly
on our own two feet made us into humans. And it seems that,
finally, women are coming into their own. All over the country,
women are loosening their girdles and tightening their abdo-
mens. Through running and swift calisthenics, they are enjoy-
ing the exhilaration of liberated bodies. Women are learning
to deliver a fast, well-paced spike in their volleyball games.
Through sweat and calluses, they are bringing weightless poise
into their gymnastic routines. In marathon races, martial arts,
or basketball, women are showing that they are not quitters,
nor creatures of inferior potential.

Of course, not everybody as yet understands that a woman,
too, was born to excel. The other day I heard for the 150th
time that the women's sports event would never enjoy sizeable
spectator support because the performances are inferior to
men's. Why should a track fan be watching a woman high
jumper clear a six foot bar, I was asked, if he can get a far
greater vicarious lift out of watching a man clear a seven foot
bar? Or take women's basketball, I was told, how boring it is.
Men's games are infinitely more dramatic! Men are taller, they
jump higher, pass the ball faster, they dive, collide, and
slamdunk.

It occurred to me that too many fans see in sports little
more than an exercise of power. But at a closer look, is the
absolute height of the bar really so important? Or does the
challenge lie in the height of the bar as it relates to the strength
and size of the individual athlete? What about the thrill of
simply watching a person defy gravity?

And where to seek the essence of basketball? Should it rest
in the supple fingertips which control the ball with the
sensitivity of a piano player? Or in the intricate cadenza of the

footwork in the lay-up? We should remember that there is no difference between the ability of men and women to acquire virtuosity in their skills.

It seems to me that the worship of size and power has taken much away from sports. Imagine judging a ballet dancer chiefly on the power of her leaps. Or a painter whose fame depends on the muscular power of his brush stroke—who else but the master who rips holes through the canvas could make it to the museum? I think people who are hung up on raw muscular superiority belong among the utilitarians who tend to reduce sports into another form of labor, and sports competition into a quasi-military contest.

Sports, however, are arts. Humans have been equipped with a wondrous range of creative movement. Motion is a basic element of life, and sports are the milieu wherein a human being can express her physical genius. Sports, like songs, make life worthy of living, and they need no utilitarian justification for their existence.

Being free and dynamic, naturally, is as much an expression of femininity as it is of masculinity. Women have finally realized that sports have never scrambled anyone's chromosomes, nor have they changed anyone's basic personality. Women know that athletics help them blossom to full womanhood rather than making them muscle-bound or infertile. They are beginning to reap the benefits of being physically active.

Having to face a physical challenge heightens a woman's sense of vitality and the awareness of her individuality. The mirror of a quest for perfection reveals to each athlete her potential and limitations that are real rather than imposed on her by an arbitrary social code. Women learn that they do not always win, but also do not always lose; they have much to lean upon and much to offer. They learn to appreciate someone's weakness without their feeling superior. Every step towards mastership of their physical frame gives them the satisfaction of an Olympic victory. And as they approach the harmonious relationship between their physical and mental beings, they learn to interact independently with the surrounding society, without being swallowed by it.

I believe we are entering an era when women will educate much of our culture to enlightened spectatorship. Through prowess in athletics they will teach the fans to appreciate individual sports for their dynamic beauty, and those who engage in them for their creativity and technical excellence. Women are beginning to confirm that the champion athlete is an artist who found his or her expression through a particular sports endeavor. Just as in other arts, thousands attempt but only a few reach the pinnacle.

It is women's task to educate the spectators towards the appreciation of the esthetic qualities along with the power display in sports. From such a sophistication will emerge a broad desire to participate. I say that women who are the guardians of life are about to become the guardians of its enjoyment.

About the Author

STEPHANIE L. TWIN, who has a Ph.D in American History from Rutgers University, is one of the few people doing scholarly work in the field of women and sports. She has presented papers on that subject at a number of conferences. Twin has worked as a sex-bias analyst and editor for the New Jersey State Department of Education, has been an inservice workshop leader for the Training Institute for Sex Desegregation of the Public Schools, and has taught college courses. She has also been a journalist and worked as a volunteer counselor for a battered women's project. Stephanie Twin lives in Brooklyn, New York, with her husband and two children.

A Note on Language

IN EDITING BOOKS, The Feminist Press attempts to eliminate harmful sex and race bias inherent in the language. In order to retain the authenticity of historical and literary documents, however, our policy is to leave their original language unaltered. We recognize that the task of changing language usage is extremely complex and that it will not be easily accomplished. The process is an ongoing one that we share with many others concerned with the relationship between a humane language and a more humane world.

Index

The numbers in italics indicate pages with photographs.

MacArthur, Douglass, 190
McCombs, Melvorne, xxix, xxxi
McGary, Ethel, xxxiii
McKim, Josephine, 148
McMillan, Kathy, 84
Mademoiselle, 157
Madison, Helene, 64
Madness in Sports, The (Beisser), xxxvi
  n40
magazines, women's sports, xxiv,
  27–28
Malone, Dudley Field, 152
Mao Tse-tung, 11
Marble, Alice, 130, 138
Marine, Michael, 205
matriarchy, xvi
masculinity: blurred concept of,
  xxxv–xxxvi; and sport, xxii–xxiii,
  93, 168, 171, 184; in women, xxv,
  xxxiv–xxxv, 4–5, 52–56, 65–68, 141
Masculinity-Femininity Quotient
  test, xxxv
Mass Leisure (Larrabee and Meyersohn), xxix n23
Masters, William H., 8
masturbation, xx
maturation, sex differences in, 14–15,
  17
Meany, Helen, 148
men: energy of, xx; records of, 7;
  sports affinity of, xxxvi. *See also*
  boys; masculinity; sex differences
menarche, 14, 15, 16, 20–21, 128
Menke, Frank G., xxviii n20
menstruation, xxviii, 4, 20, 22, 97,
  207
Metheny, Eleanor, 190
Meyer, Debbie, 7
Meyersohn, Rolf, xxix n23
Michener, James, xxxvii
Middle Ages, sport in, xxiii
middle-class: frailty concept and,
  xviii–xix; values of, xxii–xxiii. *See*
  also class; working-class women
Mills College, 24
Miss America pageant, xxx, 92, 158,
  189
modernity, women and, 43, 50
Mogel, Jerry, 7
Montagu, Ashley, 12

moral superiority, xxxvi
Morehouse, L. E., 19
Morris, Cynthia, 169
*Morris v. Michigan High School Ath-
  letic Association*, 168
Mosher, Clelia Duel, xxviii
motivation, sex differences in, 66, 211
*Motivations in Play, Games, and
  Sport* (Slovenko and Knight), xxxv
  n39
Ms. Magazine, 5, 94, 166
Munich Olympics, 85
Murphy, Lizzie, *121*
Murray, Grace Peckham, xix
muscle, 42, 45; sex differences in, 16,
  29, 46, 49, 166, 207

National Amateur Athletic Federa-
  tion, xxix, xxxii
National Association of Physical Ed-
  ucators, 179
National Organization of Women,
  165, 168
National Women's Political Caucus,
  165
NCAA, and Title IX, 176, 178
New Jersey Little League, 168
Newsweek, 5
New York City Board of Education,
  xxvii
New York Jets, xxxix
New York Times, xxxviii, 5, 85, 94
Nickerson, Elinor, 180, 181
Nineteenth Century magazine, 35
Nixon, Richard, 96, 189, 215
Nobel Peace Prize, xxv
Norelius, Martha, 148
No Sex in Education, xxiv

Oberlin College, xxxix, 182
Ogilvie, Bruce, 33–34
Ohio State University, 9, 205
Olympics, xxviii, *40*, 76–77, 94–103,
  119, 192; discrimination against
  women at, xxxi, 30, 31, 63, 97;
  women's performance at, 4, 7, 33,
  84
Olympics (Ancient Greece), xvi, 96
Olympics Medical Sub-Commission,
  xxxi

(Acknowledgments continued from page vi)

Gallico, Paul, "Gertrude Ederle." From *The Golden People* by Paul Gallico, Doubleday & Co. Inc., 1965. Reprinted by permission of Harold Ober Associates Inc. Copyright © 1964 by Paul Gallico.

Geracimos, Ann, "Memoirs of a Would–Be Swim Champ." Reprinted by permission from *womenSports* Magazine, July 1974. Copyright © 1974 by womenSports Publishing Company.

Gibson, Althea "I Always Wanted to Be Somebody." Condensation of chapters 1–3 from *I Always Wanted to Be Somebody* by Althea Gibson. Copyright © 1958 by Althea Gibson and Edward E. Fitzgerald. Copyright © 1958 by the Curtis Publishing Company. Reprinted by permission of Harper and Row Publishers, Inc.

Hart, M. Marie, "On Being Female in Sport." Revised version of an article published in *Sport in the Socio-Cultural Process* edited by M. Marie Hart (Dubuque, Iowa: William C. Brown Co.). Copyright © 1971 by M. Marie Hart. Reprinted with permission.

Hogan, Candace Lyle, "Shedding Light on Title IX." Reprinted by permission from *womenSports* Magazine, February 1976. Copyright © 1976 by womenSports Publishing Company.

Jordan, Pat, "Sweet Home—Willye B. White." Reprinted by permission of Dodd, Mead & Company, Inc. from *Broken Patterns* by Pat Jordan. Copyright © 1975, 1977 by Pat Jordan.

Scott, Jack, "A Radical Ethic for Sports." *Intellectual Digest*, July 1972. Copyright © 1972 by Jack Scott. Reprinted with permission.

Shaffer, Thomas E., M.D., "Physiological Considerations of the Female Participant." From *Women and Sport: A National Research Conference* edited by Dorothy V. Harris. © 1972 The Pennsylvania State University. Reprinted with permission.

Weiss, Paul, "Women Athletes." From *Sport: A Philosophical Inquiry*, Copyright © 1969 by Southern Illinois University Press. Reprinted by permission of Southern Illinois University Press.

Photograph Acknowledgments

Cover: © Cary Herz. *Page iv:* © Cary Herz. *Pages 2–3:* Culver Pictures. *Pages 76–77:* Joe DiMaggio, Focus on Sports. *Pages 162–163:* © Libby Friedman.

Pages 38–41. **1, 2, 3:** Photoworld. **4:** Culver Pictures. **5, 6:** Photoworld. **7, 8:** courtesy of Prints and Photographs Collection, Moorland-Spingarn Research Center, Howard University. **9:** courtesy of New York Public Library Picture Collection. **10:** Photoworld. **11.** Culver Pictures. **12.** courtesy of New York Public Library Picture Collection.

Pages 118–121. **1:** Wide World Photos. **2:** Costa Manos, Magnum Photos. **3:** Photoworld. **4:** courtesy of National Woman's Christian Temperance Union. **5:** Wide World Photos. **6, 7:** Photoworld. **8, 9, 10:** United Press International Photo. **11:** Photoworld. **12:** Culver Pictures.

Pages 192–195. **1:** © Bettye Lane. **2, 3, 4:** © Cary Herz. **5:** Eastfoto. **6:** © Cary Herz. **7:** © Bettye Lane. **8:** © Cary Herz. **9:** © Bettye Lane. **10:** © Cary Herz. **11:** © Bettye Lane.

This book was composed on the VIP *in Trump and Olive Antique by Monotype Composition Company, Baltimore, Maryland. It was printed and bound by R. R. Donnelley & Sons Company, Chicago, Illinois. The covers were printed by Algen Press, Queens, New York.*

3